$\eta \times \dfrac{5-10}{11-10}$

D0605752

DEFINING MOMENTS
THE MUCKRAKERS
AND THE
PROGRESSIVE ERA

DEFINING MOMENTS
THE MUCKRAKERS
AND THE
PROGRESSIVE ERA

Laurie Collier Hillstrom

Omnigraphics

P.O. Box 31-1640
Detroit, MI 48231

Omnigraphics, Inc.

Kevin Hillstrom, *Series Editor*
Cherie D. Abbey, *Managing Editor*

Peter E. Ruffner, *Publisher*
Matthew P. Barbour, *Senior Vice President*

Elizabeth Collins, *Research and Permissions Coordinator*
Kevin M. Hayes, *Operations Manager*

Allison A. Beckett and Mary Butler, *Research Staff*
Cherry Stockdale, *Permissions Assistant*
Shirley Amore, Martha Johns, and Kirk Kauffmann, *Administrative Staff*

Library of Congress Cataloging-in-Publication Data

Hillstrom, Laurie Collier, 1965-
   The muckrakers and the Progressive Era / by Laurie Collier Hillstrom.
      p. cm. -- (Defining moments)
   Summary: "Provides a detailed account of the muckraking movement in early twentieth-century American journalism and its contribution to progressive reforms. Explores how the muckraking tradition and progressive political ideas have continued through the modern era. Features include a narrative overview, biographies, primary sources, chronology, glossary, bibliography, and index"--Provided by publisher.
   Includes bibliographical references and index.
   ISBN 978-0-7808-1093-8 (hardcover : alk. paper) 1. Journalism—Social aspects--United States--History--20th century. 2. Social problems—Press coverage--United States. 3. Progressivism (United States politics)--History--20th century. 4. United States--Social conditions--20th century. I. Title.
   PN4888.S6H55 2009
   302.230973'09042--dc22
                                                                 2009026396

TABLE OF CONTENTS

Preface ix
How to Use This Book xiii
Research Topics for *The Muckrakers and the Progressive Era* xv

NARRATIVE OVERVIEW

Prologue 3

Chapter One: Events Leading Up to the Progressive Era 7

Chapter Two: The Role of Journalism in America 21

Chapter Three: Addressing Social Problems 35

Chapter Four: Battling the Titans of Industry 51

Chapter Five: Exposing Government Corruption 69

Chapter Six: The Muckraking Tradition Continues 85

Chapter Seven: Legacy of the Progressive Era 103

BIOGRAPHIES

Ray Stannard Baker (1870-1946) 115
Journalist and Author of Following the Color Line

S.S. McClure (1857-1949) 119
Progressive Owner and Editor of McClure's Magazine

David Graham Phillips (1867-1911) 124
Journalist Who Wrote the "Treason of the Senate" Series

Jacob Riis (1849-1914) 128
Photographer and Author of How the Other Half Lives

John D. Rockefeller (1839-1937) 132
Industrial Tycoon, Philanthropist, and Major Target of the
Muckrakers

Theodore Roosevelt (1858-1919) 137
President of the United States, 1901-1909

Upton Sinclair (1878-1968) 142
Journalist, Political Leader, and Author of The Jungle

Lincoln Steffens (1866-1936) 148
Journalist and Author of The Shame of the Cities

Ida M. Tarbell (1857-1944) 152
Journalist and Author of The History of the Standard Oil
Company

PRIMARY SOURCES

President Theodore Roosevelt Promises Progressive Reform 159

Jacob Riis Chronicles the Struggles of the Urban Poor 165

John Spargo Describes the Tragedy of Child Labor 170

Ida Tarbell Investigates the Standard Oil Trust 173

Upton Sinclair Exposes Problems in the Meatpacking Industry 178

Lincoln Steffens Reveals the Shame of the Cities 182

David Graham Phillips Blasts Corrupt U.S. Senators 188

Roosevelt Calls Crusading Journalists "Muckrakers" 192

The *Washington Post* Gives Wounded Veterans a Voice 197

Pete Hamill Explains the Importance of Investigative Journalism 206

Modern-Day Muckrakers Face Major Challenges 212

Important People, Places, and Terms 219
Chronology 225
Sources for Further Study 233
Bibliography 235
Photo and Illustration Credits 239
Index 241

PREFACE

Throughout the course of America's existence, its people, culture, and institutions have been periodically challenged—and in many cases transformed—by profound historical events. Some of these momentous events, such as women's suffrage, the civil rights movement, and U.S. involvement in World War II, invigorated the nation and strengthened American confidence and capabilities. Others, such as the McCarthy era, the Vietnam War, and Watergate, have prompted troubled assessments and heated debates about the country's core beliefs and character.

Some of these defining moments in American history were years or even decades in the making. The Harlem Renaissance and the New Deal, for example, unfurled over the span of several years, while the American labor movement and the Cold War evolved over the course of decades. Other defining moments, such as the Cuban missile crisis and the terrorist attacks of September 11, 2001, transpired over a matter of days or weeks.

But although significant differences exist among these events in terms of their duration and their place in the timeline of American history, all share the same basic characteristic: they transformed the United States' political, cultural, and social landscape for future generations of Americans.

Taking heed of this fundamental reality, American citizens, schools, and other institutions are increasingly emphasizing the importance of understanding our nation's history. Omnigraphics' *Defining Moments* series was created for the express purpose of meeting this growing appetite for authoritative, useful historical resources. This series will be of enduring value to anyone interested in learning more about America's past—and in understanding how those historical events continue to reverberate in the 21st century.

Each individual volume of *Defining Moments* provides a valuable resource for readers interested in learning about the most profound events in our nation's history. Each volume is organized into three distinct sections—Narrative Overview, Biographies, and Primary Sources.

- The **Narrative Overview** provides readers with a detailed, factual account of the origins and progression of the "defining moment" being examined. It also explores the event's lasting impact on America's political and cultural landscape.

- The **Biographies** section provides valuable biographical background on leading figures associated with the event in question. Each biography concludes with a list of sources for further information on the profiled individual.

- The **Primary Sources** section collects a wide variety of pertinent primary source materials from the era under discussion, including official documents, papers and resolutions, letters, oral histories, memoirs, editorials, and other important works.

Individually, each of these sections is a rich resource for users. Together, they comprise an authoritative, balanced, and absorbing examination of some of the most significant events in U.S. history.

Other notable features contained within each volume in the series include a glossary of important individuals, places, and terms; a detailed chronology featuring page references to relevant sections of the narrative; an annotated bibliography of sources for further study; an extensive general bibliography that reflects the wide range of historical sources consulted by the author; and a subject index.

New Feature

Each volume in the *Defining Moments* series now includes a list of research topics, detailing some of the important topics that recur throughout the volume and providing a valuable starting point for research. Students working on essays and reports will find this feature especially useful as they try to narrow down their research interests.

These research topics are covered throughout the different sections of the book: the narrative overview, the biographies, the primary sources, the chronology, and the important people, places, and terms section. This wide coverage allows readers to view the topic through a variety of different approaches.

Students using *Defining Moments: The Muckrakers and the Progressive Era* will find information on a wide range of topics suitable for conducting historical research and writing reports:

- History of American journalism from colonial era to modern times
- Economic, social, and political developments that informed the rise of the Progressive Era
- Chief areas of interest of the muckrakers, including political corruption, mistreatment of workers, the plight of immigrants, and urban misery and decay
- Various ways in which the Muckraking Era and the Progressive Era intersected—and proved mutually beneficial to one another
- Landmarks of muckraking journalism, including Ida Tarbell's exposé of Standard Oil, Upton Sinclair's investigation of the meatpacking industry, and Lincoln Steffens's "Shame of the Cities" series
- Presidency of Theodore Roosevelt and his complicated relationship with the muckrakers
- Factors leading to the close of the Muckraking Era
- Challenges facing the current generation of "muckraking" journalists
- Legacy of the muckrakers on contemporary journalists

Acknowledgements

This series was developed in consultation with a distinguished Advisory Board comprised of public librarians, school librarians, and educators. They evaluated the series as it developed, and their comments and suggestions were invaluable throughout the production process. Any errors in this and other volumes in the series are ours alone. Following is a list of board members who contributed to the *Defining Moments* series:

Gail Beaver, M.A., M.A.L.S.
Adjunct Lecturer, University of Michigan
Ann Arbor, MI

Melissa C. Bergin, L.M.S., N.B.C.T.
Library Media Specialist
Niskayuna High School
Niskayuna, NY

Comments and Suggestions

We welcome your comments on *Defining Moments: The Muckrakers and the Progressive Era* and suggestions for other events in U.S. history that warrant treatment in the *Defining Moments* series. Correspondence should be addressed to:

Editor, *Defining Moments*
Omnigraphics, Inc.
P.O. Box 31-1640
Detroit, MI 48231
E-mail: editorial@omnigraphics.com

HOW TO USE THIS BOOK

*D*efining Moments: The Muckrakers and the Progressive Era provides users with a detailed and authoritative overview of the journalistic movement that exposed social and political problems in the United States and generated public support for major reforms during the first decade of the twentieth century. The preparation and arrangement of this volume—and all other books in the *Defining Moments* series—reflect an emphasis on providing a thorough and objective account of events that shaped our nation, presented in an easy-to-use reference work.

Defining Moments: The Muckrakers and the Progressive Era is divided into three primary sections. The first of these sections, the **Narrative Overview**, provides a detailed, factual account of the muckraking movement in American journalism and its contribution to turn-of-the-century progressive reforms. It explains the transformation that occurred in the United States as a result of industrialization and traces the origins of the Progressive Era. This section also covers the development of investigative journalism in America and the rise of influential muckraking magazines like *McClure's*. It goes on to offer an in-depth look at major muckraking investigations of social problems, government corruption, and corporate influence. Finally, this section explores how the muckraking tradition and progressive political ideas have continued through the modern era.

The second section, **Biographies**, provides valuable biographical background on leading figures involved in muckraking journalism or the progressive politics of the era. Examples include S.S. McClure, the publisher who turned his namesake magazine into the nation's leading muckraking journal; Upton Sinclair, the writer who exposed horrific problems in the meatpacking industry in his classic book *The Jungle*; Ida M. Tarbell, the journalist who investigated the ruthless business practices of John D. Rockefeller and his

Standard Oil Company; and Theodore Roosevelt, the president who used muckraking revelations to advance a slate of progressive policies. Each biography concludes with a list of sources for further information on the profiled individual.

The third section, **Primary Sources**, collects essential and illuminating documents related to muckraking journalism in the Progressive Era and beyond. This diverse collection includes excerpts from *How the Other Half Lives*, Jacob Riis's groundbreaking 1890 book about the struggles of the urban poor; "The Treason of the Senate," David Graham Phillips's hard-hitting 1906 series on political corruption in the federal government; "The Man with the Muck-Rake," President Theodore Roosevelt's famous speech that coined a term for crusading journalists; and "Walter Reed and Beyond," the *Washington Post*'s Pulitzer Prize-winning 2007 report on the mistreatment of wounded veterans at U.S. military hospitals.

Other valuable features in *Defining Moments: The Muckrakers and the Progressive Era* include the following:

- A Research Topics list that provides a starting point for student research.
- Attribution and referencing of primary sources and other quoted material to help guide users to other valuable historical research resources.
- Glossary of Important People, Places, and Terms.
- Detailed Chronology of events with a *see reference* feature. Under this arrangement, events listed in the chronology include a reference to page numbers within the Narrative Overview wherein users can find additional information on the event in question.
- Photographs of the leading figures and major events associated with the Progressive Era and muckraking journalism.
- Sources for Further Study, an annotated list of noteworthy works about the muckraking era.
- Extensive bibliography of works consulted in the creation of this book, including books, periodicals, and Internet sites.
- A Subject Index.

RESEARCH TOPICS FOR THE MUCKRAKERS AND THE PROGRESSIVE ERA

Starting a research paper can be a challenge, as students struggle to decide what area to study. Now, each book in the *Defining Moments* series includes a list of research topics, detailing some of the important topics that recur throughout the volume and providing a valuable starting point for research. Students working on essays and reports will find this feature especially useful as they try to narrow down their research interests.

These research topics are covered throughout the different sections of the book: the narrative overview, the biographies, the primary sources, the chronology, and the important people, places and terms section. This wide coverage allows readers to view the topic through a variety of different approaches.

Students using *Defining Moments: The Muckrakers and the Progressive Era* will find information on a wide range of topics suitable for conducting historical research and writing reports:

- History of American journalism from the colonial era to modern times.

- Economic, social, and political developments that informed the rise of the Progressive Era.

- Chief areas of interest of the muckrakers, including political corruption, mistreatment of workers, the plight of immigrants, and urban misery and decay.

- Various ways in which the Muckraking Era and the Progressive Era intersected—and proved mutually beneficial to one another.

- Landmarks of muckraking journalism, including Ida Tarbell's exposé of Standard Oil, Upton Sinclair's investigation of the meatpacking industry, and Lincoln Steffens's "Shame of the Cities" series.

- Presidency of Theodore Roosevelt and his complicated relationship with the muckrakers.
- Factors leading to the close of the Muckraking Era.
- Challenges facing the current generation of "muckraking" journalists.
- Legacy of the muckrakers on contemporary journalism.
- Legacy of the Progressive Era in American politics.

NARRATIVE OVERVIEW

PROLOGUE

⟨⟩

They "strode like a young giant into the arena of public service," declared Progressive political leader Robert La Follette, and "assailed social and political evils in high places and low." He was describing the influential magazines that sprung up around the turn of the twentieth century and became home to a generation of investigative journalists known as the muckrakers. Although these crusading writers were mainly active during the early 1900s, their words had a profound and lasting impact on American life. In fact, many of the changes they sparked remained in effect a century later.

Writing primarily for monthly magazines, the muckrakers conducted investigations, raised public awareness of social and political problems, and generated calls for reform. They examined poverty and squalor in America's cities, as well as the long hours, low wages, and hazardous conditions faced by workers in the nation's bustling mills, factories, and mines. They revealed ruthless business practices and abuses of the public trust by large corporations and wealthy industrialists. They also exposed fraud, bribery, and corruption at all levels of government.

By bringing such issues to light, these watchdog journalists helped protect the American people—and U.S. democracy—from abuse at the hands of powerful interests. "In a mass democratic society such as ours, in which there are strong tendencies toward the concentration of power in political and economic institutions, the abuse of power has deep public consequences," noted one scholar. "It is especially important, therefore, for a vital and vigilant press to hold the leaders of such institutions accountable to preserve a dynamic and participatory democratic society."[1]

"Muckraker" may seem like an unusual name for a reporter. President Theodore Roosevelt coined the term in a famous 1906 speech. Up to that point in time, Roosevelt and the top journalists of the day had worked hand-in-hand to enact a series of progressive policies. The muckrakers brought issues to the American people's attention, and the president used the strength of public opinion to pressure Congress to pass important reforms. Together they expanded the role of the federal government in regulating business activities and addressing social problems, ushering in the Progressive Era in American history.

In 1906, however, Roosevelt grew frustrated with what he viewed as an excessively negative tone in American magazines and newspapers. He claimed that many reporters were so focused on exposing problems and scandals—or "raking through the muck"—that they ignored positive, uplifting stories. Some journalists took offense when the president called them "muckrakers," but others wore the title proudly. The word is still used today in reference to American journalists who uncover evidence of corporate greed, government corruption, and other lawlessness.

Among the many people who recognized the contributions of the muckrakers was Robert La Follette. One of the most outspoken leaders of the Progressive Era, he served as governor of Wisconsin (1901-1906), U.S. Senator from Wisconsin (1906-1924), and presidential candidate of the Progressive Party (1924). In a 1912 speech before the Periodical Publishers' Association, La Follette reflected on the accomplishments of the muckraking magazines and emphasized the vital role of a free press in American society.

> A decade ago young men trained in journalism came to see this [growing corporate] control of the newspapers of the country. They saw also an unoccupied field. And they went out and built up great periodicals and magazines. They were free.
>
> Their pages were open to publicists and scholars and liberty, and justice and equal rights found a free press beyond the reach of the corrupt influence of consolidated business and machine politics. We entered upon a new era.
>
> The periodical, reduced in price, attractive and artistic in dress, strode like a young giant into the arena of public service. Filled with this spirit, quickened with human interest, it assailed social and political evils in high places and low. It found the power of the public service corporation and the evil influences

of money in the municipal government of every large city. It found franchises worth millions of dollars secured by bribery; police in partnership with thieves and crooks and prostitutes. It found juries "fixed" and an established business plying its trade between litigants and the back door of blinking justice.

It found Philadelphia giving away franchises [contracts], franchises not supposedly or estimated to be worth $2,500,000, but for which she had been openly offered and refused $2,500,000. Milwaukee they found giving away street-car franchises worth $8,000,000 against the protests of her indignant citizens. It found Chicago robbed in tax-payments of immense value by corporate owners of property through fraud and forgery on a gigantic scale; it found the aldermen of St. Louis, organized to boodle the city with a criminal compact, on file in the dark corner of a safety deposit vault.

The free and independent periodical turned her searchlight on state legislatures, and made plain as the sun at noonday the absolute control of the corrupt lobby. She opened the closed doors of the secret caucus, the secret committee, the secret conference, behind which United States Senators and Members of Congress betrayed the public interest into the hands of railroads, the trusts, the tariff mongers, and the centralized banking power of the country. She revealed the same influences back of judicial and other appointments. She took the public through the great steel plants and into the homes of the men who toil twelve hours a day and seven days in the week. And the public heard their cry of despair. She turned her camera into the mills and shops where little children are robbed of every chance of life that nourishes vigorous bodies and sound minds, and the pinched faces and dwarfed figures told their pathetic story on her clean white pages....

No men ever faced graver responsibilities. None have ever been called to a more unselfish, patriotic service. I believe that when the final test comes, you will not be found wanting; you will not desert and leave the people to depend upon the public platform alone, but you will hold aloft the lamp of Truth, lighting the way for the preservation of representative government and the liberty of the American people.[2]

Notes

[1] Weinberg, Lila Shaffer. *The Muckrakers*. Chicago: University of Illinois Press, 2001, p. xv.

[2] La Follette, Robert M. "Speech Delivered at the Annual Banquet of the Periodical Publishers' Association," February 2, 1912. In *La Follette's Autobiography: A Personal Narrative of Political Experiences*. Madison, WI: Robert M. La Follette Co., 1913, pp. 793-797.

Chapter One

EVENTS LEADING UP TO
THE PROGRESSIVE ERA

Machines of steel and copper and wood and stone, and bookkeeping and managerial talent, were creating a new order. It looked glamorous. It seemed permanent; yet ... discontent rose in the hearts of the people.

—William Allen White

The Progressive Era developed in response to rapid changes that had taken place in American society over the course of the nineteenth century. When the Industrial Revolution swept across the United States during the 1800s, it brought remarkable advances in technology, communication, transportation, energy, and commerce. Within the space of a few decades, these innovations transformed the basic character of the nation from one of farms and rural communities to one of factories and bustling cities. Although industrialization helped lift the United States to new heights of prosperity and power, not all citizens shared in its benefits. A few talented, ambitious, and lucky individuals built vast business empires and amassed huge fortunes during this time. But their success came at the expense of millions of American workers who toiled long hours under dangerous conditions in the nation's mines, factories, slaughterhouses, and railroad yards. While the rich enjoyed lives of luxury, these workers struggled to raise families in crowded, dirty cities full of poverty, crime, and disease. By the turn of the twentieth century, a growing number of Americans insisted that this situation needed to change. They demanded that the U.S. government take action to curtail the power of big business and raise the standard of living for workers and their families.

The Industrial Revolution

The Industrial Revolution started in England in the 1700s, when inventors came up with a series of new machines that dramatically reduced the time and effort required to produce clothing, rugs, and other textile goods. Before this time, textiles had been produced in limited quantities by individuals and families working at home or in small shops. Each worker performed all of the various steps involved in making textiles, including spinning wool or cotton into threads, weaving the threads into cloth, and sewing the cloth to create clothing. The new machines made these jobs faster and easier, but they were too big and expensive for individual families to afford. As a result, most textile production moved to large, centralized mills and factories. In these facilities, each worker performed a single, specialized task in the production process over and over again. Since textile workers had to live near the factories in which they worked, cities quickly sprouted around these industrial facilities.

The advances in English textile manufacturing were followed by a number of innovations in other industries. Many of these new developments, such as the invention of the steam engine in 1769, allowed motor-powered machines to replace the muscle power of men or animals. By the early 1800s, the Industrial Revolution spread beyond the borders of England to other parts of the world. In many ways, the newly formed United States provided a perfect environment for the innovations in business and technology to take root and grow.

The United States had a number of advantages that made rapid industrialization possible. The nation possessed abundant natural resources, including fertile farmland, vast tracts of timber, a network of rivers and lakes navigable by boat, and valuable reserves of coal, iron, copper, and other minerals. The country also had a large, ambitious labor force that welcomed technological advances as an opportunity to improve their lives. Finally, the U.S. government pursued policies that promoted industrial development. Leaders of the ruling Republican Party provided tariffs to protect manufacturers and subsidies for building railroad lines and telegraph networks.

The Industrial Revolution quickly spread through the American economy, with progress in one area leading to additional innovations in another. Advances in iron mining and steel production, for example, provided the materials needed to build railroads, factories, and skyscrapers. The development of steam shipping and railways, meanwhile, allowed for the movement

When the Industrial Revolution swept across the United States in the 1800s, millions of Americans went to work in large mills and factories.

of food and manufactured goods to population centers. These transportation networks also facilitated the process of westward expansion, which opened new territory for settlement and development.

The American economy truly took off in the years following the Civil War (1861-65). By 1870 the United States trailed only England in world commerce. Dramatic improvements in manufacturing, agriculture, transportation, communication, and other industries continued over the next few decades. The United States stood as the world's leading manufacturer at the turn of the twentieth century, and the total value of all products made in the country increased by more than 200 percent between 1900 and 1920.

Impacts on American Society

The rapid industrialization of the United States had striking impacts on American life and culture. For some people, the results were overwhelmingly positive. A generation of successful businessmen emerged to take full advantage of the economic opportunities that became available during that era. Such giants of American industry and finance as J.P. Morgan, John D. Rockefeller, Cornelius Vanderbilt, and Andrew Carnegie built huge business empires and amassed great personal fortunes during the late nineteenth and early twentieth centuries. However, critics of these men called them "robber barons" who used ruthless business tactics and exploited workers for their own gain.

> *Not all American citizens enjoyed the fruits of industrialization. While the upper and middle classes enjoyed lives of luxury and comfort, millions of working-class Americans faced a daily struggle for survival.*

These business titans controlled large corporations or trusts of related companies that dominated banking, railroads, oil, mining, iron and steel production, and a variety of other industries. They used their extraordinary wealth, power, and influence to manipulate government officials, eliminate competition, command high prices, and collect huge profits. These businesses exerted a remarkable degree of control over the U.S. economy. By 1909, the top 1 percent of American business firms produced nearly half of all manufactured goods.

The leading industrialists and their families formed a rich and powerful upper class in American society. At the turn of the twentieth century, a few thousand millionaires controlled an amazing 90 percent of the nation's resources. They displayed their extreme wealth by building huge mansions and ornate offices, spending tens of thousands of dollars on lavish dinner parties, and sailing fancy yachts.

At the same time, industrialization created a sizeable middle class of business managers and other professionals. The emerging middle class built comfortable homes in safe, pleasant communities. They could afford new products and conveniences that industrialization made available, such as indoor plumbing, electric lights, telephones, preserved foods, and ready-made clothing. New department stores and retail catalogs—including Macy's, Woolworth's, and Sears & Roebuck—emerged around this time to meet their needs. Middle-class families also created a market for new leisure and recreational activities, such as sporting events, musical theater, and circuses.

Not all American citizens enjoyed the fruits of industrialization, however. While the upper and middle classes enjoyed lives of luxury and comfort, millions of working-class Americans faced a daily struggle for survival (see sidebar "Social Darwinism," p. 16). Many people in this situation were recently arrived immigrants. Earlier waves of immigrants to the United States had hailed mostly from western Europe. After 1880, however, the vast majority of immigrants came from countries in eastern and southern Europe, including Italy, Poland, and Russia. Facing food shortages and political instability in their homelands, they saw the United States as a land of opportunity. They flocked to America's shores in hopes of acquiring land for farming or finding jobs in booming factories. An incredible 14.5 million immigrants arrived in the United States between 1900 and 1915 alone.

Andrew Carnegie (front) was one of the powerful business titans who became known as "robber barons."

Problems in Cities and Factories

Immigrants and other members of the working class were most vulnerable to a number of problems that arose in the nation's cities and factories during the age of industrialization. This era saw a marked shift in American life from a rural, farming culture to an urban, industrial culture. The promise of factory jobs lured millions of people to big cities. The nation's cities grew rapidly and often haphazardly in an effort to accommodate the sudden influx of people and increase in industrial capacity. Chicago, for instance, underwent a complete transformation over a fifty-year period. "[In 1840] Chicago had been a village of log huts around Fort Dearborn holding scarcely 5,000 residents," one historian noted. "By 1890, it was a city of

11

In the early twentieth century, industrial workers like these Pennsylvania coal miners toiled long hours in difficult jobs for low wages.

165 square miles with one million residents, increasing by some 50,000 each year, transforming pastures seemingly overnight into swarming tenements."[1]

In many cities, the population explosions simply overwhelmed the resources of local governments. They were unable to plan effectively for such rapid growth and provide services for so many new residents. As a result, most large American cities were full of poverty, hopelessness, crime, and decay. Poor city dwellers often lived in crowded, dirty tenement houses and slums. Sometimes older homes that had once housed a single family were converted into tenements, with an entire family crammed into each room. The overcrowding and lack of indoor plumbing led to the spread of diseases like typhoid, cholera, and tuberculosis. Dangerous fires often swept through whole neighborhoods, and many desperate city residents became involved in prostitution and other criminal activities. The rapid growth of cities was reflected in a 300 percent increase in the nation's murder rate over the last two decades of the nineteenth century.

Going to work offered no relief for most poor residents of American cities. The sheer number of workers available to fill positions in the nation's mines and factories gave employers a great deal of power to exploit workers. Many companies demanded that their employees work long hours—commonly seventy hours per week—for very low wages. Most factory jobs required workers to perform repetitive tasks all day long in hot, dirty, and often dangerous conditions. Few laws existed to protect workers on the job, so large corporations frequently ignored safety concerns. As a result, job-related injuries and death were common. From 1880 to 1900, for example, an average of 35,000 industrial workers were killed on the job each year, and around 500,000 more were injured.

Despite the terrible working conditions, many poor Americans considered themselves lucky to have jobs because employment was so uncertain. As much as 30 percent of the urban work force was unemployed at least part of each year due to shortages of raw materials, breakdowns of machinery, seasonal changes in demand, or other reasons. In many poor families, women and children had to join the workforce in order to earn enough money to survive. By 1900 as many as three million American children were toiling at full-time jobs in mines and factories.

Early Reform Efforts

By the late 1800s, an increasing number of people recognized the negative impacts of industrialization on American society. Growth and change had occurred so rapidly that there was little time to address the difficult economic and political problems that arose. Many people noticed the enormous contrast

13

between the wealthy industrialists who controlled the powerful corporations and trusts, and the millions of industrial workers who lived in poverty and despair in the nation's cities and mining communities. Some critics blamed greed and corruption on the part of big business for the problems that had developed.

A few groups demanded that the U.S. government step in and reform the unfair practices of big business. One of the earliest organized reform efforts came from American farmers. As farming became increasingly mechanized in the 1800s, farmers experienced higher costs of production and lower prices for crops. Their problems were compounded by the high rates charged by the big railroad companies for shipping freight to and from rural areas. Many farmers went so far into debt that they lost their land to powerful banking interests. A farmers' organization called the Grange arose in direct response to these events. It pressured state governments to regulate railroad shipping rates and overhaul bank lending practices.

> *"There are real and great evils [in American business],"* declared President Theodore Roosevelt, *"and a resolute and practical effort must be made to correct these evils."*

Another group that mounted a major reform effort was organized labor. Anger about long hours, low wages, and harsh work environments led some industrial workers to form unions. Labor unions gave workers a much stronger position from which to negotiate with corporate employers. Union leaders bargained for shorter work hours, better wages and benefits, and safer working conditions. If management refused to listen to their demands, the unions could fight back with work stoppages and strikes.

One of the most famous labor-management disputes of the late nineteenth century took place in Chicago in 1894. Employees of the Pullman Palace Car Company went on strike when the company's owners sharply reduced wages—but refused to reduce rents on the company-owned homes in which the workers lived or the price of goods at company-owned stores. The strike soon spread to American Railway Union members across the country. Responding to concerns from wealthy railroad owners and community leaders about the financial impact of a railroad strike, President Grover Cleveland ordered federal troops to Illinois to break up the strike and arrest union leaders. Many people saw Cleveland's response to the Pullman strike as clear evidence that the federal government favored the interests of large corporations over those of American workers.

This 1906 political cartoon suggests that wealthy business owners gained their luxurious lifestyle at the expense of the working class.

Social Darwinism

Before the start of the Progressive Era, many influential thinkers used a theory called Social Darwinism to justify the huge gulf that existed between the richest and poorest Americans. This theory was based on the work of Charles Darwin, an English naturalist who wrote the 1859 book *On the Origin of Species.* Darwin's book said that all animal species evolved or changed over time to adapt to the conditions in which they lived. Under Darwin's theory of evolution, the animals that adapted most readily were the ones that survived to pass on their superior genetic characteristics to future generations. This idea became known as "survival of the fittest," and over time it led to improvement of the entire species.

Some people claimed that Darwin's theory explained some of the changes that took place in American society during the Industrial Revolution. The American sociologist William Graham Sumner and the English philosopher Herbert Spencer, for example, said that survival of the fittest applied to the wealth and social status acquired by human beings. Under their theory, which became known as Social Darwinism, rich people succeeded because they were genetically superior to ordinary people. Poor

In most cases, the powerful corporations and trusts of this era paid little attention to the demands of workers. Determined to maximize profits, they ruthlessly resisted unionization efforts and crushed strikes. Some skilled craftsmen managed to negotiate some improvements to their wages and working conditions, but unskilled workers generally met with less success. As a result, only one out of every ten American workers held union membership by the turn of the twentieth century.

Populists Demand Change

Although farmers and factory workers made little progress in fighting the corporate trusts, their efforts did get the attention of U.S. lawmakers. The public's growing unhappiness with the overwhelming power of big business convinced the federal government to make a few significant changes in the people, on the other hand, lacked the intelligence, drive, or other qualities necessary to thrive in the industrialized world.

Social Darwinism held a great deal of appeal for America's wealthy business owners. It made them feel as if they deserved to earn great fortunes and live luxurious lives, and it gave them an excuse to ignore the poverty and hardships suffered by others. "It is the leaders who do the new things that count," declared Andrew Carnegie, who controlled the American steel industry. "All these have been Individualistic to a degree beyond ordinary men and worked in perfect freedom; each and every one a character unlike anybody else; an original; gifted beyond most others of his kind, hence his leadership."

The Progressive Movement of the early twentieth century rejected the theory of Social Darwinism. Progressives argued that the rich gained their wealth and power not through superior genetic traits, but through greed, ruthless business practices, and exploitation of the working class. They declared that their intention was to change this situation and ensure fairness and opportunity for all Americans.

Source: Carnegie, Andrew. *The Gospel of Wealth and Other Timely Essays.* Edited by Edward C. Kirkland. Cambridge, MA: Belknap Press, 1962, p. 18.

late 1800s. In 1887, for instance, Congress passed the Interstate Commerce Act. This law created the first federal regulatory agency, the Interstate Commerce Commission (ICC), to oversee the operations of the nation's railroads. The ICC could not curb the abuses of the giant railroad corporations, however, because it had limited power to enforce its rules.

In 1890 the federal government made another attempt to reduce the power of big business by passing the Sherman Antitrust Act. This law was intended to prevent trusts from gaining monopoly control over an entire industry. It failed to accomplish this aim, however, because the U.S. Supreme Court interpreted the law in ways that were favorable to big business.

In 1891 members of farm organizations, labor unions, and other disaffected groups formed a national political party to represent their common interests.

President Theodore Roosevelt, who took office in 1901, pursued a wide range of progressive reforms.

Known as the People's Party or Populists, they wanted to limit the power of corporations, attack government corruption, and arrange for federal ownership of the nation's railroad, telegraph, and telephone industries. They also favored the passage of new tax laws and restrictions on immigration to the United States.

After claiming six seats in the U.S. Senate during the 1894 elections, the Populists endorsed Democratic candidate William Jennings Bryan in the 1896 presidential race. When Bryan lost to Republican William McKinley, however, the party's fragile coalition of interest groups fell apart. Still, the basic ideas behind the Populist Party—instituting reforms to limit the influence of big business and give the people more power in government—formed the heart of the Progressive Movement.

The Progressive Movement

Although many people recognized the need for reform in the late 1800s, it was difficult to bring diverse interest groups together to demand change. At the turn of the century, however, an increasing number of educated, middle-class Americans came to share the discontent of these groups. They recognized that the nation had reached the point where it needed to address the problems that arose out of industrialization. They believed that the problems presented important opportunities to reform American institutions and improve society for the benefit of all. When these middle-class Americans joined the fight to cure the ills affecting American society, it marked the start of the Progressive Era.

Progressives had a long list of concerns, including poverty, child labor, dangerous working conditions, government corruption, and lack of regulation of big business. They encouraged federal and state governments to take a more active role in solving these problems and spreading the benefits of economic growth more widely. Many of these goals were shared by Theodore Roosevelt (see Roosevelt biography, p. 137), who became president in September 1901, after Republican president William McKinley was shot and killed in Buffalo, New York.

At first, many people expected Roosevelt to continue the conservative policies of his predecessor. But his speeches and actions soon proved that his philosophy of governance would be dramatically different. Roosevelt recognized that the powerful corporations and trusts wielded too much power and influence in the country. He believed that the government had a responsibility to protect and serve the public interest against excessive influence from big business. "The captains of industry who have driven the railway systems across this continent, who have built up our commerce, who have developed our manufactures, have on the whole done great good to our people," Roosevelt acknowledged. "Yet it is also true that there are real and great evils [in American business] and a resolute and practical effort must be made to correct these evils"[2] (see "President Theodore Roosevelt Promises Progressive Reform," p. 159).

Notes

[1] Lukas, Anthony. *Big Trouble.* New York: Simon and Schuster, 1997, p. 305.

[2] Roosevelt, Theodore. "Theodore Roosevelt: First Annual Message," December 3, 1901. In Woolley, John T., and Gerhard Peters, *The American Presidency Project.* Available online at http://www.presidency.ucsb.edu/?pid=29542.

Chapter Two

THE ROLE OF
JOURNALISM IN AMERICA

If we can let in light and air, if the people understand ... they
will at least proceed forward.

—S.S. McClure

After taking office in 1901, President Theodore Roosevelt asked the
American people to support a long list of progressive reforms. He felt
that the U.S. government had an obligation to rein in the abuses of big
corporations and make society more fair and democratic for all its members.
Public support for these policies was strong, in part because of the work of a
generation of investigative journalists who came to prominence at this time.

Known as "muckrakers," these crusading journalists wrote long, factual-
ly detailed articles that exposed government corruption, poverty, hazardous
working conditions, child labor, wasteful use of natural resources, and other
problems facing American society. Historians Arthur and Lila Weinberg
described the muckrakers as "the press agents for the Progressive movement.
To these writers and to the fast-growing muckraking magazines goes the
credit for arousing a lethargic public to righteous indignation. They spotlight-
ed Progressivism, and gave this political movement the impetus that aided it
in the passage of social and economic legislation."[1]

The Early History of American Journalism

When German printer Johannes Gutenberg invented moveable type
and the mechanical printing press in the 1400s, people in positions of power
recognized that the printed word had the potential to influence public opin-

ion. From their first appearance in America, newspapers and magazines upheld the journalistic tradition of alerting readers to problems in government and society. During the colonial period, though, British authorities often responded to critical stories about the English crown by limiting or censoring the press.

A British printer named Benjamin Harris started the first newspaper in the American colonies in Boston in 1690. Entitled *Publick Occurrences Both Forreign and Domestick,* it was originally intended to be a monthly journal. The first edition—printed on four sheets the size of notebook paper—featured articles about a smallpox epidemic, an Indian attack, a house that caught on fire, and a local person who committed suicide. But Harris never got the chance to publish a second edition. His newspaper was immediately shut down by the governor of Massachusetts Bay Colony for publishing "doubtful and uncertain Reports."[2]

> *The muckrakers were "the press agents for the Progressive movement," according to historians Arthur and Lila Weinberg. "They spotlighted Progressivism, and gave this political movement the impetus that aided it in the passage of social and economic legislation."*

The first ongoing newspaper in the colonies was the *Boston News-Letter,* launched in 1704 by John Campbell. Campbell's paper took a serious approach to the news and often relied on reports from ships arriving in the city's harbor. Beginning in 1721, the *News-Letter* faced stiff competition from the *New England Courant,* which was published by brothers James and Benjamin Franklin. The *Courant* provided readers with a lighthearted look at current events, as a note in the first edition explained: "The main Design of the Weekly Paper will be to entertain the Town with the most comical and diverting Incidents of Humane Life."[3] But the Franklins also published editorials that criticized the Massachusetts governor. One of these pieces landed James Franklin in jail.

Despite such conflicts with British authorities, the number of newspapers in the American colonies increased steadily, especially after they started accepting paid advertising around 1750. American newspapers became much more interested in political affairs in 1765, following England's passage of the Stamp Act. This law required all legal documents, books, and newspapers printed in the colonies to appear on specially stamped paper. The only way to obtain a stamp was to pay a high tax. Since the tax hit printers the hardest, they led a furious colonial resistance to the Stamp Act.

By the turn of the twentieth century, young boys known as "newsies" could be found selling newspapers on street corners in cities across the United States.

Some American newspapers continued publishing on illegal paper after the law took effect, while others announced that they would suspend publication rather than purchase stamped paper. The day before the law took effect, William Bradford III's *Pennsylvania Journal* famously laid out its front page to look like a tombstone. No American newspapers obeyed the Stamp Act, and British lawmakers were forced to repeal it a short time later. "Such a triumph not only emboldened the newspapers to defy English authority, but also taught the political organizers and the manipulators of public opinion how useful newspapers could be to them," Frank Luther Mott wrote in his history of American journalism. "From this time forward the press was recognized as a strong arm of the Patriot movement."[4]

Colonial newspapers played an important role in shaping public opinion in the years leading up to the American Revolution. Such figures as John Adams, Samuel Adams, John Hancock, and others published politically charged essays that encouraged the colonists to rebel against English rule and fight for independence. Once the war began, newspapers helped to raise people's spirits. Thomas Paine's inspirational essay "American Crisis" first appeared in the *Pennsylvania Journal* in December 1776. "These are the times that try men's souls," Paine wrote. "Tyranny, like hell, is not easily conquered; yet we have this consolation with us, that the harder the conflict the more glorious the triumph."[5]

"We are a democracy," declared publisher Joseph Pulitzer, "and there is only one way to get a democracy on its feet in the matter of its individual, its social, its municipal, its state, its national conduct, and that is by keeping the public informed about what is going on."

In 1787, when the Founding Fathers gathered to create a Constitution for the victorious United States, they were quick to recognize the role newspapers had played in the fight for independence. The First Amendment to the Constitution guaranteed that, in America, the press would always be free to operate without government control or interference.

The Development of Modern Newspapers

Even with freedom of the press established, American newspapers suffered a decline in quality and objectivity after the war. Printing was so expensive and time-consuming that most newspapers did not earn much money. Some papers tried to attract readers by publishing sensational stories. Others were taken over by political parties or candidates and printed more propaganda than news. Still, newspapers did serve the valuable purpose of transmitting information to people in far-flung areas of the rapidly expanding United States.

The advances of the Industrial Revolution hit newspaper publishing in the 1830s. The invention of the cylinder press allowed printers to produce 1,500 newspapers per hour—a tremendous improvement over the few hundred copies per night that could be printed before. The price of newspapers dropped accordingly, from an annual subscription price of eight to ten dollars per year to just pennies per day. Combined with the movement of millions of Americans from rural areas to cities, these developments made newspapers accessible to a much larger segment of the population. Around the same time, a new generation of editors came on the scene. They emphasized news stories that held interest for the masses, such as local events, gossip, and scandals. Such changes resulted in a surge in the number of ongoing newspapers from around 1,000 in 1830 to 3,000 by 1860. About 10 percent of these papers were published daily, while the remainder appeared weekly.

Several influential modern newspapers got their starts around this time. The *New York Sun* published its first edition on September 3, 1833. Editor Benjamin H. Day explained that the *Sun,* with the motto "It Shines for All," intended "to lay before the public, at a price within the means of everyone, ALL THE NEWS OF THE DAY."[6] Within a short time the *Sun* was selling 8,000 copies per day, more than double the circulation of its nearest competitor. One historian noted that it launched "a revolution in American newspapers. The *Sun* could be bought from hawkers

William Randolph Hearst, pictured in 1904, played an important role in the development of American newspapers during the muckraking era.

on the street for a penny a copy. It stressed local news, crime reporting, and human interest; it was highly readable and full of things the readers talked to each other about.... Day created a new class of newspaper readers."[7]

The *New York Herald* published its first issue in 1835. It provided solid coverage of financial news and was also the first American paper to maintain full-time overseas news bureaus. But the *Herald* was probably most famous for the fiery editorials penned by its editor, James Gordon Bennett. Although his opinions helped increase circulation of the paper, they also incited angry readers to beat him up on many occasions. Another crusading editor was Horace Greeley, who launched the *New York Tribune* in 1841. Greeley used the pages of his paper to argue for the abolition of slavery, purer milk for children, and cleaner city streets. He influenced other newspapers to move beyond news reporting and worked to shape public opinion about the issues of the day.

Another famous New York paper was the *New York Times*. Launched in 1851, it provided readers with balanced, objective reporting of complicated news stories. During the 1870s, the paper conducted a lengthy investigation of political corruption in New York City. After combing through municipal financial records and contracts, *Times* reporters published details of how city leaders dispensed jobs and contracts in exchange for political support and bribes. Their exposure of these underhanded dealings helped put the infamous politician William "Boss" Tweed in jail.

Pulitzer and Hearst

When Joseph Pulitzer purchased the *New York World* in 1883, he promised to "expose all fraud and sham, fight all public evils and abuses [and] battle for the people with earnest sincerity."[8] Under his leadership, the *World* was the first paper to post full-time reporters in Washington, D.C., to follow the president's activities and cover news from the Capitol. Pulitzer also attracted readers with undercover reports from the daring correspondent Nellie Bly, who pretended to be insane in order to expose the terrible treatment of patients at New York City's mental hospitals.

After publisher William Randolph Hearst purchased the *New York Morning Journal* in 1892, it became known for its attention-grabbing, sensational, and often exaggerated news stories. This emphasis on shocking and scandalous news—which resembled the content of modern supermarket tabloids—became known as yellow journalism. The name came from a popular comic strip that appeared in many such newspapers, "The Yellow Kid" by Richard F. Outcault. The main character was a goofy-looking child with a bald head, big ears, a gap-toothed smile, and a yellow nightshirt. He was pictured in many situations connected with news events of the day.

The technology of newspapers continued to improve in the late 1800s. The introduction of a new printing technology called halftone reproduction allowed papers to publish clearer photographs. Many publications also increased their use of color in supplements and comic strips around this time. These changes contributed to an increase in the number of ongoing newspapers from 7,000 in 1880 to over 12,000 in 1890. Although nearly every major city in the United States was served by one or more daily newspapers, New York City remained the center of the newspaper world during this time.

The Rise of Magazines

Newspapers were not the only sources of printed information available to Americans. The first magazines appeared in the 1740s, and more than forty ongoing publications got started over the next fifty years. The nation experienced a surge in new magazine introductions during the early 1800s, including such famous titles as the *Saturday Evening Post, Godey's Lady's Book, Harper's Weekly,* and the *Atlantic Monthly.* Historians attribute the jump in magazine publishing to technological breakthroughs like the invention of the cylinder press, along with the growth of an educated, urban population with a thirst for news and entertainment. Magazines could generally present a more in-depth look at the nation's social and political life than newspapers. "American magazines were offering readers a comprehensive view of national life in the 1850s—a mirror held up to an expanding, struggling, chaotic country that was on the verge of postwar greatness."[9]

FEBRUARY, 1908   FIFTEEN CENTS

McCLURE'S MAGAZINE

Contributors to this number:
WILLIAM JAMES   GEORGE KIBBE TURNER
MAY SINCLAIR   ELLEN TERRY

McClure's, founded in 1893, was part of the new generation of general-interest monthly magazines that sold for ten cents per issue.

Improvements in printing technology, paper manufacturing, and photo reproduction contributed to an explosion of magazine publishing in the three decades following the end of the Civil War. The number of different magazines in publication in the United States grew from around 700 in 1865 to exceed 3,000 in 1885 and 5,000 by 1895. Many special-interest publications were launched during this period to represent every possible hobby and leisure activity in American life.

The end of the century saw the rise of high-quality, general-interest magazines that achieved national distribution. *Cosmopolitan* published its first issue in 1886, followed by *Collier's* in 1888, *McClure's* in 1893, and *Everybody's* in 1899. All of these monthly journals maintained a distinctive tone thanks to their editors, who took charge of hiring staff writers and selecting topics for stories. A typical issue featured in-depth, factual articles about current events, scientific discoveries, world exploration, and entertainment. These magazines also published the latest fiction and poetry by popular writers of the day, such as Robert Louis Stevenson, Rudyard Kipling, Arthur Conan Doyle, Stephen Crane, O. Henry, and Mark Twain.

This new generation of magazines expanded their influence—as well as the size of America's reading public—by charging a low price of ten cents per issue. "With *Munsey's, McClure's,* and *Cosmopolitan* selling at half the rates of the *Century, Harper's,* and *Scribner's,* the die was cast—the country was to be the empire of the low-priced, heavily illustrated, advertisement-laden, popular monthlies with their contents emphasizing youthful optimism, self-improvement, and success,"[10] one historian noted.

> *"The magazine press, and especially McClure's, [became] a forum for new questions about the nature and direction of American society and government,"* one historian noted.

The Muckrakers Arrive

The rise of high-interest national magazines coincided with Theodore Roosevelt's presidency. Roosevelt spearheaded the Progressive Movement by calling attention to the government corruption and corporate greed underlying the nation's surface prosperity. His reform efforts received a great deal of reinforcement from the work of the investigative journalists known as muckrakers. They conducted extensive research into a variety of political and social problems, then detailed their findings in compelling feature articles that appeared mainly in the popular magazines of the era. "What was new and makes the muckraking era unique," according to the Weinbergs, "is that for the first time there was a group of writers and a concentration of magazines hammering away at the ills they found in society. Neither before nor since has there been in periodical literature anything which can compare to the relentless drive for exposure."[11]

The muckrakers enjoyed a number of advantages that increased the impact of their work. First, in an era when television and the Internet had not yet been invented, their magazines were the only news source that was distributed nationally and reached wide audiences. Second, their readership included many educated, middle-class people who possessed a thirst for

Professional journalists, like the men pictured in this photo, aggressively pursued stories about the problems facing American society during the muckraking era.

knowledge and a sense of civic responsibility. "The muckrakers had a powerful effect on the middle class, arousing its concern about social ills and shabby politics," one historian explained. "Before they launched their attacks, voices of dissent and disenchantment had been heard, but the expert journalists who wrote for the ten-cent [magazines] cut through the national confusion and gave Americans a full report on what was happening to them without their knowledge or consent."[12]

Finally, the muckrakers had the guidance and support of brilliant editors and publishers who shared their concerns about the problems facing American society. Joseph Pulitzer once described the public responsibility of newspapers and magazines by saying that "We are a democracy, and there is only one way to get a democracy on its feet in the matter of its individual, its social, its municipal, its state, its national conduct, and that is by keeping the public informed about what is going on. There is not a crime, there is not a dodge, there is not a

S.S. McClure's Famous January 1903 Editorial

Many historians pinpoint the January 1903 issue of *McClure's* magazine as the start of the muckraking journalism movement. That issue featured three groundbreaking investigative reports about abuses of power and disrespect for the law in American business, government, and society. In the editorial excerpted below, publisher S.S. McClure famously calls readers' attention to the situation.

Concerning Three Articles in This Number of *McClure's*, and a Coincidence That May Set Us Thinking

How many of those who have read through this number of the magazine noticed that it contains three articles on one subject? We did not plan it so; it is a coincidence that the January *McClure's* is such an arraignment of American character as should make every one of us stop and think. How many noticed that?

The leading article, "The Shame of Minneapolis," might have been called "The American Contempt of Law." That title could well have served for the current chapter of Miss Tarbell's *History of Standard Oil*. And it would have fitted perfectly Mr. Baker's "The Right to Work." All together, these articles come pretty near showing how universal is this dangerous trait of ours.

trick, there is not a swindle, there is not a vice that does not live by secrecy. Get these things out in the open, describe them, attack them, ridicule them in the press, and sooner or later public opinion will sweep them away."[13]

The reports of the muckrakers shocked the American people and inspired them to demand change. In this way, the writers fed the fires of Roosevelt's progressive reform efforts. "They turned local issues into national issues, local protests into national crusades," one writer explained. "They didn't preach to the converted; they did the converting."[14] Of course, the magazines also benefited from the muckraking crusades, in the form of increased advertising sales and circulation. By 1906, when the muckrakers reached the height of their

Miss Tarbell has our capitalists conspiring among themselves, deliberately, shrewdly, upon legal advice, to break the law so far as it restrained them, and to misuse it to restrain others who were in their way. Mr. Baker shows labor, the ancient enemy of capital, and the chief complainant of the trusts' unlawful acts, itself committing and excusing crimes. And in "The Shame of Minneapolis," we see the administration of a city employing criminals to commit crimes for the profit of the elected officials, while the citizens—Americans of good stock and more than average culture, and honest, healthy Scandinavians—stood by complacent and not alarmed.

Capitalists, workingmen, politicians, citizens—all breaking the law, or letting it be broken. Who is left to uphold it?... There is no one left; none but all of us....

We all are doing our worst and making the public pay. The public is the people. We forget that we all are the people; that while each of us in his group can shove off on the rest the bill of today, the debt is only postponed; the rest are passing it on back to us. We have to pay in the end, every one of us. And in the end the sum total of the debt will be our liberty.

Source: Weinberg, Arthur, and Lila Weinberg, eds. *The Muckrakers*. Champaign: University of Illinois Press, 2001, p. 4.

popularity and influence, annual circulation of the top ten magazines that focused on investigative journalism totaled three million.

Although the muckrakers tackled a wide variety of topics—from unsanitary conditions in meatpacking plants to poverty in the nation's cities—their work centered around one major theme: betrayal. "America's citizens had been betrayed by those who had supposedly made the country what it was, by the men who had built the great corporations and who had made the free market a national religion," John Tebbel and Mary Ellen Zuckerman wrote in *The Magazine in America, 1741-1990*. "In this betrayal, they had been abetted and aided by politicians at every level, but particularly those in the highest positions of power. Reading these revelations, most Americans felt both shock and outrage, and as one exposé followed another, they developed a fascination for what was being told to them and were scarcely able to wait for the next revelation."[15]

McClure's Magazine Leads the Movement

Although dozens of magazines and newspapers published investigative articles in the early 1900s, *McClure's* magazine is generally credited with launching the muckraking movement. When publisher S.S. (Samuel Sidney) McClure (see McClure biography, p. 119) founded his namesake magazine in 1893, he told readers that his goal was to present "articles of timely interest" about "what is newest or most important in every department of human activity."[16]

What set *McClure's* apart from other monthly journals of the era was its stable of talented, passionate young journalists. McClure paid his writers a generous monthly salary, rather than a rate based on how many words or inches of type they produced. This policy freed the journalists to spend weeks or even years researching and writing articles. McClure expected his writers to meet high standards of factual accuracy and write in an engaging style.

From its first issue, *McClure's* offered readers in-depth articles about the most important events of the day, from international conflicts to revolutionary new inventions. The magazine distinguished itself by analyzing these events and putting them into perspective for Americans. It challenged readers to think about the nation, and its place in the world, in different ways. "The magazine press, and especially *McClure's,* [became] a forum for new questions about the nature and direction of American society and government,"[17] one historian noted. The formula proved very popular, and the magazine's circulation grew from 60,000 copies per monthly issue in 1894 to 250,000 in 1896 to over 350,000 by the turn of the century.

Many historians trace the birth of the muckraking era to the January 1903 issue of *McClure's.* In addition to the usual short stories, poems, and news articles, the issue featured three groundbreaking investigative reports that exposed serious problems in American business, government, and society. One of these reports, by correspondent Ida M. Tarbell, was part of a series on the history of the Standard Oil Company. It detailed some of the ruthless business tactics used by its owner, the phenomenally wealthy John D. Rockefeller, in building the powerful trust. Another article, by Ray Stannard Baker, reported on appalling working conditions and violent labor-management conflict in the Pennsylvania coal mining industry. In the third report, Lincoln Steffens examined rampant political corruption in the city government of Minneapolis, Minnesota.

McClure and his writers noticed that these three reports offered variations on the same theme: a general contempt for law in American society. McClure identified the theme for readers in an editorial that appeared in the January 1903 issue (see sidebar "S.S. McClure's Famous January 1903 Editorial," p. 30). And from that point forward, *McClure's* and many other magazines increasingly turned their focus toward publishing hard-hitting investigative reports on the various problems facing American society. Years later, McClure claimed that he had not intended to launch a reform-journalism movement. He said that the January 1903 issue "came from no formulated plan to attack existing institutions, but was the result of merely taking up in the magazine some of the problems that were beginning to interest the people a little before the newspapers and the other magazines took them up."[18]

Publisher S.S. McClure and his stable of talented writers made *McClure's* a leading muckraking journal.

In any case, the shocking exposés ignited calls for reform among the American people. "It was no new game to lift the rocks in twentieth-century America and watch the bugs scramble for cover, but what was new was the expertise and authority of the writing,... and the challenge accepted by Theodore Roosevelt in the White House," wrote one historian. "The country was quickly fragmenting into militant economic interest groups bent upon class warfare.... By documenting this perilous national situation, by giving it reality, drama, and human interest, the January *McClure's* was ensured a success."[19]

Notes

1 Weinberg, Arthur, and Lila Weinberg, eds. *The Muckrakers.* Champaign: University of Illinois Press, 2001, p. xxii.

[2] Quoted in Mott, Frank Luther. *American Journalism: A History 1690-1960.* New York: Macmillan, 1962, p. 9.

[3] Quoted in Mott, p. 16.

[4] Mott, p. 107.

[5] Quoted in Mott, p. 91.

[6] Quoted in Serrin, Judith, and William Serrin, eds. *Muckraking: The Journalism That Changed America.* New York: New Press, 2002, p. 307.

[7] Serrin, p. 307.

[8] Quoted in Mott, p. 434.

[9] Tebbel, John, and Mary Ellen Zuckerman. *The Magazine in America, 1741-1990.* New York: Oxford University Press, 1991, p. 13.

[10] Wilson, Harold S. *McClure's Magazine and the Muckrakers.* Princeton, NJ: Princeton University Press, 1970, p. 64.

[11] Weinberg, p. xxii.

[12] Tebbel, p 111.

[13] Quoted in Jensen, Carl. *Stories that Changed America: Muckrakers of the 20th Century.* New York: Seven Stories Press, 2000, p. 21.

[14] Dorman, Jessica. "Where Are Muckraking Journalists Today?" *Nieman Reports,* Summer 2000, p. 55.

[15] Tebbel, p. 111.

[16] Quoted in Wilson, p. 104.

[17] Wilson, p. v.

[18] McClure, Samuel Sidney, with Willa Cather. *My Autobiography.* New York: Frederick A. Stokes, 1914, p. 246.

[19] Wilson, p. 146.

Chapter Three

ADDRESSING
SOCIAL PROBLEMS

⚊⚊⚋⚋⚋⚊⚊

The journalist is a true servant of democracy. The best journalist of today occupies the exact place of the prophets of
old: he cries out the truth and calls for reform.

—Ray Stannard Baker, 1906

Although investigative journalism existed before the turn of the twentieth century, the rise of mass-circulation, general-interest magazines
brought it to the forefront of American life at that time. Muckraking
turned into a movement that promoted progressive reform of a wide range of
social, political, and economic institutions. Investigative reports helped raise
public awareness of problems like poverty and squalor in the nation's rapidly
growing cities, the struggles of newly arrived immigrants, and the exploitation of child labor. The work of the muckrakers also helped create a climate
favorable to recognizing and addressing other social issues, like women's
rights, racial equality, and environmental protection. "It didn't take great
insight to recognize that poverty, vice, electoral fraud, unsafe foods, monopolistic practices, segregation, child labor exploitation, and civil rights viola-
tions were leading to the disintegration of society," noted one historian. "But
it did take some courageous individuals who saw the problems to dedicate
their lives and talents to solving them."[1]

Poverty and Squalor in the Cities

The rapid industrialization of the late nineteenth century led to explosive
growth in the population of American cities. The availability of work in facto-

ries convinced millions of people to move from rural to urban areas. Poor whites left hardscrabble farms behind in search of better lives in big cities like New York, Chicago, Philadelphia, and Detroit. In addition, millions of African Americans migrated to these northern regions from the South, where their opportunities were strictly limited by the discriminatory system of laws and unwritten rules of conduct known as Jim Crow. "As long as Jim Crow ruled the South, that system of segregation, subordination, and terror created powerful incentives for leaving and staying away,"[2] one historian acknowledged.

Meanwhile, twelve million immigrants arrived on American shores between 1870 and 1900. While some immigrants headed inland from the major port cities to establish farms on the frontier, millions of others joined the competition for jobs and housing in already overcrowded urban areas. "Once settled, immigrants looked for work. There were never enough jobs, and employers often took advantage of the immigrants," noted one study. "Men were generally paid less than other workers, and women less than men. Social tensions were also part of the immigrant experience. Often stereotyped and discriminated against, many immigrants suffered verbal and physical abuse because they were 'different.'"[3] To minimize the hardships of adapting to a new land, many immigrants settled in ethnic enclaves with others who spoke the same language and followed the same customs (see sidebar "Anti-Immigrant Sentiments in America," p. 41).

Between migration and immigration, most American cities grew very rapidly. In fact, the percentage of Americans who lived in the nation's sixty largest cities increased from 37 percent in 1900 to 50 percent by 1930. In many cases, such rapid expansion outstripped the availability of jobs, housing, waste disposal, and other services. As a result, poor and working-class urban residents often lived in overcrowded and unsanitary conditions. The concentrated industrial facilities and overtaxed municipal sewage systems dumped pollution into the air and water, contributing to the spread of cholera and other deadly diseases. "A single blast furnace, a single dye works may easily have its effluvia absorbed by the surrounding landscape: twenty of them in a narrow area effectively pollute the air or water beyond remedy,"[4] one scholar noted.

Some of the worst living conditions were found in the tenement houses. Owned and operated by greedy landlords with political connections, these filthy, airless buildings were packed to the rafters with poor and working-

Cleaning up crowded and unsanitary tenement districts, like Mulberry Street in New York City, was a high priority for social reformers.

class people. In many cases, more than a dozen members of an extended family would share a single room. They rarely had electricity or indoor plumbing, and they usually relied on coal-fired furnaces or fireplaces for heat. Factory workers received such low wages—and the landlords of nicer facilities charged such high rents—that the tenements were the only option available for many poor families. They could not afford to find cleaner, safer accommodations within the city or to move out to the comfortable, middle-class suburbs. The miserable living conditions in the tenements provided an ideal environment for criminal activity, excessive alcohol consumption, and the spread of disease.

Several prominent muckraking journalists addressed the problems of poverty and squalor in their work. One of the best-known writers to investigate the problems facing poor and working-class residents of American cities was Jacob Riis (see Riis biography, p. 128). Riis had arrived in the United States in 1870 as an immigrant from Denmark. He eventually got a job as a police reporter for the *New York Tribune*. His job frequently took him into the tenement districts on the Lower East Side of Manhattan in New York City. Riis wandered through the slums for years, recording his observations in a notebook and taking photographs of the residents and their surroundings. In 1890 he published the results of his work in a powerful book called *How the Other Half Lives* (see "Jacob Riis Chronicles the Struggles of the Urban Poor," p. 165).

> *"They gave up all thought of joyful living, probably in the hope that by tremendous exertion they could overcome their poverty; but they gained while at work only enough to keep their bodies alive,"* sociologist Robert Hunter wrote in Poverty (1904). *"Theirs was a sort of treadmill existence with no prospect of anything else in life but more treadmill."*

Riis's investigation found 37,000 tenement buildings in New York City housing over one million residents. Thanks to inconsistent employment, low wages, and high rents, many of these people lived in terrible poverty and faced the threat of starvation. Riis was disgusted by the dirty, overcrowded conditions he saw in the tenements. He recognized that people forced to live in such conditions often became so desperate that they resorted to begging and crime in order to survive. "In the tenements all the influences make for evil," he wrote, "because they are the hot-beds of the epidemics that carry death to rich and poor alike; the nurseries of pauperism and crime that fill our jails and police courts; that throw off a scum of 40,000 human wrecks to the island asylums and workhouses year by year; that turned out in the last eight years a round half million beggars to prey upon our charities; that maintain a standing army of 10,000 tramps with all that that implies; because, above all, they touch the family life with deadly moral contagion."[5]

Riis's book forced middle-class Americans and government officials to confront the problems facing people in the nation's urban slums. His exposé of New York City tenements led to the establishment of the Tenement House Commission to improve the design of urban housing and provide safe and sanitary living conditions for the poor. "Tenement-house reform holds the key to the problem of pauperism in the city," he declared. "We can never get rid of either the tenement or the pauper. The two will always exist together in

This famous photograph by Jacob Riis shows poor immigrant children sleeping on a city street.

New York. But by reforming the one, we can do more toward exterminating the other than can be done by all other means together that have yet been invented, or ever will be."[6] Riis also helped to build playgrounds and improve public schools in the cities.

Riis's work, which is frequently cited as one of the earliest examples of muckraking journalism, inspired many other reformers to address the problems faced by the urban poor. Some of the most effective assistance for poor immigrants came from the settlement house movement. Reformer Jane Addams founded one of the first settlement houses, Hull House, in Chicago in 1889. It offered a variety of services to help immigrant families adjust to life in the United States, including English-language instruction, citizenship guidance, an employment bureau, recreational activities, and day care for working mothers. By 1910 Hull House had become the model for a network of 500 settlement houses in the nation's largest cities. These facilities fought to improve living conditions for working-class families by passing new health and safety codes for tenements, modernizing sanitation and sewage systems, offering libraries and social programs, and providing welfare benefits for widows and orphans.

Sociologist Robert Hunter worked closely with settlement houses and charities in the tenement districts of both Chicago and New York City. In 1904 he published an influential book called *Poverty* that offered middle-class Americans a detailed description of the plight of the nation's urban poor. Hunter pointed out that the low wages and difficult jobs available to working-class people ensured that most of them would never rise above a minimal level of existence. "The wages were so low that the men alone often could not support their families, and mothers with babies toiled in order to add to the income," he wrote. "They gave up all thought of joyful living, probably in the hope that by tremendous exertion they could overcome their poverty; but they gained while at work only enough to keep their bodies alive. Theirs was a sort of treadmill existence with no prospect of anything else in life but more treadmill."[7]

Child Labor

A related social issue that the muckrakers addressed was child labor. Many poor families had no choice but to send all members out in search of employment. Around the turn of the century, many factories, textile mills, and coal mines relied on child labor for their operations. Children were cheaper to hire and easier to discipline or fire than adult workers, and their small stature proved valuable in industries like mining, where workers often had to fit into tight spaces.

Although children had worked to help their families in the past—farm children helped harvest crops, for instance, while children of merchants helped stock shelves—industrial jobs proved to be far more difficult and dangerous for young workers. "Children have always worked, but it is only since the reign of the machine that their work has been synonymous with slavery," declared muckraking journalist John Spargo in his 1906 book *The Bitter Cry of the Children*. "The craftsman was supplanted by the tireless, soulless machine. The child still worked, but in a great factory throbbing with the

Anti-Immigrant Sentiments in America

Millions of immigrants to America settled in communities that welcomed them with open arms. Once they passed through Ellis Island and other gateways into the United States, immigrants frequently made their way to neighborhoods and towns with similar ethnic and cultural ties to the ones they left behind. Italian immigrants settled in New York City's "Italian" district, Swedish immigrants traveled to the Swedish-American farming communities of Minnesota, and so on.

Immigrants chose these destinations not only out of considerations of familiarity and comfort, but also because many Americans disliked and distrusted the new arrivals. This hostility was displayed by both native-born Americans and immigrants who had already found homes and jobs in the New World. Such cold attitudes toward new immigrants had many sources. Some people opposed the presence of the newcomers because they felt that the wave of immigration was overwhelming America's land and other natural resources. Others worried—in some cases for good reason—that the new immigrants posed a threat to their jobs or wages. And still others feared that the influx of newcomers, with their unfamiliar languages, cultural practices, and appearance, might ruin the stability and safety of the communities in which they lived.

Vicious racial and ethnic prejudice, though, was at the root of much anti-immigrant sentiment. Many critics of immigration in the late nineteenth and early twentieth centuries viewed newcomers from southern and eastern Europe as lazy, stupid, and immoral people. These opponents of immigration saw the people streaming through Ellis Island as a disease that threatened the health of America's political, economic, and social systems, and they treated the newcomers accordingly.

Sources:

Handlin, Oscar. *The Uprooted.* 1951. Reprint. Philadelphia: University of Pennsylvania Press, 2002.

Tichenor, Daniel J. *Dividing Lines: The Politics of Immigration Control in America.* Princeton, NJ: Princeton University Press, 2002.

This 1909 photograph by Lewis Hine documents the use of child labor in a Georgia textile mill.

vibration of swift, intricate machines. In place of parental interest and affection there was the harsh, pitiless authority of an employer ... looking not to the child's well-being and skill as an artificer, but to the supplying of a great, ever-widening market for cash gain."[8]

Spargo's book *The Bitter Cry of the Children* was one of several works that condemned child labor during the muckraking era (see "John Spargo Describes the Tragedy of Child Labor," p. 170). The author came to the United States from England in 1901. England had recently instituted reforms to address the exploitation of children in its cities and industries. Spargo was shocked to find that similar conditions existed in his new home. In conducting a study of factories and other industrial facilities, he found children as young as four years old working in New York City canneries, and as young as five working in cotton mills in the South.

Spargo found it difficult to compile accurate statistics on the use of child labor in America. Many children, as well as their parents, lied about their ages because their families were so desperate for additional income. Still, he estimated that in New York alone, 76,000 children under the age of fifteen missed the entire year of school in 1900. "It is impossible for any one who is at all conversant with the facts to resist the conclusion that, after making all possible allowances for other causes, by far the larger part of these absentees are at work," he wrote. "Thousands find employment in factories and stores; others find employment in some of the many street trades, selling newspapers, peddling, running errands for small storekeepers, and the like."[9]

Some of the muckrakers evoked sympathy and outrage in readers by describing the terrible conditions faced by children working in industrial facilities. These boys and girls often performed repetitive tasks in hot, noisy factories full of dangerous machines for ten to twelve hours per day. Investigative journalist Edwin Markham detailed the grim existence of the 50,000 children who worked in the textile mills of the South in the September 1906 edition of *Cosmopolitan*. "Think of the deadly drudgery in these cotton mills," he wrote. "Children rise at half-past four, commanded by the ogre scream of the factory whistle; they hurry, ill fed, unkempt, unwashed, half dressed, to the walls which shut out the day and which confine them amid the din and dust and merciless maze of the machines. Here, penned in little narrow lanes, they look and leap and reach and tie among acres and acres of looms. Always the snow of lint in their faces, always the thunder of machines in their ears."[10]

The work of Spargo, Markham, and other writers helped bring the issue of child labor to the attention of middle-class Americans and government policymakers. In 1907 the National Child Labor Committee (NCLC) was chartered by an act of Congress. The organization hired anthropologist and

> *"Think of the deadly drudgery in these cotton mills," wrote Edwin Markham. "Children rise at half-past four, commanded by the ogre scream of the factory whistle; they hurry, ill fed, unkempt, unwashed, half dressed, to the walls which shut out the day and which confine them amid the din and dust and merciless maze of the machines."*

Women fought for a number of progressive reforms, including the right to vote.

photographer Lewis Hine to further document the plight of impoverished children in the nation's cities. His work generated support for the passage of numerous state laws restricting the use of child labor and promoting compulsory education. National pressure from the NCLC eventually led to federal legislation banning most forms of child labor.

Women's Issues

The social problems targeted by the muckrakers held particular interest for many women. Moved to take action by the articles they read in *McClure's* and other magazines, middle-class women joined the progressive reform movement in large numbers in the early 1900s. Since few middle-class women worked outside the home in those days, they were able to dedicate their time and talents to various issues that affected families less fortunate than their own. Some women reformers helped the poor by working with churches or charities. Others campaigned to end child labor or to improve housing, sanitation, and educational opportunities in urban areas. Still others launched some of the first U.S. campaigns to abolish prostitution and pornography or promote family planning through sex education and birth control. In 1899 activist Florence Kelley founded the National Consumers' League, an organization which fought to pass food safety laws and to end the exploitation of female workers.

One of the main muckraking journalists to tackle women's issues was Rheta Childe Dorr. Born in Nebraska in 1863, Dorr made her way to New York City with the goal of becoming a writer. She experienced gender and pay discrimination in a series of jobs with newspapers and magazines. For instance, Dorr went undercover to investigate working conditions for women in a variety of industrial and retail jobs, only to have *Everybody's* magazine publish her exposé under the byline of a male colleague. In 1910 Dorr published an influential book about the growing movement for women's rights called *What Eight Million Women Want*. She went on to become a war correspondent and a prominent supporter of women's suffrage.

Many activists understood that gaining the right to vote, or suffrage, was key in bringing women's issues to the forefront. The women's suffrage movement had actually started before the Civil War. It got new life during the Progressive Era, however, thanks to the efforts of women reformers. A number of male political leaders, including Theodore Roosevelt, came to believe that granting women the right to vote would make it easier to pass progressive legislation. By 1910 seven western states had extended voting rights to women. The women's suffrage movement became increasingly militant during the 1910s. Using confrontational protest methods like picket lines and hunger strikes, the activists finally won the long battle. American women gained the right to vote in 1920, with the passage of the Nineteenth Amendment to the Constitution.

Women activists also played a leading role in the Progressive Era campaign against excessive alcohol consumption. Some reformers believed that the abuse of alcohol contributed to the social problems that affected American families, especially the poverty, crime, and immorality they saw in large cities. Some argued for moderation or temperance, while others fought for an outright ban on or prohibition of the use of alcohol. "If cities were choking in

Progressive reformers worked to conserve America's natural resources, which were increasingly used to fuel industrial growth.

industrial smoke and shameful immorality, if strange new peoples and alien languages and political philosophies cast an eerie cloud over traditional America, there had to be reasons," one historian explained. "If economic misery strangled the nation, if families split apart, if crime increased and suicides were on the rise, there had to be answers. For many the greatest of the reasons was liquor; the most urgent of the answers was to wipe it out."[11]

Groups like the Women's Christian Temperance Union helped make prohibition a topic of spirited debate in the early 1900s. Although many politicians approached the issue carefully, it gradually gained support during the Progressive Era. Several states passed laws against alcohol during the 1910s, and in 1920 the Eighteenth Amendment to the Constitution banned the manufacture, distribution, or sale of alcohol throughout the United States. Prohibition proved to be nearly impossible to enforce, however, and alcohol remained widely available. Generally recognized as a failure, Prohibition was repealed in 1933 with the passage of the Twenty-First Amendment to the Constitution.

Environmental Protection

Another social issue that drew the attention of the muckrakers and progressive reformers was the environment. Industrialization had led to a significant increase in the consumption of—and transfer of control over—America's natural resources. As part of their investigations of the power and influence of big corporations and trusts, the muckrakers revealed that banks, mining companies, railroads, logging companies, and other business interests had gained control of huge swaths of public land.

These muckraking reports prompted increased public questioning of government policies that "had always been to open up the country for private development as rapidly as possible," said one environmental historian. "The developers, ranchers, mining and lumber interests, mostly in the West, saw no reason to alter things."[12] But conservation-minded Americans seized on the work of the muckrakers to press for new environmental protection laws.

The burgeoning conservation movement found a sympathetic ear in Roosevelt. "The idea that our natural resources were inexhaustible still obtained [when I took office], and there was as yet no real knowledge of their extent and condition," he recalled in his autobiography. "The relation of the conservation of natural resources to the problems of National welfare and National efficiency had not yet dawned on the public mind."[13] But as activists and muckrakers stirred up public support for conservation, Roosevelt took action to protect remaining wilderness areas from logging, mining, and development. As president, he added 50 million acres to the national forest system and established 51 wildlife refuges, 18 national monuments, and 5 national parks.

Racial Equality

Progressive reformers and their muckraking allies in the press made progress in addressing such pressing social problems as poverty, squalor, child labor, and women's rights. They were considerably less successful, however, in dealing with the issue of racial equality. "Progressives showed little fear in dealing with problems of gender, family, class, and economy—but not of race,"[14] one scholar acknowledged. At the turn of the century, African Americans in the South lived under Jim Crow laws that kept them segregated from whites. They were denied access to many public facilities, like restaurants, theaters, hotels, and swimming pools. They were forced to sit in the back of railroad cars and attend inferior schools.

Black citizens who did not obey the rules, or failed to show sufficient humility and respect in their dealings with whites, faced a constant threat of violence. Lynching (hanging of African Americans by gangs of whites) was a common tactic used to intimidate African Americans and keep them in what was said by some to be "their place." Blacks who migrated to northern cities found conditions somewhat better, although they still had fewer educational and employment opportunities than whites and endured ugly discrimination on a daily basis.

African-American activists, such as Ida B. Wells, fought to enlist the support of the muckrakers and other progressive reformers in bringing an end to racial segregation and violence. The middle-class whites who led the charge for progressive reform recognized the need to address racial tension and violence against blacks. But few went so far as to promote true social and legal equality for African Americans. A notable exception was Ray Stannard Baker (see Baker biography, p. 115), whose 1908 book *Following the Color Line: An Account of Negro Citizenship in the American Democracy* explored racial prejudice in the United States. "The white man is in undisputed power in this country," he wrote. "The Negro ... is like a child in the house of a harsh parent. All that stands between him and destruction is the ethical sense of the white man. Will the white man's senses of justice and virtue be robust enough to cause him to withhold the hand of unlimited power? Will he see, as Booker T. Washington says, that if he keeps the Negro in the gutter he must stay there with him?"[15]

Many progressive lawmakers felt reluctant to push for African-American civil rights. They needed the support of Southern lawmakers in order to pass progressive reforms, and they knew that most of these officials favored segregation. Black leaders of the era resented such attitudes and argued that the treatment of African Americans as second-class citizens conflicted with basic American values. Many historians view the timid approach to racial issues as one of the major failures of the Progressive Era.

Notes

1 Jensen, Carl, ed. *Stories That Changed America: Muckrakers of the 20th Century.* New York: Seven Stories Press, 2000, p. 15.

2 Gregory, James N. *The Southern Diaspora: How the Great Migrations of Black and White Southern-ers Transformed America.* Chapel Hill: University of North Carolina Press, 2007, p. 23.

3 Library of Congress. "Rise of Industrial America: Immigration to the United States, 1851-1900." Available online at http://www.loc.gov/teachers/classroommaterials/presentationsandactivities /presentations/timeline/riseind/immgnts/immgrnts.html.

4 Mumford, Lewis, and Bryan S. Turner. *The Culture of Cities.* New York: Routledge, 1997, p. 162.

5 Riis, Jacob. *How the Other Half Lives.* New York: Scribner's, 1890, p. 3.

6 Quoted in Shapiro, Bruce, ed. *Shaking the Foundations: 200 Years of Investigative Journalism in America.* New York: Thunder's Mouth Press/Nation Books, 2003, p. 58.

7 Hunter, Robert. *Poverty.* New York: Macmillan, 1904, p. 325.

8 Spargo, John. *The Bitter Cry of the Children.* New York: Macmillan, 1906, p. 129.

9 Spargo, p. 145.

10 Markham, Edwin. "The Hoe-Man in the Making." *Cosmopolitan,* September 1906.

11 Bruns, Roger A. *Preacher: Billy Sunday and Big-Time American Evangelism.* New York: W.W. Nor-ton, 1992, p. 161.

12 Tebbel, John, and Mary Ellen Zuckerman. *The Magazine in America, 1741-1990.* New York: Oxford University Press, 1991, p. 118.

13 Roosevelt, Theodore. *Theodore Roosevelt: An Autobiography.* New York: Macmillan, 1913, p. 410.

14 McGerr, Michael. *A Fierce Discontent: The Rise and Fall of the Progressive Movement in America.* New York: Oxford University Press, 2005, p. 6.

15 Baker, Ray Stannard. *Following the Color Line: An Account of Negro Citizenship in the American Democracy.* New York: Doubleday, 1908, p. 299.

Chapter Four

BATTLING THE TITANS OF INDUSTRY

—————

Murder it was that went on there upon the killing-floor, systematic, deliberate and hideous murder. They were slaughtering men there, just as certainly as they were slaughtering cattle; they were grinding the bodies and souls of them, and turning them into dollars and cents.

—Upton Sinclair, *The Jungle*

One of the main goals of the Progressive Movement was to reduce the power and influence of large corporations over workers, political leaders, and other aspects of American society. The muckrakers helped by exposing some of the unfair business practices used by the large corporations or "trusts" that dominated most industries at that time. Journalists chronicled the ways in which these industrial giants exploited workers by demanding long hours and exhausting labor in hazardous conditions in exchange for low wages and dehumanizing treatment. They also detailed many cases in which big business took advantage of American consumers by selling products that were spoiled, dangerous, or did not deliver on their promised benefits. Muckraking articles and books about abuses of public trust by large corporations generated outrage among both middle-class and working-class Americans. They responded by pressuring state and federal governments to step in to limit the power of big business and protect the interests of small businesses, workers, and consumers.

Investigating the Trusts

The turn of the twentieth century saw a tremendous consolidation of American business in the hands of a few wealthy men. Most industries were dominated by a few large corporations. The U.S. Steel Corporation, for instance, controlled 80 percent of all steel production nationwide, while the Standard Oil Company controlled 90 percent of U.S. oil production. These companies grew into huge monopolies by acquiring smaller competitors or forcing them out of business. In the late 1890s and early 1900s, for example, more than 4,000 independent companies were consolidated into about 250 large corporations or trusts. The corporations then used their tremendous power and influence to negotiate favorable contracts with other businesses, command high prices for their products, demand concessions from their workers, derail proposed government regulations, and build huge fortunes for their owners.

> *"Muckraking was what people wanted to hear," wrote columnist Walter Lippmann. "There is no other way of explaining the quick approval which the muckrakers won.... There must have been real causes for dissatisfaction, or the land notorious for its worship of success would not have turned so savagely upon those who had achieved it."*

Several prominent muckraking journalists went behind the scenes to investigate the business practices of the trusts. They pored through financial records and legal documents, spoke with employees and competitors, and prowled the factories and railroad yards they owned. Their investigations uncovered countless examples of underhanded deals and secret alliances among the large corporations. The exposés angered middle-class Americans and transformed wealthy industrial magnates like J.P. Morgan, John D. Rockefeller, Cornelius Vanderbilt, and Andrew Carnegie into enormously controversial figures. In some parts of America, in fact, these captains of industry became known as "robber barons" for their ruthless business tactics and willingness to exploit workers and consumers for personal gain. "Muckraking was what people wanted to hear," wrote influential columnist Walter Lippmann in 1914. "There is no other way of explaining the quick approval which the muckrakers won. They weren't voices crying in a wilderness, or lonely prophets who were stoned. They demanded a hearing; it was granted. They asked for belief; they were believed. They cried that something should be done and there was every appearance of action. There must have been real causes for dissatisfaction, or the land notorious for its worship of success would not have turned so savagely upon those who had achieved it."[1]

One of the earliest and most famous muckraking attacks on the trusts was journalist Ida M. Tarbell's groundbreaking investigation of the Standard

Oil Company (see Tarbell biography, p. 152). This company was so big and powerful—and its reach extended into so many different areas of business—that it was known as "The Octopus." Tarbell started working on a history of the massive company owned by John D. Rockefeller (see Rockefeller biography, p. 132) in 1901, around the time that Theodore Roosevelt took office as president of the United States. She spent a year gathering information, tracking down leads, and reviewing documents. The first story in the series, "The Birth of an Industry," appeared in *McClure's* magazine in November 1902, and eight more installments followed.

Muckraking journalist Ida M. Tarbell, pictured in 1905, is best known for exposing the ruthless business practices of John D. Rockefeller's Standard Oil Company.

Tarbell told readers how Rockefeller had gotten started in the oil business in Pennsylvania in 1863, shortly after oil was first discovered there. From there, she chronicled how Rockefeller formed Standard Oil in 1870 and then used every possible means to expand its power and influence. The company secretly negotiated favorable prices from the railroads, for instance, which allowed it to reduce its shipping costs far below its competitors. This advantage made it impossible for smaller businesses to compete, which allowed Rockefeller to pressure them to sell their operations to him at less than their true value. Tarbell also charged that Standard Oil officials had resorted to bribery, threats, and even sabotage to cover up these shady dealings.

Tarbell made her case against Standard Oil patiently and systematically. She was careful to criticize the business practices employed by Standard Oil, rather than the size and power of the company. "I was willing that they should combine and grow as big and rich as they could, but only by legitimate means,"[2] she explained.

Tarbell's series for *McClure's* proved so fascinating to readers that circulation of the magazine increased by 100,000 copies during its run. She continued the story in a second series of articles that appeared in *McClure's* between December 1903 and October 1904. Tarbell eventually published her work in

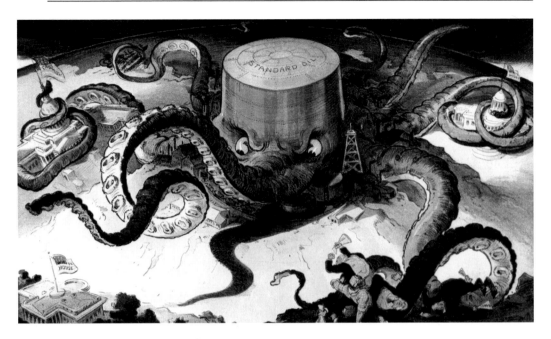

This political cartoon depicts the Standard Oil Company as an octopus, with its tentacles wrapped around various industries and branches of the U.S. government.

book form as *The History of the Standard Oil Company* (see "Ida Tarbell Investigates the Standard Oil Trust," p. 173). Throughout the publication of these reports, Rockefeller and other Standard Oil Company officials never challenged the accuracy of Tarbell's work. Rockefeller generally followed a policy of not responding to critics. But historians also note that Tarbell had convincing evidence to back up most of her claims.

At any rate, Tarbell's revelations helped shift public opinion squarely against Rockefeller. He turned into a symbol of ruthlessness and greed in the minds of many Americans. Rockefeller and his defenders thought that the attacks were unfair. Supporters claimed that he was simply an extraordinary businessman, and they pointed out that he gave millions of dollars to charity. Still, it took decades for his image to recover from the damage inflicted by the muckrakers.

Uncovering the Exploitation of Workers

Most of the large corporations that dominated American industries took advantage of their economic power and political influence to treat their workers poorly. The wealthy owners of mining operations, steel mills, textile factories, slaughterhouses, and other industrial facilities believed that they had the right to run their businesses as they pleased. Their main goal was to earn profits, and their relentless pursuit of this goal often led them to exploit workers.

Even as the owners of large corporations amassed great personal wealth, they barely paid subsistence wages to the workers in their mills and factories. The average annual salary for workers in manufacturing industries was only $435 in 1900, and some workers earned considerably less. The average salary for coal miners was only $340 per year, for instance, while farmhands received an average of $180 per year plus room and board.

To make matters worse, many industrial jobs were exhausting, requiring workers to perform repetitive tasks for hours on end without breaks. Many jobs were outright dangerous. Mine workers faced a constant threat of explosions or cave-ins, for example, while thousands of factory workers were killed or injured by machines each year. In addition, many workers in the nation's paper and steel mills, slaughterhouses, and mining operations were exposed to hazardous levels of toxic chemicals, fumes, or dust. This exposure contributed to numerous health problems, including asthma and tuberculosis (see sidebar "Alice Hamilton, Occupational Health Pioneer," p. 56). Most employers did little to protect workers from such hazards or to compensate them if they became unable to work.

Working-class Americans had very little power to resist or change this situation. Anyone who complained about long hours or dangerous working conditions—or tried to organize fellow workers in protest—ran a high risk of being fired. Since most working-class people depended on their meager income to support their families, they could not afford to jeopardize their jobs. In addition, workers in many industries were forced to live in "company towns" where all the homes, shops, schools, and other facilities were owned by their employer. Workers in these situations risked losing their homes as well as their jobs if they voiced any objections. As a result, many turn-of-the-century workers simply accepted long hours, low wages, and difficult working conditions as a fact of life.

Other workers, however, rebelled against these conditions. Workers in some industries organized labor unions to bargain with employers for higher wages, shorter hours, safer work environments, and other benefits. A few unions made progress in improving working conditions for their members. For the most part, though, American workers remained at the mercy of the

Alice Hamilton, Occupational Health Pioneer

Industrial workers in turn-of-the-century America spent long hours toiling in hot, dirty, noisy factories for low wages. Yet these hardships were often not the worst that they endured. Millions of workers in the nation's mines, mills, and factories were exposed to dangerous levels of toxic chemicals, fumes, or dust on the job. Many of them suffered from chronic illnesses or deadly diseases as a result. Most employers made no effort to educate workers about the health hazards they faced or to compensate them if they became disabled. Occupational health and safety thus became a big issue for progressive reformers.

One of the pioneers of this field of study was Alice Hamilton. Born in 1869, Hamilton received a medical degree from the University of Michigan in 1893. Following postgraduate study in Germany and at Johns Hopkins University, she became a professor of pathology at the Women's Medical School of Northwestern University in 1897. During her time in Chicago, she became acquainted with Hull House, a settlement house dedicated to improving the lives of the urban poor. Hamilton eventually opened a well-baby clinic for poor families in the neighborhood. Her work brought her into contact with countless immigrants and other working-class parents who were suffering from pains, tremors, and illnesses triggered by workplace conditions. She also learned of the sudden or unexplained deaths of dozens of industrial workers.

Hamilton realized that little was known or understood about these problems, and she grew determined to apply her medical knowledge to the new field of occupational health. In 1908 she was appointed as the managing director of the Illinois Commission on Occupational Diseases, a state organization charged with investigating industrial poisoning from

big corporations. In the absence of laws protecting organized labor, mine and factory owners could simply fire any employees who attempted to form a union. If workers arranged a work stoppage or strike, a company could hire replacement workers. In some cases, businesses resorted to intimidation and violence to suppress union activities.

lead and other materials. In this role, Hamilton conducted an extensive survey on industrial illnesses and their social consequences. She inspected factories, spoke with workers and their families, examined hospital records, and performed laboratory research. She issued a series of ground-breaking reports showing that the majority of industrial workers in the state faced life-threatening hazards on the job.

Hamilton's work connected a number of common diseases with specific occupations. She found that steelworkers often suffered from carbon monoxide poisoning, for instance, while workers in hat-making facilities faced high rates of mercury poisoning. She also identified many kinds of repetitive stress injuries among industrial workers, such as "dead fingers" syndrome among workers who used jackhammers. Illinois legislators found Hamilton's report so persuasive that they passed sweeping reforms that set occupational safety standards and improved the health of workers.

Hamilton continued her work on a national scale as a special investigator for the U.S. Bureau of Labor from 1911 to 1919. She then accepted a position as Assistant Professor of Industrial Medicine at the Harvard Medical School, becoming the first woman to join the faculty of that prestigious institution. In 1925 she published the first American textbook on the subject of industrial toxicology, *Industrial Poisons in the United States*. Following her retirement from Harvard in 1935, Hamilton became a consultant to the U.S. Division of Labor Standards and served as the president of the National Consumers League. She published her autobiography, *Exploring the Dangerous Trades*, in 1943.

Hamilton died in 1970 at the age of 101. The U.S. Centers for Disease Control (CDC) named a laboratory after her in Cincinnati, Ohio. Research in the field she pioneered continues in the twenty-first century through the CDC's National Institute for Occupational Safety and Health.

Although the labor unions shared many goals with the larger progressive movement, many Americans considered them to be too radical. They worried that union leaders wanted to overthrow America's system of capitalism and replace it with socialism. The main idea behind socialism—collective ownership of businesses and other property—appealed to some supporters of the working class, but most middle-class Americans still believed in the capitalist system of private property and free enterprise. Therefore, most progressive reformers wanted to use the power of the U.S. government to end the exploitation of workers by large corporations. They favored establishing new regulations at the city, state, and federal levels to limit the power of the trusts and improve conditions for workers. The muckrakers helped increase public demand for such regulations and put pressure on political leaders to take action.

Creating Sympathy for the Working Class

A number of muckrakers chronicled the poor working conditions and unfair labor practices endured by industrial workers. One famous article, "Old Age at Forty" by John A. Fitch, appeared in the March 1911 issue of *American Magazine*. Fitch investigated working conditions at steel mills and discovered that most workers were required to put in twelve-hour shifts each day. At the end of each week, when the day and night shifts switched places, one group of workers was forced to remain on the job for twenty-four hours straight. Fitch found that working such long hours in physically demanding jobs took a huge toll on the steelworkers, their families, and the community.

Although many other industries had instituted an eight-hour workday by this time, Fitch argued that the big steel operations "have inaugurated labor policies that are undemocratic and destructive. They have taken more and more of the day from their workmen; they have demanded more and more of their strength; they have taken from them individual freedom; they have robbed the home of a father's time and care, and from the citizenship of the mill towns they have sapped the virility and aggressiveness necessary to democracy."[3]

While Fitch and other writers raised awareness of poor industrial working conditions, several incidents occurred that brought national attention to the issue. In May 1911 a deadly fire broke out in a New York City textile mill owned by the Triangle Company. The facility produced a type of tailored women's blouse called a shirtwaist. Hundreds of young women, most of them immigrants, toiled there in sweatshop conditions. Factory managers routinely locked the doors to prevent the workers from leaving during their shift or stealing material. When the factory caught on fire, many employees were trapped inside. In all, the tragedy took the lives of 146 young women.

Reporter William G. Shepherd of United Press was on the scene and watched dozens of workers jump to their death from the factory windows rather than die in the inferno. He described the horrific scene to his editors over the telephone: "The floods of water from the firemen's hose that ran into the gutter were actually stained red with blood. I looked upon the heap of dead bodies and I remembered that these girls were the shirtwaist makers. I remembered their great strike of last year in which these same girls had demanded more sanitary conditions and more safety precautions in the shops. These dead bodies were the answer."[4] In the wake of the tragedy, the State of New York passed several new laws that reduced work hours for women and improved workplace safety conditions.

This cover of *Frank Leslie's Illustrated Weekly* depicts a violent confrontation between striking workers and corporate security guards outside a steel mill owned by Andrew Carnegie.

Another shocking incident occurred in April 1914 in Ludlow, Colorado. Ludlow was the home of miners who worked for the Colorado Fuel and Iron Company, owned by John D. Rockefeller. The miners went on strike to protest the long hours, low wages, and poor working conditions they received from the company. Following a series of minor confrontations, Colorado National Guard troops under the direction of company management attacked a tent city full of striking miners and their families. Twenty people were killed in the mining camp, including two women and eleven children. This violent incident, which became known as the Ludlow Massacre, drew renewed public attention to labor-management issues and generated political support for such reforms as a national eight-hour workday and a ban on child labor.

Raising Concerns about Food Safety

Freelance writer Upton Sinclair (see Sinclair biography, p. 142) set out to expose the hardships endured by workers in the meatpacking industry. As it turned out, though, middle-class Americans were even more appalled by his descriptions of the disgusting, unsanitary conditions in which meat was processed. His work created a tremendous public outcry that led directly to the passage of federal laws aimed at improving food safety.

> *"There was never the least attention paid to what was cut up for sausage,"* Upton Sinclair wrote in **The Jungle**. *"There would be meat stored in great piles in rooms; and the water from leaky roofs would drip over it, and thousands of rats would race about on it."*

In 1904 Sinclair received an assignment to investigate slaughterhouse operations in Chicago and write a series of muckraking articles for a magazine called *Appeal to Reason*. Chicago was the center of the nation's meat production at that time. Trainloads of cattle, pigs, and sheep from farms and ranches across the Midwest arrived in the city's rail yards each day. A continuous stream of livestock was herded into slaughterhouses and meatpacking facilities owned by three powerful corporations: Armour, Swift, and Morris.

Once inside, the animals were killed and processed by an assembly line of workers. Each worker performed a single, repetitive task in the process of turning live animals into saleable cuts of meat. The workers were known by descriptive titles—such as knockers, stickers, skinners, boners, trimmers, and luggers—based on the jobs they did over and over, day after day.

Sinclair conducted an undercover investigation over the course of seven weeks. Dressed in shabby work clothes and carrying a lunchbox, he slipped into Chicago meatpacking plants unnoticed. By pretending to be a worker, he was able to observe the meatpacking operations firsthand. Sinclair even lived at a settlement house in the nearby tenement district known as Packingtown. He spoke with other workers and their families and developed a clear understanding of the challenges and hardships they faced.

In order to make the problems in the meatpacking industry seem more immediate to readers, Sinclair decided to weave his observations into a story about a fictional worker named Jurgis Rudkos. Rudkos was a Lithuanian immigrant who worked in Packingtown and endured everything Sinclair had witnessed in the plants and the surrounding neighborhood. At the end of the

Muckraker Upton Sinclair investigated conditions in Chicago meatpacking plants for his best-selling book *The Jungle*.

story, Rudkos joins the Socialist Party, which promises to bring fairness to workers by spreading ownership of the nation's factories among all citizens. Sinclair hoped that readers would share his view that socialism could help

61

solve the problems of modern industry and raise the standard of living for working-class Americans.

Sinclair's series of articles drew a great deal of attention and helped increase the circulation of *Appeal to Reason*. In 1906 he revised and shortened the series and published it as a book called *The Jungle* (see "Upton Sinclair Exposes Problems in the Meatpacking Industry," p. 178). It became a best-seller, was translated into seventeen languages, and turned Sinclair into a worldwide celebrity. Still, the author was disappointed that many readers focused on his revelations about food safety, rather than his message about socialism. "I aimed at the public's heart, and by accident I hit it in the stomach,"[5] he admitted.

Readers of *The Jungle* were shocked and disgusted by Sinclair's descriptions of unsanitary slaughterhouse and meatpacking operations. They were particularly appalled to learn that diseased animals, spoiled meat, and even rats routinely made their way into the nation's food supply. "There was never the least attention paid to what was cut up for sausage," he revealed. "There would be meat stored in great piles in rooms; and the water from leaky roofs would drip over it, and thousands of rats would race about on it.... These rats were nuisances, and the packers would put poisoned bread out for them; they would die, and then rats, bread, and meat would go into the hoppers together. This is no fairy story and no joke; the meat would be shoveled into carts, and the man who did the shoveling would not trouble to lift out a rat even when he saw one—there were things that went into the sausage in comparison with which a poisoned rat was a tidbit."[6]

The large corporations that controlled the meatpacking industry insisted that their operations were clean and sanitary, and that they had inspections and other precautions to ensure that no tainted meat ever reached American consumers. *The Jungle* created such public outrage, however, that Roosevelt sent federal investigators to Chicago to review the situation. The inspectors not only confirmed Sinclair's findings, but in some cases found conditions even worse than those detailed in *The Jungle*. Roosevelt threw his weight behind efforts to craft strong new regulations for the meatpacking industry, and Congress responded by passing the Pure Food and Drug Act of 1906.

Protecting Consumers from Patent Medicines

The Pure Food and Drug Act also addressed another industry of concern to American consumers: patent medicines. Patent medicines were mysterious pills and potions that promised to cure a wide variety of illnesses and ailments. The companies that manufactured these remedies advertised heavily in newspapers and magazines. Their slick ads often included glowing testimonials from people who were miraculously restored to good health by using the product. In fact, patent medicine makers spent more money on advertising than they did on manufacturing. They spent so much money for ad space that they were often able to dictate terms to newspaper and magazine publishers. In many cases, the patent medicine companies inserted clauses in these contracts that prohibited publications from running any articles that were critical of their business.

Nevertheless, a few muckraking magazines conducted investigations of the patent medicine industry. They found that most of the popular remedies were not healthy at all. In fact, many of the products contained dangerous ingre-

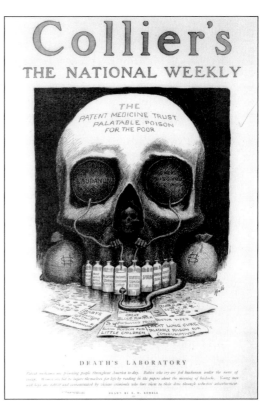

In 1905 *Collier's* magazine published a year-long series of muckraking articles about the health risks associated with patent medicines.

dients, including alcohol, narcotics, stimulants, and depressants. A few included addictive drugs like morphine and cocaine, which created dependence in consumers and ensured that they would keep buying the product.

Several magazines published articles and editorials condemning the patent medicine industry as a dangerous fraud perpetrated on American consumers. Muckraker Samuel Hopkins Adams wrote a year-long series called "The Great American Fraud" for *Collier's* magazine in 1905. He charged that the American people paid $75 million per year to patent medicine manufacturers for products that did nothing to improve their health. Edward Bok, the editor of *Ladies' Home Journal,* told his magazine's readers that "It is not by any means putting the matter too strongly to say that the patent medicine habit is one of the gravest curses, with the most dangerous results, that is

Frank Norris Condemns
Greedy Railroad Barons in *The Octopus*

Another classic work of muckraking literature that condemned corporate greed and its impact on the lives of working-class Americans was *The Octopus* by Frank Norris. Published in 1901, this novel centered around a deadly real-life confrontation between railroad barons and a group of settlers over land rights in California's San Joaquin Valley.

When the Transcontinental Railroad was completed in 1869, it suddenly became possible to travel from one side of the continent to the other in a matter of days. Over the next few years, several major railroad companies entered into a fierce competition to develop additional rail lines across California. In most cases, these companies received grants of land from the federal government along the routes where they planned to lay tracks. Each rail line that was constructed opened up new areas for settlement, ranching, and agriculture by ensuring that farm products could be shipped back east to market.

Many people settled along the rail lines, with the understanding that the railroad companies would eventually turn over ownership of the federal land grants to homesteaders at a fair market value. The settlers generally improved the land by building houses, barns, corrals, and irrigation systems. Many families established homes and lived there for years, thinking that they were gradually gaining property rights, when in actuality the railroad companies retained title to the land.

inflicting our American national life."[7] Other magazines revealed that the patent medicine companies used their financial power to limit negative media attention and government regulatory efforts.

American consumers were outraged by the deceptive and dangerous practices of the patent medicine industry. They demanded that political leaders take action to protect them from unhealthy products and false advertising. In the resulting uproar, many magazines and newspapers announced that they would no longer accept advertisements for patent medicines. In addi-

This situation had dire consequences for settlers of land granted to the Southern Pacific Railroad Company in the San Joaquin Valley. In 1880, when the railroad company decided to sell its parcels, it set the price per acre ten times higher than the settlers had been led to expect. Railroad executives justified the price increase by saying that it reflected the value of the improvements the settlers had made. When the settlers were unable to pay, the railroad company forced them to vacate the property. In many cases, railroad employees and backers then stepped in to purchase the improved land.

Some settlers got together to challenge the Southern Pacific's actions in court, but the railroad company used its financial strength and political connections to ensure that all of the lawsuits were decided in its favor. Devastated at the loss of everything they had worked to build, one group of angry settlers got into an armed confrontation with railroad employees and law enforcement officers who had been sent to evict them from the disputed land. Six settlers were killed in the resulting gunfight, which became known as the Battle at Mussel Slough.

This tragic incident forms the centerpiece of Norris's novel. *The Octopus* raised public awareness of the abuses of the railroad companies and generated calls for progressive reforms. Still, some historians claim that Norris presented a more sympathetic picture of wealthy industrialists and large corporations than many other muckrakers.

tion, several state medical societies disavowed the products and state legislatures banned their sale. Reinforcing the concerns about food safety raised by *The Jungle*, the pressure to reform the patent medicine industry contributed to the passage of the Pure Food and Drug Act of 1906.

Busting the Trusts

Muckraking exposés about the large corporations that dominated American industry at the turn of the century had a dramatic impact on public opinion (see sidebar "Frank Norris Condemns Greedy Railroad Barons in *The Octopus*," p. 64). Millions of middle-class citizens called for the federal government to take steps to limit the power and influence of large corporations and promote the welfare of workers. The influence of the muckrakers was "evident in the growth of the federal government's regulatory power over railroads, packing houses, and the food and drug industries," according to one historian. "The public demand that produced this result was unquestionably inspired and maintained primarily by the magazine muckrakers."[8]

By raising public awareness of the abuses of industry, the muckrakers helped increase support for President Roosevelt's progressive reforms. Roosevelt believed that the role of government needed to expand in order to address the many problems brought on by rapid industrialization. He wanted to take action to improve conditions for the poor and working class and restore the American people's faith in democracy.

> The influence of the muckrakers was "evident in the growth of the federal government's regulatory power over railroads, packing houses, and the food and drug industries," according to one historian.

One of Roosevelt's main concerns was labor-management relations, which was a frequent muckraking topic. He intervened on behalf of labor unions in several high-profile disputes with management during his presidency, and he launched an aggressive trust-busting campaign. In 1902, for example, Roosevelt stepped in to help resolve a bitter strike by United Mine Workers members against the large corporations that controlled Pennsylvania coal mines. The president threatened to put the mining operations under federal government control if management did not agree to settle the dispute through arbitration. Once the two sides appeared before an impartial party, the miners received a wage increase and other concessions that they had demanded. Roosevelt's handling of the strike put other large corporations on notice that his administration would not automatically side with industry in labor disputes. "The federal government, for the first time in its history, had intervened in a strike not to break it, but to bring about a peaceful settlement," noted one historian. "The great anthracite strike of 1902 cast a long shadow."[9]

Roosevelt also took action to stop or reverse the monopolistic business practices of the trusts. In 1902, for instance, he used the Sherman Antitrust Act to prevent financier J.P. Morgan from executing a plan to control all railroad transport between Chicago and the West Coast. Following the election of 1904, which he won in a landslide with 57 percent of popular vote, Roosevelt stepped up his trust-busting activities even further. In 1906 he pushed the Hepburn Act through Congress, which empowered the Interstate Commerce Commission (ICC) to increase its regulation of the railroads. The agency set reasonable shipping rates, ensured that the railroads did not make unethical deals that favored big companies, and forced the railroads to sell off their interests in unrelated industries.

Roosevelt prosecuted more than forty antitrust cases against corporate giants during his second term in office. The most prominent trust-busting effort involved Rockefeller's Standard Oil Company. Following a lengthy investigation and legal battle that did not conclude until two years after Roosevelt left office, the Department of Commerce and Labor used the Sherman Antitrust Act to break up the trust. Rockefeller was forced to sell off thirty-eight different pieces of his holdings. Some of these companies went on to become successful oil industry players on their own, including Amoco, Chevron, Exxon, and Mobil. The proceeds from these sales made Rockefeller the richest man in the world. Still, the breakup of Standard Oil was cited by a national panel of historians and journalists as one of the top 100 historic events that changed America during the twentieth century.

Notes

1 Lippmann, Walter. *Drift and Mastery: An Attempt to Diagnose the Current Unrest.* H. Holt and Company, 1914, p. 4.
2 Tarbell, Ida M. *All in the Day's Work.* New York: 1938, p. 230.
3 Fitch, John A. "Old Age at Forty." *American Magazine,* March 1911.
4 Shepherd, William G. "Eyewitness at Triangle." United Press, May 27, 1911.
5 Sinclair, Upton. *The Jungle: A Norton Critical Edition.* Edited by Clare Virginia Eby. New York: W. W. Norton, 2003, p. 351.
6 Sinclair, Upton. *The Jungle.* New York: 1906, p. 162.
7 Bok, Edward. "The Patent-Medicine Curse." *Ladies' Home Journal,* 1904.
8 Tebbel, John, and Mary Ellen Zuckerman. *The Magazine in America, 1741-1990.* New York: Oxford University Press, 1991, p. 114.
9 Reynolds, Robert L. "The Coal Kings Come to Judgment." *American Heritage,* April 1960.

Chapter Five

EXPOSING GOVERNMENT CORRUPTION

—◆◆◆—

If the whole picture is painted black there remains no hue
whereby to single out the rascals ... from their fellows.

—Theodore Roosevelt, April 14, 1906

As progressive reformers worked to pass new laws addressing poverty and other social issues, reducing the power of large corporations, and improving conditions for industrial workers, they often found their efforts stalled by corrupt politicians. Many officials at all levels of government had close ties to the wealthy industrialists who benefited from lax oversight of their business activities. These businessmen used all of their political and economic influence to resist regulatory reforms. In order to promote progressive reforms in other areas, therefore, the muckrakers turned their attention to exposing political corruption. "Legislation was necessary to protect woman and child workers, to clean up slums, improve housing, and control the great corporations, but first government itself had to be reformed," one historian noted. "And to do that it was necessary to rescue the democratic process from interest groups whose only concern was in increasing their power and profits."[1]

Bringing Shame on Corrupt City Governments

At the turn of the twentieth century, political corruption drove the government of virtually every major American city. Municipal jobs and contracts were routinely awarded on the basis of connections, bribery, and political favors rather than merit or cost efficiency. Citizens, merchants, and bankers who needed city services usually had to pay the political "boss" or his repre-

Muckraker Lincoln Steffens exposed government corruption in his "Shame of the Cities" series for *McClure's*.

sentatives in order to get things done. The most notorious example was William M. "Boss" Tweed, the leader of a corrupt political machine that controlled New York City and stole millions of dollars from its residents. Most people simply accepted the fact that their city leaders operated on the principles of fraud and greed instead of the age-old values of honesty and hard work. They viewed corruption as a necessary evil in a fast-growing, modern, industrial city.

Such attitudes began to change during the Progressive Era, when corrupt city governments came under investigation by muckraking journalists. By bringing bribery, backroom deals, and political favors into the open, the muckrakers provoked public outrage at the unfairness and inefficiency of civic corruption. Their work led to a series of reforms aimed at improving the performance and responsiveness of city governments across the country.

One of the earliest and best-known muckraking attacks on city corruption is the "Shame of the Cities" series that appeared in *McClure's*. Its author, Lincoln Steffens (see Steffens biography, p. 148), joined the staff of the magazine in 1902. Shortly after Steffens' arrival, publisher S.S. McClure put him on a train headed west with instructions to find important stories to cover. Steffens followed a lead to St. Louis, Missouri, where he found a newly elected district attorney fighting a lonely battle against political corruption in the city.

The attorney, Joseph Folk, told Steffens how political boss Ed Butler directed every aspect of city business for the financial and political gain of himself and his followers. Butler demanded payment from anyone who wanted a city contract or city services, from public transportation and road improvements to garbage collection and zoning. He guaranteed votes on the city council for a certain price. Folk told Steffens that millions of dollars in bribes exchanged hands, with much of the money ending up in Butler's pockets. No one dared complain about the situation, however, because the boss's reach extended into every area of life in the city. He used intimidation and coercion to silence critics and maintain his influence.

Steffens was shocked and disgusted by the extent of political corruption in St. Louis. He was also amazed that so few residents of the city seemed to share his outrage. Steffens hired a local reporter to research and write an article detailing Butler's abuse of the public trust, then returned to the *McClure's* offices in New York. When he received the article, however, Steffens noticed that the local reporter had left out the most damaging information about the boss's activities. Steffens revised the story, adding some of the disturbing facts he had learned from Folk. But the local newsman reacted with panic when he saw the new version. He demanded that Steffens issue the story under his own name because "he could not live and work in St. Louis if the article was printed as I had edited it,"[2] Steffens recalled. This incident helped convince the *McClure's* staff that only outside reporters could expose local problems without fear of retribution.

"Tweed Days in St. Louis," the first installment in Steffens' "Shame of the Cities" series, appeared in the October 1902 issue of *McClure's* (see "Lincoln Steffens Reveals the Shame of the Cities," p. 182). Steffens showed readers how the political corruption in St. Louis and other cities was related to the social and economic problems facing the United States. "Before Steffens, urban-reform reporting focused narrowly on corrupt acts of office," wrote one historian. "Steffens connected the dots, showing the bargains between political machines and corporate interest."[3]

"Legislation was necessary to protect woman and child workers, to clean up slums, improve housing, and control the great corporations, but first government itself had to be reformed," one historian noted.

The article generated a tremendous response from readers. Many people wrote letters to the magazine describing similar problems in their own municipal governments. These letters confirmed the suspicions of Steffens and other *McClure's* staff members that the situation in St. Louis was part of a pattern of rampant political corruption in American cities. "Evidently you could shoot me out of a gun fired at random," Steffens told S.S. McClure, "and wherever I lighted, there would be a story, the same way."[4]

The Boss

This 1906 cartoon from *Collier's* magazine shows a corrupt political boss controlling the lives of city residents.

  Steffens immediately began investigating reports of political bosses and corrupt officials controlling the governments of other major cities. He published another exposé on the topic, "The Shame of Minneapolis: The Rescue and Redemption of a City That Was Sold Out," in the famous January 1903 issue of *McClure's* that helped launch the muckraking movement. This installment in the series followed the story of Albert Alonzo "Doc" Ames, the corrupt mayor of Minneapolis. At one time a popular and respected local physician, Ames turned into an exceptionally greedy political boss once he was elected to office. "He set out upon a career of corruption which for deliberateness, invention, and avarice has never been equaled. It was as if he had made up his mind that he had been careless long enough, and meant to enrich his last years," Steffens wrote. "Immediately upon his election, before he took office, he organized a cabinet and laid plans to turn the city over to outlaws who were to work under police direction for the profit of his administration."[5]

Steffens followed up with stories about corruption and reform efforts in such cities as Philadelphia, Pittsburgh, Chicago, and New York. In 1904 he published seven of his reports together in book form as *The Shame of the Cities*. His work increased public awareness of civic corruption and led to the removal of many dishonest officials from office across the country. "The articles had an enormous impact, resulting in reform for the individual cities he reported on," noted one historian. "They also had a cumulative effect. Political and corporate crime was no longer a local issue—it was a national problem. Steffens raised America's social consciousness and his exposés paved the way for reform programs at all levels, from the cities to the federal government."[6]

With his exposés on political corruption, Lincoln Steffens "raised America's social consciousness and ... paved the way for reform programs at all levels, from the cities to the federal government."

Exposing Corporate Influence over the U.S. Senate

The muckrakers' exposure of corruption in city governments led to further investigations at the state and federal levels. Not surprisingly, these investigations uncovered widespread problems with corporate trusts and wealthy industrialists exercising undue influence over elected officials. Powerful business interests often hand-picked candidates for office, financed their election campaigns, and then controlled their votes on proposed legislation that would reform or regulate their activities.

Some of the worst cases of corporate influence over elected officials were found in the U.S. Senate. The method used to elect members of the Senate at that time was particularly vulnerable to manipulation by business interests. When the United States was founded in 1776, the framers of the Constitution provided for senators to be elected by state legislatures rather than by popular vote. This system made it easy for powerful political and financial figures in the state to control the choice of senators for their own benefit. "The Senate was a chamber of bosses with one senator from each state representing the political machine in his state, and the other senator representing the leading businessmen," charged one historian. "Together, they victimized the ordinary citizens."[7]

Muckraking journalist David Graham Phillips attacked government corruption in his "Treason of the Senate" series for *Cosmopolitan.*

In the early 1900s, a number of prominent members of the Senate came under investigation and were convicted of fraud and other crimes. Many progressives, such as newspaper owner William Randolph Hearst, argued that the only way to end such corruption was to provide for the direct election of U.S. Senators by popular vote. "The people will never be protected against the trusts by a Senate in which the trusts occupy many seats and control a majority,"[8] Hearst declared in an editorial. When Hearst purchased the muckraking journal *Cosmopolitan* in 1905, he made exposing corruption in the Senate one of his first orders of business. He assigned David Graham Phillips (see Phillips biography, p. 124), a veteran reporter who had also written popular novels with an anti-corruption theme, to prepare a series of articles on the subject.

The first installment in Phillips' nine-part series, "The Treason of the Senate," appeared in the March 1906 issue of *Cosmopolitan* (see "David Graham Phillips Blasts Corrupt U.S. Senators," p. 188). Hearst promoted it heavily with advertising and sensational headlines, and its popularity helped increase circulation of the magazine by 50 percent. Phillips started out by explaining to readers how the Senate played a significant role in deciding how the nation's prosperity would be shared: "The laws it permits or compels, the laws it refuses to permit, the interpreters of laws [judges] it permits to be appointed—these factors determine whether the great forces which modern concentration has produced shall operate to distribute prosperity equally or with shameful inequality and cruel and destructive injustice."[9]

Phillips went on to profile twenty-one senators whom he claimed had inappropriate relationships with corporate interests. He questioned, for instance, the common practice of senators accepting paid positions on corporate boards—and then voting on legislation affecting those businesses. Phillips warned that such links often caused members of the Senate to act against the best interests of the American people. "Treason is a strong word, but not too strong, rather too weak, to characterize the situation in which the Senate is the eager, resourceful, indefatigable agent of interests as hostile to the American people as any invading army could be, and vastly more dangerous," he declared. "Interests that manipulate the prosperity produced by all; whose growth and power can only mean the degradation of the people."[10]

Enacting Political Reforms

Phillips' "Treason of the Senate" series alarmed American voters and generated a chorus of calls for reform. Progressives targeted political corruption and corporate influence at all levels of government with new vigor in the wake of his articles. One of the top priorities for these reformers was changing the way senators were elected. They launched a campaign to pass a constitutional amendment providing for the direct election of senators by popular vote. They felt that taking the responsibility for choosing senators out of the hands of state legislatures and political parties would help reduce the influence of corporate interests over the process.

Although it took several years, the campaign was ultimately successful. The Seventeenth Amendment to the U.S. Constitution was ratified on April 8, 1913, and voters elected senators directly in the following year's elections. In the meantime, Phillips' series led to increased public scrutiny of Senate votes on various reform issues. This attention contributed to the passage of a number of progressive laws regarding railroad rates, meat inspection, employer liability, and other issues.

Reform-minded governors like Hiram Johnson of California and Robert M. La Follette of Wisconsin also sponsored measures to combat political corruption at the state and municipal levels of government. The main idea behind these measures was to increase citizen participation in the electoral process. Reformers believed that if voters played a stronger role in choosing their representatives and shaping legislation, they would remove corrupt lawmakers from office and reduce the influence of powerful corporate interests.

One important reform measure was the direct primary election. This measure allowed voters, rather than political machines, to narrow the field of candidates to appear on the ballot for a general election. Another reform measure, the secret ballot, enabled citizens to cast their votes without fear of retribution from political bosses. Many cities and states also enacted measures

Criticism of corporate influence over the U.S. Senate—represented by the overbearing political bosses in this cartoon—led to a Constitutional amendment providing for the direct election of senators.

providing for recall elections, which gave voters a way to remove corrupt officials from office. Two other reform measures that found strong support at this time were the initiative and the referendum. The initiative gave voters the ability to bypass state legislatures and pass their own laws through special elections. The referendum, on the other hand, gave voters a means to repeal unpopular laws passed by state legislatures.

The efforts of the muckrakers in exposing political corruption also led to greater enforcement of some long-ignored laws. For example, the Pendleton Act of 1883 was intended to prevent political leaders from appointing their friends and supporters to fill government jobs at the expense of more qualified applicants. The Pendleton Act established a system of open testing, similar to the modern civil service exam, to determine job applicants' qualifications. It also made it illegal for elected officials to require government employees to contribute to or help with their campaigns. During the Progressive Era, pressure from muckrakers and other reformers resulted in much stricter federal enforcement of these provisions.

Trying Roosevelt's Patience

Although the "Treason of the Senate" series encouraged lawmakers across the country to enact important political reforms, it also severely strained the relationship between Roosevelt and the muckrakers. For three years the journalists and the president had generally worked as partners in the drive for progressive reform. The muckrakers raised public awareness of the problems facing American society and increased the pressure for change. Roosevelt used the resulting public support to convince Congress to back the policies and programs he devised to address the problems.

For much of his presidency, Roosevelt maintained a respectful and even friendly relationship with the muckrakers, especially with the staff of *McClure's*. "I have learned to look to your articles for real help," he once wrote to Ray Stannard Baker. "You have impressed me with your earnest desire to be fair, with your freedom from hysteria, and with your anxiety to tell the truth rather than to write something that will be sensational."[11]

During his last years in office, however, Roosevelt voiced growing concerns about the trends he saw in American journalism. As muckraking became a movement with dozens of publications competing for readers, the president felt that the articles grew more sensational, unfair, bitter, and personal. Roosevelt worried that by exaggerating some problems, the muckrakers would cause readers to lose faith in the foundations of American democracy and capitalism. He also resented some writers' insistence that wealthy business owners were responsible for all the problems in American society. Roosevelt did not appreciate some writers' calls for a working-class revolution to install a socialist system.

On a few occasions, Roosevelt complained about what he viewed as an excessively negative tone in the muckraking journals. In a 1905 letter to S.S. McClure, he asked the publisher to strive for more balanced coverage. "It is an unfortunate thing to encourage people to believe that all crimes are connected with business, and that the crime of graft is the only crime. I wish very much that you could have articles showing up the hideous iniquity of which mobs are guilty, the wrongs of violence by the poor as well as the wrongs of corrup-

During his last years in office, President Theodore Roosevelt voiced growing concerns about the negative tone of American journalism.

tion by the rich," the president wrote. "Put sky in the landscape, and show, not incidentally but of set purpose, that you stand as much against anarchic violence and crimes of brutality as against corruption and crimes of greed."[12]

McClure and a few other magazine publishers took Roosevelt's suggestion to heart. Partly because they recognized that the American people were growing weary of a steady diet of bad news, some journals made efforts to include more positive stories. "I think you are right," McClure told Ray Stannard Baker, "that we should in some way offset the critical campaign of the magazine by some articles that would show the real and conquering American in his true character and aspect. It is, of course, a little difficult to formulate such articles."[13]

The End of the Muckraking Era

By the time *Cosmopolitan* published the "Treason of the Senate" series in 1906, however, Roosevelt had reached the end of his patience. Phillips' account of political corruption in the federal government targeted a number of the president's friends, allies, and supporters. Roosevelt had counted on these people to help him win reelection in 1904, and he needed them to help push his policies of progressive reform. Combined with other articles—including a series by Lincoln Steffens suggesting that the corruption reached all the way to the White House—the attack convinced Roosevelt that the muckrakers had finally crossed the line and become more of a hindrance than a help to his legislative agenda.

In early 1906, Roosevelt launched a counterattack. He made a number of statements criticizing the leading muckraking journals. He also characterized the crusading journalists as dangerous radicals who threatened to destroy American society. The president did not go out of his way to differentiate between the writers whose work he felt had merit, and those whose work he felt was irresponsible. Upon learning that Roosevelt planned to make a speech outlining his views on the subject, Baker sent the president a letter asking him to reconsider. "Even admitting that some of the so-called 'exposures' have been extreme, have they not, as a whole, been honest and useful?" he wrote. "Would not a speech, backed by all of your great authority, attacking the magazines, tend to give aid and comfort to these very rascals, besides making it more difficult in the future not only to get the truth told but to have it listened to?"[14]

Roosevelt brushed aside Baker's concerns. Instead, he expressed his feelings in an address before the Gridiron Club in April 1906. Although this speech—delivered in a private setting—was off the record, parts of it appeared in the press. The president repeated the sentiments in another speech delivered at a ceremony laying the cornerstone for a new congressional office building on April 14 (see "Roosevelt Calls Crusading Journalists 'Muckrakers,'" p. 192).

It was in these public statements that Roosevelt coined the term "muckraker" to describe the investigative journalists (see sidebar "Origin of the Term 'Muckraker,'" p. 80). He suggested that the writers were so busy raking through the muck looking for problems to expose that they were incapable of seeing anything admirable about the country. "There is filth on the floor," Roosevelt declared, "and it must be scraped up with the muck-rake, and there

"The man who never does anything else, who never thinks or speaks or writes save of his feats with the muck-rake, speedily becomes, not a help to society, not an incitement to good, but one of the most potent forces of evil," thundered President Theodore Roosevelt in a 1906 speech.

79

Origin of the Term "Muckraker"

Ever since President Theodore Roosevelt made his famous 1906 speech criticizing the investigative journalists of his era, the word "muckraker" has been applied mainly to people who work to expose corruption and wrongdoing. On occasion, it has been used to describe people who spread gossip or sensational stories. Modern readers may be surprised to learn that the term "muckrake" originally applied to a tool that resembled a pitchfork and was used to clean barns.

Roosevelt drew his unusual use of the word "muckraker" from a classic work of English literature called *The Pilgrim's Progress* by John Bunyan. The book, which was written in the seventeenth century, follows the spiritual journey of a character named Christian. After beginning his travels at the City of Destruction, Christian must overcome a series of trials and temptations in order to reach the Celestial City. His route passes through the Valley of the Shadow of Death, for instance, and requires him to climb the Hill of Difficulty. Christian's journey represents the earthly existence of man, and his destination represents heaven or the kingdom of God.

One of the characters in *The Pilgrim's Progress* is called the Man with the Muckrake. When a crown from heaven appears above this man's head,

are times and places where this service is the most needed of all the services that can be performed. But the man who never does anything else, who never thinks or speaks or writes save of his feats with the muck-rake, speedily becomes, not a help to society, not an incitement to good, but one of the most potent forces of evil."[15]

Some of the best-known journalists of the era took offense at the president's speech and rejected his use of the term "muckraker." They believed that their work promoted the interests of all Americans by holding industrial and political powers accountable for their actions. They worried that being dismissed as radical troublemakers by a popular president would cause their work to be marginalized. Lincoln Steffens, for one, declared that Roosevelt had effectively put an end to the investigative reporting that had formed the he continues looking downward and raking through the dirt at his feet. Bunyan offers the character as an example of someone who is so focused on the riches of earthly existence that he fails to notice the path to heaven that is open to him. The encounter teaches Bunyan's pilgrim the value of living a simple life: "Whereas it was also showed thee that the man could look no way but downwards, it is to let thee know that earthly things, when they are with power upon men's minds, quite carry their hearts away from God."

Roosevelt knew that *The Pilgrim's Progress* was familiar to most Americans of that era. He figured that his audience would understand his reference to the Man with the Muckrake. He described the investigative journalists who exposed the inequity and corruption in America as muckrakers because he felt they were too busy picking through the nation's problems to notice any positive things about the country. Yet many historians argue that the president distorted Bunyan's character for his own purposes. In *The Pilgrim's Progress,* the muckraker is too obsessed with earthly wealth to worry about spiritual redemption. Given this fact, some scholars claim that the word could more accurately be used to describe the robber barons and corrupt officials whom the "muckrakers" targeted.

Source: Bunyan, John. *The Pilgrim's Progress.* London: 1678.

basis for his rise to power. Some journalists, on the other hand, embraced the muckraker label and wore it proudly. They felt that angering the nation's powerful corporate and government leaders was part of their job description. They figured that earning enemies was a natural consequence of exposing uncomfortable truths.

Still, Roosevelt's criticism seemed to resonate with the American people. After 1906, public interest diminished in the type of investigative reporting that the muckraking journals offered. Sales of *McClure's* and other muckraking magazines underwent a decline. Some historians, however, assert that Roosevelt's stance was not much of a factor in this downturn. Instead, they point to public weariness of reading about the problems in American society. Another factor in the decline, say historians, was the rise of marketing and public relations functions in the world of business. Many large corporations hired professionals to put a positive spin on their activities and improve their public images. These efforts helped them to counteract muckraking reports and create uncertainty about the facts in the public mind.

By the time Roosevelt made his speech, some observers even questioned whether the most successful muckraking magazines were being hypocritical when they criticized big business. *McClure's,* for instance, had expanded over the years to become a large corporation like those it investigated. As it grew, the magazine depended on advertising revenue to cover its soaring production costs. As a result, its editors became more cautious about criticizing the companies that purchased ad space within its pages.

Citing differences in editorial philosophy with publisher S.S. McClure, half a dozen prominent staff writers (including Baker, Steffens, and Tarbell) left the magazine during the summer of 1906. They founded their own journal, *American Magazine,* and released its first issue in October 1906. Although they still planned to publish exposés, the group announced that the new magazine would focus on stories that "reflect a happy, struggling, fighting world in which, as we believe, good people are coming out on top."[16] *American Magazine* went on to publish muckraking articles on such topics as race relations, church corruption, West Coast politics, and efforts to abolish the twelve-hour workday before it folded in 1916.

As the twentieth century entered its second decade, the growing threat of World War I captured the interest of the American people as well as the attention of the nation's major magazines and newspapers. By 1912, as one historian noted,

> Muckraking was plainly going out of style. The radicals were certain that 'the interests' had killed it, but later historians agree that the muckrakers had simply worn out their welcome. For nearly a decade they had delivered successive hammer blows on the public skull, creating a colossal national headache, and now people were beginning to sense how good they would feel when it stopped.... Not that the muckraking magazines were without merit. They threw a strong spotlight on the most serious of America's social ills and alarmed the government enough to cause it to make an attempt at setting up a regulatory check

on laissez-faire capitalism [an economic philosophy that advocates limiting government intervention and allowing market forces to take their own course]. Further, they invented the kind of journalism we now call investigative reporting, thus fulfilling what the architects of the First Amendment expected the press to be: a force able to make government accountable to the governed and to provide constant fuel to the democratic machine by means of free inquiry.[17]

Notes

1 Traxel, David. *Crusader Nation: The United States in Peace and the Great War, 1898-1920.* New York: Alfred A. Knopf, 2006, p. 6.

2 Steffens, Lincoln. *The Autobiography of Lincoln Steffens.* New York: Harcourt, Brace and Company, 1931, p. 372.

3 Shapiro, Bruce, ed. *Shaking the Foundations: 200 Years of Investigative Journalism in America.* New York: Thunder's Mouth Press/Nation Books, 2003, p. 71.

4 Steffens, p. 392.

5 Steffens, Lincoln. "The Shame of Minneapolis," *McClure's,* January 1903. In Shapiro, Bruce, ed. *Shaking the Foundations: 200 Years of Investigative Journalism in America.* New York: Thunder's Mouth Press/Nation Books, 2003, p. 75.

6 Jensen, Carl, ed. *Stories That Changed America: Muckrakers of the 20th Century.* New York: Seven Stories Press, 2000, p. 42.

7 Jensen, p. 42.

8 Quoted in Serrin, Judith, and William Serrin, eds. *Muckraking: The Journalism That Changed America.* New York: New Press, 2002, p. 105.

9 Quoted in Serrin, p. 106.

10 Quoted in Serrin, p. 106.

11 Dorman, Jessica. "Where Are Muckraking Journalists Today?" *Nieman Reports,* Summer 2000, p. 55.

12 Quoted in Wilson, Harold S. *McClure's Magazine and the Muckrakers.* Princeton, NJ: Princeton University Press, 1970, p. 179.

13 Quoted in Wilson, p. 166.

14 Dorman, p. 55.

15 Roosevelt, Theodore. "The Man with the Muck-Rake." *Putnam's Monthly and the Critic,* October 1906, p. 42.

16 Baker, Ray Stannard. *American Chronicle: The Autobiography of Ray Stannard Baker.* New York: Charles Scribner's Sons, 1945, p. 226.

17 Tebbel, John, and Mary Ellen Zuckerman. *The Magazine in America, 1741-1990.* New York: Oxford University Press, 1991, p. 120.

Chapter Six

THE MUCKRAKING
TRADITION CONTINUES

As long as the public was well informed and well led, the muckrakers retained faith that the state would uphold the public welfare and morality; it would indeed impose the general will upon all the disintegrating facets of American life.

—Harold S. Wilson,
McClure's Magazine and the Muckrakers

Although the first decade of the twentieth century is considered the heyday of muckraking journalism, the media has continued to serve as a watchdog of public interests ever since. Some of the same social and political problems that confronted Ida Tarbell, Lincoln Steffens, Upton Sinclair, Ray Stannard Baker, and other early muckrakers remained issues in American life. Large corporations continued to exploit workers and mislead consumers, for instance, and powerful government leaders spun webs of lies and corruption. But new generations of investigative journalists arrived on the scene to expose such abuses and inspire reforms, even as journalism expanded beyond newspapers and magazines to radio, television, documentary films, and the Internet (see "Pete Hamill Explains the Importance of Investigative Journalism," p. 206).

In this way, they kept the muckraking tradition alive. "Independent, aggressive journalism strengthens American democracy, improves the lives of its citizens, checks the abuses of powerful people, supports the weakest members of society, connects us all to one another, educates and entertains us,"[1] declared one historian.

American Journalism Since the Muckrakers

When World War I broke out in Europe in 1914, the muckraking era in American journalism came to an end. Newspapers and magazines across the United States dedicated large amounts of space to war coverage, and domestic problems received much less attention. Some periodicals, especially evening newspapers, saw their circulation grow during the war years. But wartime increases in the price of paper, ink, and printing machinery caused many small newspapers to go out of business or sell their operations to larger concerns.

This consolidation of newspaper publishing continued during the post-war period, as successful owners bought out competing publications to create chains or syndicates. By the mid-1920s, for example, William Randolph Hearst owned twenty-eight newspapers in eighteen different cities. Successful newspaper groups such as Gannett, Booth, and Ridder (later Knight-Ridder) also got their starts during this time. The postwar period also saw the rise of pulp magazines that focused on dramatic, action-oriented fiction, like *True Story* and *All-Story*.

Yet some magazines continued to focus on news and current events. Henry Luce introduced the weekly newsmagazine *Time* during the 1920s and used it as the foundation to build a huge publishing empire. During the 1930s, the development of portable, 35-millimeter cameras and improvements in photographic reproduction led to the rise of photojournalism, and to the creation of such photo-heavy magazines as *Life* and *Look*.

Printed sources of news and information faced increasing competition from the new medium of radio during the period between World Wars I and II. The number of radio receivers in the United States increased from a few hundred thousand in 1920 to reach 14 million in 1930 and 44 million in 1940. Concerned about the potential impact of this new communication technology on circulation, a number of newspaper publishers launched their own radio broadcasting arms. Still, the American people continued to rely on newspapers and magazines as their main source of news.

During the Great Depression of the 1930s, the total daily circulation of newspapers nationwide actually increased. Magazines experienced strong sales, as well, and more than twenty different magazines could claim circulation over one million by 1940. When the United States entered World War II the following year, American newspapers and magazines sent hundreds of war correspondents overseas to provide coverage. Radio networks also

This 1906 political cartoon shows some of the leading writers of the muckraking era—including Ray Stannard Baker, Lincoln Steffens, and Ida Tarbell—marching into battle under the banner of influential magazines.

offered extensive war reporting, and the American people watched newsreel features on theater screens. Many historians consider World War II coverage to be a high point in American journalism.

After the war ended in 1945, the new medium of television arose to challenge newspapers and magazines. Ownership of television sets increased from 10 million nationwide in 1950 to reach 50 million by 1960. Meanwhile, the number of broadcast TV stations grew from about 100 to more than 500 during this same decade. Although television newscasts could not provide the volume of information available in print sources, they gave stories an immediacy and visual appeal that newspapers and magazines often lacked. "As a conduit for information, television is a joke compared with a newspaper. The full text of a network evening-news telecast takes up about one-third of the front page of a regular newspaper," one analyst noted. But "whenever television wants to be first with a story, it can be. It doesn't matter how well or poorly television has covered the story."[2] During the 1950s and 1960s, legendary broadcast journalists like Walter Cronkite, David Brinkley, and Mike Wallace anchored popular network TV newscasts.

The 1970s saw investigative journalism reach heights not seen since the muckraking era. A new generation of young, idealistic publishers took the reins of several major newspapers. They encouraged their reporters to question authority, and the reporters responded by uncovering shocking information about the inner workings of the U.S. government. These revelations contributed to the resignation of President Richard Nixon and the withdrawal of American military forces from Vietnam.

During the 1980s, the American people gained more media options with the introduction of cable TV news channels like CNN. Facing high production costs and declining readership, many newspapers and magazines either failed or consolidated into giant media companies. However, some observers complained that the quality of American journalism suffered during this period. Viacom, Time Warner, and other media giants were often criticized for focusing on profits at the expense of quality products.

During the 1990s, the Internet brought about a major shift in the way Americans received news and information. It challenged the dominance of traditional media, like television and print journalism, by giving people access to a huge variety of news sources at all times. As Americans increasingly turned to online information sources, the nation's daily newspapers suffered severe declines in circulation. A number of major newspapers were forced to reduce their reporting staffs, limit their delivery schedules, or even close their doors. Some media critics worried that the technological changes might spell the end of traditional investigative journalism. "By now, everyone who cares about journalism and its role in society understands that the business model that for four decades handsomely supported large metropolitan newspapers has crumbled as readers and advertisers flock to the Internet," noted one analyst. "The result is a curious mixture of glut and shortage: an explosion of certain kinds of information available instantly and free of charge on the Web—spot news, stock prices, weather, sports, the latest doings of celebrities and, most of all, opinion—offset by an accelerating shrinkage of foreign reporting and in-depth investigation."[3]

Muckraking in the Second Half of the Twentieth Century

Despite all the changes that have taken place in American journalism since the muckraking era, the media has continued to serve a vital function in society. On many notable occasions throughout the years, determined reporters have picked up and carried the muckraking torch. They have conducted investigations, uncovered problems, raised public awareness, and generated calls for reform. In this way, investigative journalists have protected the public interest against powerful political and economic forces (see sidebar "The Muckraking Movies of Michael Moore," p. 98).

Historians rank CBS News correspondent Edward R. Murrow among the best investigative journalists of the twentieth century.

One of the most famous examples of muckraking journalism during the second half of the twentieth century came during the early years of television news. It involved Edward R. Murrow, a legendary newsman who had first gained fame during World War II for broadcasting radio reports from London rooftops in the middle of German bombing raids. In 1951 Murrow launched a television program called *See It Now* for CBS News. The show tackled a wide range of controversial issues, from political corruption to nuclear weapons, and set long-lasting standards for excellence in TV news reporting.

In 1954 Murrow dedicated eleven episodes of *See It Now* to challenging Senator Eugene McCarthy of Wisconsin. McCarthy was one of the most powerful and feared figures in the country at that time. Taking advantage of widespread concerns about the spread of communism following World War II, in the early 1950s McCarthy launched an anti-communist witch hunt. Using his authority as chairman of a special congressional committee on "un-American activities," he terrorized celebrities, intellectuals, and anyone who disagreed with his political views. His charges of disloyalty cost many of his victims their reputations and jobs. But few people dared to speak out against McCarthy because they worried about becoming the next target of his crusade.

Murrow felt that McCarthy's campaign posed a threat to American democracy. He was determined to expose the senator's dangerous motivations and unfair tactics. On the March 9, 1954, episode of *See It Now,* Murrow put together clips of McCarthy speaking at campaign rallies and during hearings of his investigating committee. He used the senator's own words to condemn him before the American people. "The line between investigation and persecution is a very fine one, and the junior senator from Wisconsin has stepped over it repeatedly," Murrow concluded. "We must not confuse dissent with disloyalty. We must remember always that accusation is not proof and that conviction depends upon evidence and due process of law."[4]

"We must not confuse dissent with disloyalty," Edward R. Murrow declared in a famous 1954 news program condemning McCarthyism.

The program generated tens of thousands of viewer responses, nearly all of them supporting Murrow. His courageous stand helped turn public opinion against McCarthy. The Senate officially censured McCarthy for his conduct in December 1954, and his political career ended a short time later. "Murrow's March 9, 1954, broadcast has come to be known as 'television's finest hour,'" noted one historian. "It revealed the power of the medium to fight evil by telling the people what was really happening."[5]

Taking On Large Corporations

Like the turn-of-the-century muckrakers, some modern-day writers have famously challenged the health and safety practices of large corporations. One prominent example is biologist Rachel Carson, whose 1962 book *Silent Spring* exposed the environmental damage resulting from the unregulated use of pesticides. During the 1950s, chemicals like dichloro-diphenyl-trichloroethane (DDT) were commonly sprayed on food crops and in homes to get rid of unwanted "pests" like insects, rodents, and weeds. The U.S. government promoted the use of DDT to help reduce insect-borne disease and increase food production. The large chemical companies that manufactured DDT and other pesticides insisted that they were safe. But Carson's research showed that these chemicals were toxic to birds, fish, and other creatures—including humans. In *Silent Spring,* she explained how DDT accumulated in soil, water, and the tissues of animals over time, causing terrible environmental damage.

The chemical companies attacked Carson, questioning her data and challenging her qualifications as a scientist. Nevertheless, her book became a best-seller and brought national attention to the dangers of pesticides. *Silent Spring* created such a public outcry that the U.S. Congress formed a special committee to investigate the use of the chemicals. The committee agreed with Carson's findings and recommended passing new laws to regulate pesticides. In 1972 Congress banned DDT from use in the United States. Carson's work is widely credited with raising public awareness about pollution and helping to launch the American environmental movement.

Another writer who famously took on powerful corporate interests was Ralph Nader. An admirer of the muckrakers, Nader claimed that his efforts to improve American society were inspired by reading Upton Sinclair's book *The Jungle*. After training to be a lawyer, Nader often found himself representing the victims of car accidents. His growing interest in automobile safety led to a job researching the issue for the U.S. Department of Labor in the 1960s.

In 1965 Nader published the results of his research in a book called *Unsafe at Any Speed: The Designed-In Dangers of the American Automobile.* He told readers that highway accidents took the lives of over 50,000 Americans each year and cost the nation an estimated $8 billion in property damage, medical expenses, lost wages, and insurance payments. He claimed that large automobile manufacturers like General Motors (GM) knowingly sold vehicles that endangered consumers. Nader insisted that GM and other automakers chose not to install costly safety equipment because it would reduce their profits. "A great problem of contemporary life is how to control the power of economic interests which ignore the harmful effects of their applied science and technology," he wrote. "The automobile tragedy is one of the most serious of these manmade assaults on the human body."[6]

GM sent private investigators after Nader in an attempt to discredit him, but the corporation's efforts backfired. Nader sued GM for invasion of privacy and ended up winning a large monetary settlement and a public apology. His book became a best-seller and generated intense public concern about automobile safety. The U.S. Congress investigated Nader's claims and addressed the problem by passing the Traffic and Motor Vehicle Safety Act of 1966. Nader's work thus led to the introduction of mandatory safety equipment like seatbelts and federal crash testing to ensure that new vehicles met basic safety standards.

Following his initial success, Nader went on to found dozens of consumer advocacy groups. His work helped spark the establishment of federal agencies to oversee the health and safety practices of large corporations, including the Consumer Product Safety Commission (CPSC), the Occupational Safety and Health Administration (OSHA), and the Environmental Protection Agency (EPA). "Ralph Nader started changing America in 1965 with *Unsafe at Any Speed*," wrote one historian. "The book was the landmark event of a new public interest movement focused on consumer affairs."[7]

Revealing Military Abuses

During the 1960s and early 1970s the United States became involved in the Vietnam War. More than 58,000 Americans lost their lives in this failed effort to prevent Communist-led North Vietnam from taking over South Vietnam, which was led by a U.S.-supported government. Over time, the Vietnam War became deeply unpopular with the American people, in part because journalists uncovered troubling information about the U.S. military's policies and conduct of the war.

One of the most shocking revelations about the Vietnam War came from Seymour Hersh, who is often mentioned among America's best investigative journalists. Fascinated with news gathering from an early age, Hersh started his career as a copy boy and police reporter in Chicago. After serving in the U.S. Army as a journalist and speechwriter, he joined the Associated Press in 1963 and was assigned to cover the U.S. Department of Defense. As he wandered around the Pentagon looking for stories, he began to realize that military leaders did not always tell the American people the truth about events in Vietnam.

In 1969 Hersh heard a rumor that a U.S. Army officer named William Calley had led a murderous attack on innocent civilians in a Vietnamese village called My Lai 4. He found Calley at Fort Benning, Georgia, where he was secretly being court-martialed for his actions. Hersh conducted an exclusive interview with Calley and got the full story of what became known as the My Lai massacre. He learned that American soldiers had raided the village and killed an estimated 500 people, many of them women, children, and old men. Members of Calley's platoon burned down huts with entire families inside and threw hand grenades into protective bunkers that were crammed full of unarmed villagers. At one point, Calley ordered his men to

Journalist Seymour Hersh won a Pulitzer Prize for his investigation of the My Lai massacre, a Vietnam War incident in which American soldiers killed hundreds of civilians.

push about 75 civilians into a drainage ditch and shoot them to death. "Seconds after the shooting stopped, a bloodied but unhurt two-year-old boy miraculously crawled out of the ditch, crying," Hersh related. "He began running toward the hamlet. Someone hollered, 'There's a kid.' There was a long pause. Then Calley ran back, grabbed the child, threw him back in the ditch and shot him."[8]

Hersh wrote a news story about the My Lai massacre, but the atrocities he described were so horrific that the editors of several major newspapers and magazines refused to believe that the incident really happened. He finally convinced a friend to distribute the article through the small, independent Dispatch News Service. Before long, the My Lai tragedy had become front-page news across the country, and Hersh ended up winning a Pulitzer Prize for investigative reporting. He expanded upon the story in two books, *My Lai*

4: A Report on the Massacre and Its Aftermath and *Cover-Up: The Army's Secret Investigation of the Massacre of My Lai 4.*

Hersh continued working as an investigative reporter and uncovered a number of problems with U.S. military and intelligence operations over the years. While working for the *New York Times* in the 1970s, for instance, he exposed an illegal domestic spying operation conducted by the Central Intelligence Agency (CIA). More recently, he gained attention for his criticism of the planning and conduct of U.S.-led wars in Iraq, and for his efforts to improve the treatment of U.S. military veterans.

> *"Watergate became an example for the ages, a classic case when journalism made a difference," one historian noted. "Good journalism does not often topple a president, but it frequently changes the lives of citizens, both grand and ordinary."*

Another major revelation about the Vietnam War took place on June 13, 1971, when Neil Sheehan of the *New York Times* broke the story of the existence of the Pentagon Papers. This 7,000-page report was a secret U.S. military study about the development of U.S. policy in Southeast Asia and the causes of the Vietnam War. It showed that U.S. government and military leaders had misled the American people for years about their decision-making processes in Vietnam. "The Pentagon researchers ... examined not only the policies and motive of American administrations, but also the effectiveness of intelligence, the mechanics and consequences of bureaucratic compromises, the difficulties of imposing American tactics on the Vietnamese, the governmental uses of the American press, and many other tributaries of their main story," Sheehan wrote. "The authors reveal, for example, that the American intelligence community repeatedly provided the policy makers with what proved to be accurate warnings that desired goals were either unattainable or likely to provoke costly reactions from the enemy."[9]

A former Pentagon advisor named Daniel Ellsberg, who had grown disillusioned with U.S. conduct in the war, leaked a copy of the Pentagon Papers to Sheehan. President Richard M. Nixon immediately went to court to prevent the *New York Times* from publishing the documents. Three weeks later, the U.S. Supreme Court ruled that the newspaper could proceed under the U.S. Constitution's guarantee of freedom of the press. The publication of the Pentagon Papers increased public mistrust of the government and hastened the end of U.S. involvement in Vietnam. One historian

Washington Post reporters Carl Bernstein (left) and Bob Woodward uncovered the Watergate scandal, which led to the resignation of President Richard Nixon in 1974.

described it as an "investigative coup" and "the single most consequential 'leak' on record."[10]

Uncovering the Political Scandal of the Century

Probably the most famous case of investigative journalism in American history is the Watergate scandal uncovered by Bob Woodward and Carl Bernstein of the *Washington Post*. In June 1972, the young reporters were assigned to cover a suspicious break-in at the offices of the Democratic National Committee, located inside the Watergate Hotel building in Washington, D.C. Woodward and Bernstein quickly learned that the burglars had connections to the Republican Party. "One of the five men arrested early Saturday in the attempt to bug the Democratic National Committee headquarters is the salaried security coordinator for President Nixon's reelection committee," they revealed. "The five suspects, well-dressed, wearing rubber surgical gloves and unarmed, were arrested about 2:30 a.m. Saturday when they were surprised by Metropolitan police inside the 29-office suite of the Democratic headquarters on the sixth floor of the Watergate. The suspects had extensive photographic equipment and some electronic surveillance instruments capable of intercepting both regular conversation and telephone communication."[11]

Suspecting that the crime was politically motivated, Woodward and Bernstein launched an investigation that lasted more than two years, produced a series of 225 news articles, and earned them a Pulitzer Prize. Based on tips from sources inside the White House, they eventually discovered that President Nixon and high-ranking members of his administration had tried to cover up the crime and their knowledge of it. The *Washington Post* articles led to the appointment of a U.S. Senate committee to investigate the matter. Nixon resigned from office in 1974 rather than face impeachment for his role in the scandal, and twenty-two members of his administration ended up going to prison.

Woodward and Bernstein wrote a best-selling book about their investigations called *All the President's Men*. The movie version, starring Robert Redford and Dustin Hoffman, won an Academy Award as Best Picture. The story demonstrated the power of the press and inspired a new generation of Americans to pursue careers as investigative journalists. "Watergate became an example for the ages, a classic case when journalism made a difference," one historian noted. "Good journalism does not often topple a president, but it frequently changes the lives of citizens, both grand and ordinary."[12]

Revisiting Familiar Muckraking Themes

Even as the twenty-first century approached and the American media underwent significant changes, investigative journalists drew attention to some of the same issues that the muckrakers addressed almost one hundred years earlier. In his 1997 book *One World, Ready or Not*, for instance, William Greider explained how globalization brought old problems like child labor and exploitation of factory workers to the doorsteps of American consumers.

Greider told about a terrible fire that destroyed a toy factory in Thailand in 1993, killing more young female workers than had died in the 1911 Triangle Shirtwaist factory fire. Although the Thai facility mostly produced toys for large American companies—like Fisher-Price, Hasbro, and Tyco—the incident was almost completely ignored by the U.S. media. "Americans worried

In 2004 modern-day muckraking journalists exposed the abuse of Iraqi prisoners by U.S. military personnel at Abu Ghraib Prison in Baghdad.

obsessively over the everyday safety of their children, and the U.S. government's regulators diligently policed the design of toys to avoid injury to young innocents," he wrote. "Yet neither citizens nor government took any interest in the brutal and dangerous conditions imposed on the people who manufactured those same toys, many of whom were mere adolescent children themselves. Indeed, the government position, both in Washington and Bangkok, assumed that there was no social obligation connecting consumers with workers, at least none that governments could enforce without disrupting free trade or invading the sovereignty of other nations."[13]

In 2001, meanwhile, journalist Eric Schlosser investigated America's modern meatpacking industry in *Fast Food Nation: The Dark Side of the All-American Meal.* Schlosser visited slaughterhouse operations and encountered many of the same terrible working conditions that famed muckraker Upton

The Muckraking Movies of Michael Moore

In addition to newspapers, magazines, television, and the Internet, documentary films provide a venue for modern-day muckrakers to raise public awareness of problems facing the nation. The best known—and most controversial—muckraking filmmaker in America is Michael Moore. Moore was born on April 23, 1954, in Flint, Michigan, an industrial town that was home to several factories that produced automobiles for General Motors (GM). Many members of Moore's family worked on the assembly line and belonged to the United Auto Workers (UAW) union.

Moore launched his career as a muckraking journalist at the age of twenty-two. After dropping out of college at the University of Michigan-Flint, he founded an alternative weekly newspaper called *The Michigan Voice.* The paper shut down in 1986 when Moore accepted a position as the editor of *Mother Jones,* a liberal political magazine. After only a few months on the job, however, he was fired over disagreements about content. Moore filed a lawsuit for wrongful dismissal and received an out-of-court settlement of $58,000. He used this money to make his first documentary film.

Roger and Me, released in 1989, chronicles the decline of Flint and the struggles of city residents after GM relocated its assembly plants—and thousands of jobs—to Mexico. The film centers around Moore's fruitless efforts to arrange a face-to-face meeting with Roger Smith, the former president of GM, to discuss the situation. Moore's next film, *Bowling for Columbine* (2002), examines the issues of gun ownership and violence in the United States. It was inspired by the 1999 tragedy at Columbine High School in Colorado, in which two students went on a shooting rampage that took the lives of thirteen people.

Sinclair had written about a century earlier in *The Jungle.* Schlosser reported that the majority of the workers were recent immigrants from developing countries. They worked long hours in grueling jobs for low wages. Under constant pressure to keep up with high-speed production lines, they faced a high likelihood of job-related injuries. Many of these injuries went unreported, and the workers did not receive health care or other benefits.

Moore also wrote and directed *Fahrenheit 9/11,* a 2004 documentary about the impact of the terrorist attacks of September 11, 2001, on U.S. government policy and American society. The film was highly critical of the George W. Bush administration and its decision to invade Iraq. In 2007 Moore released *Sicko,* a documentary which exposed problems in the American health care system. He has also written several best-selling books that offer his opinions about U.S. politics and culture, including *Downsize This!, Stupid White Men,* and *Dude, Where's My Country?*

Moore's work has earned him many awards and millions of fans. *Bowling for Columbine* won an Academy Award as Best Documentary Feature of 2002. *Fahrenheit 9/11* earned $200 million in box-office receipts worldwide, making it the highest-grossing documentary film of all time. In 2005, *Time* magazine featured Moore on its list of the 100 Most Influential People in the United States. Admirers of the filmmaker claim that he sheds light on important political, economic, and social problems and looks out for the interests of ordinary Americans.

At the same time, though, Moore's work has made him one of the most reviled figures in America. A number of rival documentary filmmakers have released movies that criticize and attempt to discredit Moore, such as *Michael and Me, Michael Moore Hates America,* and *Manufacturing Dissent.* In addition, there are numerous Web sites and blogs dedicated to pointing out factual errors, omissions, or misleading information in Moore's films. Moore's critics claim that he ignores data that contradicts his preconceived ideas, edits interviews in a way that slants the subjects' meaning, and otherwise distorts the truth. Moore defends his methods and his message on his own Web site, www.michaelmoore.com.

Modern-day muckrakers also continued to expose military abuses and government cover-ups in the twenty-first century (see "The *Washington Post* Gives Wounded Veterans a Voice," p. 197). In 2004, for instance, American magazines, newspapers, and television news programs revealed the systematic abuse of Iraqi prisoners by U.S. soldiers at Abu Ghraib prison in Baghdad. A number of military police officers took photographs of themselves torturing or humiliating prisoners at the facility. When these photographs came to the attention of U.S. Army authorities in 2003, they conducted a secret investigation and charged several people involved under the Uniform Code of Military Justice. But the matter did not become public knowledge until months later, when the photographs were broadcast on *60 Minutes II* and Seymour Hersh published a report in the *New Yorker.* Some Americans expressed anger about the journalists who publicized these embarrassing events, but others rushed to defend Hersh and other reporters who exposed the conditions at Abu Ghraib. "The most patriotic role the press can play is to fulfill its constitutionally protected duty to aggressively probe and question those who have the power to make the decisions that can affect our security and our liberty,"[14] declared one advocate.

Challenges for Future Muckrakers

Although investigative journalists continued to expose problems in American government and society into the twenty-first century, the rapidly changing media environment has created significant challenges for would-be muckrakers. Faced with declining circulation and budget crises, most major newspapers have reduced their reporting staffs and the amount of space dedicated to national and international news (see "Modern-Day Muckrakers Face Major Challenges," p. 212).

At the same time, instantaneous access to news and information on cable TV and the Internet has driven a significant decline in viewership for network television newscasts. Local TV news has become more sensational and crime-oriented in an effort to attract viewers, while several networks have dropped their national news telecasts in favor of talk shows emphasizing celebrity and entertainment features. Television newsmagazines that once focused on in-depth, investigative reports—like *60 Minutes, Dateline NBC,* and *PBS Frontline*—have found this mission increasingly difficult in the face of budget cuts and audience fragmentation. "It's risky, it's expensive, it takes huge resources and talent, and with much of the press owned by large corporations, I think there's a certain reluctance to do that [sort of reporting],"[15] explained Bill Buzenberg, director of the Center for Public Integrity.

The spread of new information technology like the Internet has contributed to the decline of traditional media. As more news and information has become available through alternative sources, competition for reading and viewing audiences has increased. But while the Internet has made a large quantity of information available, some critics question whether the quality of news gathering and reporting has declined as a result. "The best journalism—much of it produced by a small number of newspapers—now reaches more Americans than ever on the newspapers' Internet sites and through their relationships with, and influence on, the best news programs on television and radio," noted one analyst. "[But] too much of what has been offered as news in recent years has been untrustworthy, irresponsible, misleading or incomplete.... Too many of those who own and lead the nation's news media have cynically underestimated or ignored America's need for good journalism, and evaded their responsibility to provide it."[16]

Other media critics, however, believe that the Internet can play an important role in extending the reach of independent, muckraking journalism. It provides ordinary citizens with an opportunity to express minority viewpoints and organize opposition to powerful political and corporate interests. The Internet gives millions of people around the world the power to become citizen journalists—providing photos and eyewitness accounts of news events, posting comments on mainstream media sites, or contributing insights through blogs.

A number of independent media centers and investigative journalism nonprofits sprung up in the early 2000s to take advantage of the Internet's capacity for spreading news and information. Such organizations as the Center for Public Integrity, the Pulitzer Center on Crisis Reporting, the Center for Investigative Reporting, and ProPublica are often compared to the early muckrakers because they view journalism as an important tool in exposing problems and promoting change.

Notes

1 Downie, Leonard Jr., and Robert G. Kaiser. *The News about the News: American Journalism in Peril.* New York: Knopf, 2002, p. 13.

2 Andrews, Peter. "The Press." *American Heritage,* October 1994, p. 36.

3 Steiger, Paul E. "Going Online with Watchdog Journalism." *Nieman Reports,* Spring 2008, p. 30.

4 Bliss, Edward Jr. *In Search of Light: The Broadcasts of Edward R. Murrow.* New York: Knopf, 1967, p. 247.

5 Jensen, Carl. *Stories That Changed America: Muckrakers of the 20th Century.* New York: Seven Stories Press, 2000, p. 136.

6 Nader, Ralph. *Unsafe at Any Speed.* New York: Grossman, 1965.

7 Jensen, p. 224.

8 Hersh, Seymour. *My Lai 4: A Report on the Massacre and Its Aftermath.* New York: Random House, 1970, p. 64.

9 Sheehan, Neil, and Hedrick Smith. "Vast Review of War Took a Year." *New York Times,* June 13, 1971.

10 Shapiro, Bruce, ed. *Shaking the Foundations: 200 Years of Investigative Journalism in America.* New York: Thunder's Mouth Press/Nation Books, 2003, p. 353.

11 Woodward, Bob, and Carl Bernstein. "GOP Security Aide among Five Arrested in Bugging Affair." *Washington Post,* June 17, 1972.

12 Downie and Kaiser, p. 3.

13 Greider, William. *One World, Ready or Not.* New York: Simon and Schuster, 1997, p. 333.

14 Giles, Bob. "The Vital Role of the Press in a Time of National Crisis." *Nieman Reports,* Winter 2002, p. 96.

15 Quoted in Guthrie, Marisa. "Investigative Journalism under Fire." *Broadcasting and Cable,* June 23, 2008, p. 10.

16 Downie and Kaiser, p. 9.

Chapter Seven

LEGACY OF THE PROGRESSIVE ERA

—◆◆◆—

The test of our progress is not whether we add more to the
abundance of those who have much; it is whether we provide enough for those who have too little.

—Franklin D. Roosevelt

Although the Progressive Era came to an end in the late 1910s, many of
the changes that took place during that time had an impact on American life for generations to come. Progressive leaders put a number of
safeguards in place to reduce corruption in politics and make government
more accountable to the people. They also established government agencies
and commissions to regulate the activities of big business and to protect both
workers and consumers from the worst abuses of powerful corporations.
Finally, they took steps to help the poor and to address some of the social
problems that had arisen from rapid industrialization.

Since the close of the Progressive Era, American politics has shifted back
and forth between periods dominated by progressive and conservative ideas.
Several times in the twentieth century, the nation has responded to major
social and economic problems by expanding the role of government and
instituting progressive reforms. During the 1930s, for instance, President
Franklin D. Roosevelt's New Deal programs helped Americans survive the
Great Depression. In between these periods, though, the nation has chosen
leaders who advocated reducing the role of government in citizens' lives,
deregulating industry, and promoting economic growth through free-market
capitalism. Some observers have speculated that the 2008 election of President Barack Obama might herald the beginning of a new Progressive Era.

Lasting Achievements of the Progressive Era

By the time President Theodore Roosevelt left office in 1908, the Progressive Era was in full swing. With the muckrakers generating public support for his policies, Roosevelt had launched a slate of reforms that broke the monopoly power of trusts, outlawed a variety of unfair business practices, improved the lives of poor and working-class Americans, protected consumers from unsafe food and drugs, and conserved vast areas of land and natural resources.

Roosevelt's successor, fellow Republican William Howard Taft, recognized that the American people still had a thirst for reform when he took office. Taft continued to pursue popular policies aimed at reducing the power of big business in society and government. His efforts received support from a coalition of Democrats and progressive Republicans that formed a majority in the U.S. Congress.

One of the most significant pieces of legislation to pass during the Taft administration was the Mann-Elkins Act of 1910. It imposed federal regulations over the growing telephone, telegraph, and cable industries and also strengthened regulations over the railroad industry. Trust-busting efforts continued under Taft as well, including the breakup of John D. Rockefeller's Standard Oil Company in 1911. Finally, two important Constitutional amendments passed Congress during Taft's term: the Sixteenth, which established a federal income tax; and the Seventeenth, which provided for the direct election of U.S. senators. Both amendments were ratified by the necessary number of states in 1913.

By the time Taft's first term ended in 1912, the Progressive Movement had achieved many of its goals. "In just nine years, between 1903 and 1912, with the muckraking magazines providing the public opinion behind political action, the Sherman Anti-Trust Act had become the instrument to attack monopoly, the Interstate Commerce Commission was serving as a model for other regulatory commissions, the Pure Food and Drug Act was safely on the books, and, for the first time, conservation was a national issue. From the exposure of corruption in the senate came the popular election of senators," one historian noted. "Moreover, there was agitation to eradicate the evils of child labor, to give working women more equality, and to shorten the hours of workers. All these and other social reforms were, in part, the result of the investigative reporting done by the muckrakers in the ten-cent magazines."[1]

Despite the changes that had continued to take place under Taft, though, Roosevelt grew impatient with the pace of reform. In 1912 he decided to run for president as the candidate of the newly formed Progressive Party (also known as the Bull Moose Party). Progressive Republicans divided their votes between Roosevelt and Taft, however, which handed the election to Democrat Woodrow Wilson.

During Wilson's first term in office, progressives in Congress passed a number of significant reforms. The Federal Reserve Act of 1913, for instance, regulated the banking industry and helped stabilize the value of the dollar. The Clayton Antitrust Act of 1914 outlawed a variety of unfair business practices and protected the rights of workers to organize unions and conduct peaceful labor protests. The Federal Trade Commission Act of 1914 created a new government regulatory agency to enforce the provisions of the Clayton and Sherman Antitrust Acts. Finally, the Adamson Act of 1916 established an eight-hour work day for employees of railroads that crossed state lines.

Since the close of the Progressive Era, American politics has shifted back and forth between periods dominated by progressive and conservative ideas.

The End of the Progressive Era

By the mid-1910s, the Progressive Movement had addressed many of the most pressing problems caused by rapid industrialization. The federal government had adopted measures aimed at reducing political corruption, assumed greater regulatory control over large corporations, and established agencies and programs to improve the lives of poor and working-class Americans. In the meantime, however, international events began to capture a larger share of public attention. World War I broke out in Europe in 1914 between the Allies (mainly England, France, and Russia) and the Central Powers (primarily Germany, Turkey, and Austria-Hungary). The war's impact on the United States triggered a backlash against some of the underlying ideas of the Progressive Era.

Progressive leaders were divided over whether the United States should get involved in the war. Some opponents of U.S. involvement worried that entering the war would distract people from the problems still facing American society. They also expressed concern that the wartime production of military equipment would restore too much power to American industry. Supporters of involvement, on the other hand, argued that helping the Allies defeat the

President Franklin Delano Roosevelt—a distant cousin of President Theodore Roosevelt—instituted a wide range of progressive reforms in the 1930s through his New Deal programs.

Central Powers would "make the world safe for democracy" and allow the spread of progressive ideas around the globe.

Once the United States entered the war in 1917, Wilson continued to expand federal authority. He instituted an unpopular military draft, and he convinced Congress to pass sweeping measures designed to limit antiwar activities. The Wilson administration spied on citizens who openly criticized the war effort, for instance, and placed restrictions on civil liberties. Many people resented the loss of their basic freedoms and viewed it as an indication that the federal government had taken too much control over American society.

At the same time, the war changed many people's opinion of the large corporations that dominated the American economy. Business leaders threw the nation's industrial might squarely behind the war effort. Factories churned out military arms and equipment that turned the tide in favor of the Allies, and the war ended with Germany's surrender in 1918. By helping to win the war, the large corporations once again came to be viewed as valuable assets—rather than threats—to the nation's well-being.

Finally, some middle-class Americans felt less sympathy for workers, immigrants, and other progressive groups during and after World War I. At a time when the nation emphasized patriotism and worried about the spread of communism, people who spoke out against government corruption, corporate greed, and social injustice increasingly came to be regarded as dangerous radicals.

Progressives won a couple of final battles immediately following World War I. When the Eighteenth Amendment to the Constitution took effect in 1920, it banned the manufacture, sale, and transportation of alcohol in the United States. Later that year, American women gained the right to vote in national elections following the passage of the Nineteenth Amendment. On the whole, though, support for progressive causes dwindled. The election of pro-business Republican Warren G. Harding to the presidency in 1920 marked a shift back toward conservative political ideas.

The New Deal Brings Back Progressive Ideas

In 1929 a sudden drop in the value of the U.S. stock market pitched the nation into the Great Depression. This terrible economic downturn was marked by widespread bank failures, financial losses, business closures, and unemployment. By the early 1930s, 25 percent of the American workforce was without jobs, and rates of hunger and homelessness were soaring.

Many people blamed the policies of Republican President Herbert Hoover, who took office in 1929, for worsening the Depression. Hoover supported giving tax breaks and some public assistance to struggling workers and farmers. But he also believed that local relief agencies and charities—rather than the federal government—should take primary responsibility for helping people through the crisis. Because some people viewed Hoover as uncaring, the shantytowns full of poor and desperate people that sprung up in many American cities became known as Hoovervilles.

Discontent with Hoover's response to the crisis led to the election of Democrat Franklin D. Roosevelt to the presidency in 1932. A distant cousin of Theodore Roosevelt, he believed that active intervention by the federal government could lift the nation out of the Depression. Roosevelt convinced Congress to pass an array of progressive reforms designed to help struggling Americans and stimulate the economy. These programs, which were collectively known as the New Deal, reflected the spirit of the Progressive Era. In fact, the New Deal achieved several policy goals that Theodore Roosevelt and his Progressive Party had included in their platform twenty years earlier.

President Franklin D. Roosevelt believed that active intervention by the federal government could lift the nation out of the Great Depression. He convinced Congress to pass an array of progressive reforms designed to help struggling Americans and stimulate the economy.

A number of New Deal programs were intended to help American farmers. The Agricultural Adjustment Act of 1933, for instance, paid subsidies to farmers for voluntarily reducing their production by keeping land idle. The Farm Security Administration, created in 1937, gave farmers loans to help them relocate from marginal land to more productive acreage. Many other New Deal programs tried to improve conditions for industrial workers. For example, the National Industrial Recovery Act of 1933 abolished child labor and established a minimum wage and a maximum work week. The National

Labor Relations Act of 1935, also known as the Wagner Act, required employers to recognize labor unions.

A big priority for Roosevelt was putting unemployed Americans back to work. He believed that providing people with jobs would not only lift their spirits and enable them to support their families, but also give them money to spend and help improve the economy. Accordingly, the New Deal created several work relief agencies that provided people with jobs in public works projects. One successful agency, the Tennessee Valley Authority, built dams throughout the South to control flooding and bring electricity to rural areas. Another such agency, the Civilian Conservation Corps, put millions of young men to work on conservation projects in national parks and other public lands. Similarly, the Works Progress Administration employed over two million workers building roads, bridges, airports, and government offices across the country.

The New Deal also reformed U.S. tax laws and increased regulation of the banking industry and stock market. The Securities and Exchange Commission was created in 1934 to oversee the stock market and protect investors from unfair and fraudulent dealings. Similarly, the Federal Deposit Insurance Corporation was created to restore faith in the banking industry by placing a federal guarantee on bank deposits. Finally, the New Deal saw the passage of a progressive income tax that charged wealthy Americans higher tax rates.

Probably the most important legislation to come out of the New Deal was the Social Security Act of 1935. It created a "safety net" of federal assistance for poor, disabled, and elderly Americans. This net consisted of a pension system, funded by income tax payments, to provide financial assistance for retired workers. It also established unemployment insurance to help workers who lost their jobs. Finally, Social Security offered aid to disabled people and to children whose parents died or were unable to work.

The New Deal helped many people survive the Great Depression. It established a number of regulatory agencies and social programs that continue to protect Americans in the twenty-first century. Yet Roosevelt did not solve all of the country's problems, and the economy did not recover completely until World War II. In addition, his policies were very unpopular among business leaders and conservatives. Some critics argued that the increased regulation of business, combined with higher taxes and government spending, actually prolonged the Depression. Others claimed that Social Security and other relief

The New Deal's work relief programs, such as the Civilian Conservation Corps, provided jobs for unemployed Americans during the Great Depression.

programs reduced the incentives for people to work hard and instead encouraged them to depend on the government for their financial security. When the nation entered a period of prosperity following World War II, such views contributed to a return to conservative principles of government.

Shifts in American Political Thought

Since Roosevelt's death in 1945, American political thought has swung back and forth like a pendulum between progressive and conservative ideas. In general, conservatives believe that too much government regulation of business reduces individual initiative and hampers economic growth. They also distrust government interference in American society, arguing that it diminishes personal liberty and individual responsibility. Progressives, on the other hand, feel that government involvement is sometimes necessary to further the interests of the American people and help the nation prosper.

109

President Lyndon B. Johnson's Great Society programs marked a return to progressive ideas in the 1960s.

The next major era of progressive reform came in the 1960s. Led by Democratic President Lyndon B. Johnson, the federal government launched a number of progressive reforms that came to be known as the Great Society programs. African Americans fought for equality in the civil rights movement, and the federal government responded with such important legislation as the Civil Rights Act of 1964 and the Voting Rights Act of 1965. Poor and elderly Americans received greater access to affordable medical care during this time through the establishment of Medicare and Medicaid. The government also provided educational opportunities for a generation of military veterans through the G.I. Bill, which had been passed a few years earlier.

Following the social upheaval of the 1960s and 1970s, the nation shifted back toward conservative values with the election of Republican Ronald Reagan to the presidency in 1980. Reagan famously declared that "Government is not a solution to our problem; government is the problem." During his eight

Proclaiming that "Government is the problem," President Ronald Reagan shifted the nation back toward conservative ideas.

years in office, he launched a number of initiatives designed to shrink the size of the federal government, cut taxes, and reduce federal regulations on business. Reagan also cut government spending on social programs, arguing that they had created a "welfare state" in which people became excessively dependent on federal assistance.

The two decades after Reagan left office in 1988 were marked by political stalemates. Both conservatives and progressives enjoyed periods of advantage, but the shifts were less pronounced than in earlier eras. Through much of the 1990s, for instance, Democrat Bill Clinton—who generally supported progressive policies—held the White House, while conservative Republicans controlled both houses of Congress.

Some observers predicted that the election of President Barack Obama marked the beginning of a new Progressive Era in American politics.

A New Progressive Era?

In 2008, however, the U.S. economy entered into the worst recession in recent history. Many Americans blamed the conservative policies of President George W. Bush, whose administration cut taxes on the wealthy and reduced federal regulation of banks and other businesses. Such attitudes contributed to the election of Democrat Barack Obama to the presidency.

Upon taking the reins of government in early 2009, the Obama administration faced a number of significant challenges, including a severe economic downturn, growing inequality between rich and poor, business crises resulting from deregulation, and expensive military involvement in overseas wars. Some observers saw parallels between these circumstances and those that applied in earlier eras when progressive ideas took hold. They predicted that Obama's response to the problems facing the country might mark the beginning of a new Progressive Era. "The stars have aligned to give progressives a chance to permanently shift the conversation about America's values," one article noted. "The question before us now is, do today's progressives have what it takes to do what FDR [Franklin D. Roosevelt] and his allies accomplished 75 years ago—seize the new politics, take on the big challenges, and usher in a new era?"[2]

Notes

[1] Tebbel, John, and Mary Ellen Zuckerman. *The Magazine in America, 1741-1990.* New York: Oxford University Press, 1991, p. 110.

[2] Rosenberg, Simon, and Peter Leyden. "The 50-Year Strategy: A New Progressive Era." *Mother Jones,* October 31, 2007.

BIOGRAPHIES

Ray Stannard Baker (1870-1946)
Journalist and Author of Following the Color Line

Ray Stannard Baker, who also wrote under the name David Grayson, was born in Lansing, Michigan, on April 17, 1870. He was the first of six children born to Joseph Stannard Baker, who worked as a land agent, and Alice (Potter) Baker. They raised their children in an environment that emphasized the importance of literature and religious faith, and their eldest son carried these lessons with him for the rest of his life.

Baker graduated from Michigan Agricultural College (now Michigan State University) in 1889, and also briefly studied law at the University of Michigan. His career as a newspaper journalist began at the *Chicago News-Record*, which he joined in 1892 after a couple of years of work in his father's business. He spent six years at the newspaper, providing a wide range of stories on the city's political, economic, and social problems. During this period, Baker's attitudes about the poor and uneducated men, women, and children that populated Chicago's sprawling tenement slums underwent a dramatic change.

Awakening of a Social Reformer

When Baker first took the job with the *News-Record*, he believed that most of the impoverished people of Chicago had only themselves to blame for their troubles. But as the years went by, he began to question his assumptions. In 1893 he covered a march of jobless men known as Coxey's Army to Washington, D.C., where they organized protests against unemployment. One year later he was assigned to cover the Pullman Strike, a major labor strike by railroad workers who walked off the job in protest when their wealthy employer slashed their wages. As he wrote about these and other stories of industrial unrest and urban decay, Baker became convinced that the problems of poverty, exhausting and dangerous workloads, and disillusionment that faced working Americans were not always the result of personal failures. He also came to believe that their complaints should be treated more seriously by politicians and management.

Still, Baker's development into a full-fledged "muckraker" was a gradual one. In the summer of 1898 he left the *Chicago News-Record* for a staff position with *McClure's Magazine*. During Baker's first three years at *McClure's*, his most notable contributions to the magazine were highly positive feature stories on powerful men in American politics and industry, like politician Theodore Roosevelt and banking tycoon J.P. Morgan. In 1902, though, he was assigned to cover a major strike of unionized coalminers in eastern Pennsylvania. This assignment changed the course of Baker's career forever.

Despite his earlier experiences in Chicago, Baker still retained faith in America's capitalist system—and the basic fairness and decency of most corporate management toward workers—when he arrived in Pennsylvania. And the report he submitted criticized union leaders for committing violence against workers who crossed picket lines. But his investigation also revealed the low wages, terrible working conditions, and dehumanizing treatment that had led to the strike. When Baker returned to *McClure's* editorial offices, his story painted a grim picture of corporate greed and desperate miners. "Baker was a first-class reporter of formidable integrity," summarized one historical account. "He did not selectively gather facts to support his bias [toward management] but tore away the top layers of the labor situation to expose the appalling conditions in the mine fields."[1]

Baker's story on the Pennsylvania coal strike appeared in the January 1903 issue of *McClure's*. The same issue also featured explosive articles by Ida Tarbell on the ruthless practices of the Standard Oil Company and by Lincoln Steffens on political corruption in Minneapolis. Together, these three articles on American greed and division packed a huge punch, and their joint appearance in *McClure's* has frequently been described as the birthplace of the muckraking era. "It was no new game to lift the rocks in twentieth-century America and watch the bugs scramble for cover, but what was new was the expertise and authority of the writing,"[2] wrote one historian.

A Leading Voice of the Muckrakers

McClure's remained at the forefront of American journalism throughout the muckraking era. During this time, Baker emerged as one of the magazine's most famous writers. He contributed investigative reports on abusive treatment of workers and corruption in the garment, beef, and railroad industries, and he wrote sympathetically about the goals of organized labor unions. Baker's writing voice in all of these articles was calm and factual. His cool style infuriated at least one *McClure's* reader, who asked him why he did not tear into corrupt politicians and greedy business executives in his articles. Baker replied that "If I got mad, you wouldn't."[3]

In 1906 Baker and several of his colleagues at *McClure's* left the magazine to buy another periodical called *Leslie's Monthly Magazine*. They renamed it *American Magazine* and set about creating a publication that would blend muckraking articles with more uplifting stories about various aspects of American life and society. Baker remained on the staff of *American Magazine* for the next nine years, but his status as an investigative reporter enabled him to raise his family far from the periodical's New York offices. He and his wife Jessie Irene Beal (whom he married in 1896) and their four children lived in Baker's hometown of Lansing and also in Amherst, Massachusetts, during this period.

During his time at *American* and beyond, Baker's career took two different paths. On the one hand, he continued to be a part of the muckraking tradition of investigative reporting with books like *Following the Color Line* (1908), which explored racial prejudice in the United States. He also contributed articles to *American* on political reform movements and events like the textile strike of 1912 in Lawrence, Massachusetts. Baker also became a friend and ally to Senator Robert M. La Follette, one of the most fiercely progressive political figures of the early twentieth century. Despite all this, however, Baker never joined some of his other reform-minded colleagues who allied themselves with socialism and other left-wing political movements.

Instead, Baker launched a completely different writing career during this time that purposely avoided the world of politics. Writing under the name David Grayson, Baker produced a series of fanciful essays about wandering through the countryside, where he enjoyed nature's simple pleasures and the generosity of rural people. The "Grayson stories" were so enormously popular with the reading public that Baker wrote a total of nine books using the Grayson pen name from 1907 to 1942.

Biographer of Woodrow Wilson

In the mid-1910s Baker became a committed "Wilsonian"—a supporter of Democratic President Woodrow Wilson. When the United States entered

World War I in 1917 he worked as both a diplomat and press representative for the Wilson administration. His advocacy for Wilson's political positions and causes continued long after Wilson's 1921 retirement from office. In fact, during the 1920s and 1930s, Baker became one of the country's leading scholars on Wilson and his presidency. He wrote the three-volume *Woodrow Wilson and World Settlement* (1922) and joined with William E. Dodd to edit the six-volume *Public Papers of Woodrow Wilson* (1925-1927).

In the early 1920s Wilson agreed to let Baker write a biography of his life and presidency. He gave Baker access to his private papers and submitted to interviews with the journalist. Wilson died in 1924, but three years later Baker published the first of his biographical volumes. Baker eventually published eight volumes of *Woodrow Wilson: Life and Letters* from 1927 to 1939. The series was awarded a Pulitzer Prize for biography in 1940.

Baker withdrew from investigative reporting during the 1920s and 1930s, but he still occasionally commented on current affairs and political controversies. In the 1940s he was slowed by poor health, but he still managed to publish two autobiographies, *Native American: The Book of My Youth* (1941) and *American Chronicle: The Autobiography of Ray Stannard Baker* (1945). Baker died of a heart attack in Amherst on July 12, 1946.

Sources:

Baker, Ray Stannard. *American Chronicle: The Autobiography of Ray Stannard Baker.* New York: Scribner, 1945.

Bannister, Robert C., Jr. *Ray Stannard Baker: The Life and Thought of a Progressive.* New Haven, CT: Yale University Press, 1966.

Wilson, Harold S. *McClure's Magazine and the Muckrakers.* Princeton, NJ: Princeton University Press, 1970.

Notes

[1] Tebbel, John, and Mary Ellen Zuckerman. *The Magazine in America: 1741-1990.* New York: Oxford University Press, 1991, p. 112.

[2] Wilson, Harold S. *McClure's Magazine and the Muckrakers.* Princeton, NJ: Princeton University Press, 1970, p. 147.

[3] Quoted in Tebbel, p. 192.

S.S. McClure (1857-1949)
Progressive Owner and Editor of McClure's Magazine

Samuel Sidney McClure was born on February 17, 1857, in Frocess, County Antrim, Ireland. His father, Thomas McClure, was a carpenter and farmer. His mother, Elizabeth (Gaston) McClure, divided her time between farm work and caring for Samuel and his three younger brothers. In 1865 Thomas McClure died in an accident while working in a shipyard. His sudden death threatened the future of the rest of the family, which had depended on his earnings for basic food, clothing, and shelter. The circumstances of McClure's family steadily worsened, and in 1866 Elizabeth McClure fled to America—where four of her siblings had already immigrated—with her four sons.

Entering the World of Magazine Publishing

The McClure family settled on a small farm outside of Valparaiso, Indiana. Their first months in America were a terrible struggle, but in 1867 Elizabeth McClure married a fellow Irish immigrant named Thomas Simpson. They had four more children together before his death from typhoid fever in 1873.

Young Samuel attended school in Valparaiso, and by the time he graduated from high school he was known to classmates by his initials, "S.S." In 1874 McClure enrolled at Knox College in Galesburg, Illinois, where he distinguished himself as the editor of the school newspaper (the *Knox Student*) and the founder of the Western College Associated Press. During his time at Knox, McClure developed an intense romantic attachment to Harriet Hurd, the daughter of one of his professors. The relationship appeared to end after McClure's graduation in 1882. McClure fled to Boston after Hurd rejected him in response to intense pressure from her disapproving family.

Within a year, though, McClure had established himself in the world of magazine publishing by co-founding the highly successful magazine *Wheelman* with famed bicycle maker Albert Pope. McClure's success with *Wheelman* enabled him to make another bid for Harriet Hurd's hand in marriage, and this time her family grudgingly consented to the union. They were married on September 4, 1883, and eventually had five children.

Setting a New Course

In 1884 McClure and his wife left Boston for New York City, where he worked briefly at a printing company and at *Century* magazine. Late in the year, however, he launched his own business, which he called the McClure Syndicate. This syndicate—one of the first of its kind established in the United States—sold articles and short stories by popular writers to magazines and newspapers across the country. By the late 1880s McClure was working with some of the world's leading writers, including Rudyard Kipling, Robert Louis Stevenson, Henry James, Walt Whitman, Stephen Crane, and Jack London.

In 1893 McClure used his syndicate earnings to launch his own national periodical, called *McClure's Magazine*. The first issues were released at the height of a serious economic downturn in the United States, and the magazine barely survived its first year. But the high quality of its content and its low price—10 cents an issue at a time when most other magazines cost 25 or 35 cents—brought steady increases in readership. McClure compensated for the low price of the magazine by relying on advertising revenue. Other magazines followed suit, and the percentage of space devoted to advertising in many U.S. periodicals swiftly rose.

By 1900 *McClure's Magazine* enjoyed a circulation of more than 350,000 and a national reputation for publishing top-notch fiction and journalism. Several famous writers and reporters on the staff, including Ida Tarbell, Willa Cather, and Lincoln Steffens, first came to the attention of American readers in the pages of *McClure's*. In addition, McClure continued to place work from talented new fiction writers alongside contributions from some of the country's leading literary figures. His blend of news coverage, investigative reports, and high-quality fiction became the envy of nearly every other magazine in America.

Flagship of the Muckraking Movement

McClure's Magazine rose to prominence at a turbulent time in U.S. history. Industrialization, free-market capitalism, and settlement of the West had ushered in an exciting era of economic expansion across much of the country. But the gap between America's rich business class and its millions of working poor seemed to be growing wider with each passing year. A so-called Progressive Movement rose up to protest against this state of affairs, as well as other perceived problems in American society such as political corruption, urban squalor, and mistreatment of laborers.

As the first decade of the twentieth century unfolded, American newspapers and magazines contributed to these calls for governmental and economic reform by publishing hard-hitting investigative reports detailing outrageous examples of consumer fraud, government corruption, and immoral behavior by powerful corporations and individuals. These "muckraking" reports, as they came to be known, became a specialty of several national magazines, including *Collier's, Cosmopolitan, Munsey's,* and *The Independent.* But S.S. McClure's magazine became the most famous of the muckraking magazines of the Progressive Era.

McClure's emergence as the flagship magazine of the muckraking movement is usually traced to its January 1903 issue, which featured three explosive investigative reports by Tarbell, Steffens, and muckraking journalist Ray Stannard Baker. Tarbell's piece on the ruthless practices of Standard Oil—the third installment in an entire series of Tarbell articles on Standard that was published by *McClure's*—was one of the most famous reports of the entire muckraking era. But the articles by Steffens and Baker—on political corruption and vicious lawlessness in the Pennsylvania coal fields, respectively—had a similarly momentous impact on public opinion. Together, the three investigative pieces amounted to a scathing attack on the state of American politics, business, and society. Today, the publication of the January 1903 issue of *McClure's* is often cited as one of the most important events in the history of American journalism.

As the muckraking movement gained momentum, McClure and his talented stable of writers and editors maintained a leading role. They were progressives themselves, and they saw the magazine as a tool that could help bring about much-needed reforms to American factories, tenements, boardrooms, and legislative chambers. As one historian observed, "McClure and his staff were very conscious of participating in a political and economic movement intent upon reshaping many of the country's institutions."[1]

This dedication to the reform cause led McClure and his editors to fill issue after issue with reports and analyses of various problems in American society. Meanwhile, the magazine's lively and daring tone and its beautiful covers and illustrations attracted a broad cross-section of readers. By 1905 it was almost universally regarded as the finest general-interest magazine in the country. "*McClure's* was a supernova in the journalistic firmament," confirmed one scholar. "Besides a talent for picking writers, McClure could talk almost anyone into working for him, and when he did, he gave them a free hand. He plowed his profits back into the magazine and thought nothing of spending thousands of dollars on one story."[2]

The Decline of *McClure's*

The fortunes of *McClure's Magazine* and its colorful owner changed dramatically in 1906. Over the course of that year, President Theodore Roosevelt publicly condemned the muckrakers for being excessively negative about American life and society. Even more importantly, McClure lost the services of Tarbell, Baker, and Steffens. Each of these writers had become frustrated by the publisher's careless financial stewardship of *McClure's*. In addition, they were angered by the fact that he was framing the magazine as a guardian of public and business morality at the same time that he was carrying out multiple extramarital affairs.

The simultaneous resignation of the magazine's three top journalists was a terrible blow to McClure—he once described it as the greatest tragedy of his life—but it was made even worse by the fact that they decided to establish their own magazine. When the trio left *McClure's* to form their own publication, called *American Magazine,* they took many readers with them. McClure and chief editor Willa Cather tried several strategies to reverse his magazine's sliding sales, but none of them worked.

In 1912 McClure lost financial control of the magazine. In 1914 he published his autobiography, but the book was actually written by Cather (who later went on to become a Pulitzer Prize-winning novelist). McClure spent the next several years supporting himself as a writer, and in 1922 he returned to *McClure's* for a three-year stint as the magazine's managing editor. He then left the public spotlight almost entirely, and in 1929 his namesake magazine went out of business. McClure spent his final years living quietly in New York City, where friends and relatives reportedly gave him financial assistance. He died of a heart attack on March 21, 1949.

Sources:
Cather, Willa. *The Autobiography of S.S. McClure.* Lincoln: University of Nebraska Press, 1997.

Lyon, Peter. *Success Story: The Life and Times of S.S. McClure.* New York: Scribner's, 1963.
Wilson, Harold S. *McClure's Magazine and the Muckrakers.* Princeton, NJ: Princeton University Press, 1970.

Notes

1 Wilson, Harold S. *McClure's Magazine and the Muckrakers.* Princeton, NJ: Princeton University Press, 1970, p. 191
2 Woodress, James. *Willa Cather: A Literary Life.* Lincoln: University of Nebraska Press, 1989, p. 185.

David Graham Phillips (1867-1911)
Journalist Who Wrote the "Treason of the Senate" Series

David Graham Phillips was born in Madison, Indiana, on October 31, 1867. He was one of five children born to David Graham Phillips Sr., a banker, and Margaret (Lee) Phillips. Even as a youngster, Phillips had a strong interest in literature. This passion was encouraged by his parents, who placed great value on education and the arts. By the time he enrolled at Indiana's Asbury College (now Depauw University) in the early 1880s, Phillips was focused on a writing career. In 1885 he transferred to Princeton University in New Jersey, and he graduated two years later.

Newspaperman from Cincinnati to London

In 1888 Phillips secured his first newspaper job, working as a reporter for the *Cincinnati Times-Star.* Within two years, though, he had moved on to a more prestigious position with the *New York Sun.* Phillips quickly cemented his reputation within the New York newspaper world as a gifted journalist. In 1893 the *New York World*, which was owned by famed publisher Joseph Pulitzer, hired him as its chief correspondent in London.

Phillips stayed with the *World* for the next nine years. During this time he filed stories and investigative reports from all across Europe and the United States, and even spent time in charge of the newspaper's editorial page. As time passed, though, Phillips became disenchanted with the constant deadlines and hurried pace of newspaper work. In 1901 Phillips published his first novel, *The Great God Success,* and a year later he decided to leave the paper for a life of novel-writing and investigative reports for magazines. He stayed in New York City, though. He lived in the city's Gramercy Park neighborhood with one of his sisters, Carolyn, who edited and organized much of his writing.

Phillips enjoyed a very successful career as a novelist, in part because he put in such long hours at his craft. He wrote twenty-two novels and plays in the space of ten years, including *The Deluge* (1905), *The Plum Tree* (1905), *Light-Fingered Gentry* (1907), *The Fashionable Adventures of Joshua Craig* (1909) and *The Hungry Heart* (1909). His best-known novel was probably *Susan Lenox: Her Fall and Rise* (1917), which was published six years after his death thanks to the tireless efforts of Carolyn. In 1931 *Susan Lenox*, which told the story of a brave but downtrodden young woman trying to lift herself out of a life of prostitution, was made into a motion picture starring Greta Garbo and Clark Gable.

"The Treason of the Senate"

Many of the novels that Phillips produced focused on themes of political corruption, corporate greed, and oppression of women and the poor. These same issues dominated the muckraking investigative reports that he wrote for *Cosmopolitan*, the *Saturday Evening Post*, *Success*, and other national magazines during the early 1900s. His hard-hitting investigations of greed and lawlessness by industrial tycoons and politicians earned Phillips many enemies, but they also vaulted him to the forefront of the muckraking movement.

Phillips's most famous contribution to the muckraking cause came in 1906, when he wrote a nine-part series for *Cosmopolitan* magazine known as "The Treason of the Senate." This series, which was later published in book form, uncovered widespread fraud and corruption in the U.S. Senate. The journalist took aim at numerous senators. He accused them of taking bribes from industrial interests to pass business-friendly laws and of selecting corrupt allies of industry for open senate seats.

Phillips used harsh and angry language throughout "The Treason of the Senate." He described New York Senator Thomas Collier Platt, for example, as someone with a "long and unbroken record of treachery to the people in legislation of privilege and plunder." But the prime target of his muckraking series was Nelson Aldrich, a powerful Republican senator from Rhode Island. Phillips charged that under Aldrich's corrupt leadership, rich Americans were accumulating wealth and power at the expense of the nation's poor and powerless. "Property is concentrating in the hands of the few," wrote Phillips, "and the little children of the masses are being sent to toil in the darkness of mines, in the dreariness and unhealthfulness of factories instead of being sent to school."[1]

Many corporate leaders and national lawmakers, including President Theodore Roosevelt, rejected the accusations leveled by Phillips. They claimed that "Treason of the Senate" was riddled with misleading and untrue charges. The publication of Phillips's series has even been cited as a major factor behind Roosevelt's decision to issue a stern 1906 speech condemning muckraking journalism for eroding the American people's faith in the country's public and business institutions. Nonetheless, the series also was hailed by thousands of reformers and ordinary citizens for exposing corruption and decay at the highest levels of American government. "Glory Hallelujah!" declared one *Cosmopolitan* reader. "You have found a David who is able and willing to attack this Goliath of a Senate!"[2]

"Treason of the Senate" also gave new momentum to a reform campaign to have U.S. senators elected by the American public. When the United States was first formed, the Constitution provided for the election of senators by individual state legislatures. Many people believed that this system was undemocratic and rife with abuse and fraud, but calls for reform floundered until Phillips's series came along. As public anger intensified, lawmakers realized that they had to respond with meaningful legislation. In June 1911 the U.S. Senate approved a constitutional amendment providing for the direct election of U.S. senators by American voters. Eleven months later, the House of Representatives approved the amendment as well. It then went to the states for ratification, and in April 1913 the Seventeenth Amendment to the U.S. Constitution was ratified.

Phillips did not live to see the Seventeenth Amendment become law, however. On January 23, 1911, a mentally ill man named Fitzhugh Goldsborough shot Phillips on a New York street. Goldsborough had become obsessed by the idea that Phillips's 1909 novel *The Fashionable Adventures of Joshua Craig* included veiled insults toward members of Goldsborough's family. After shooting Phillips, the murderer then turned the gun on himself and committed suicide. Phillips was rushed to a hospital, but he died one day later.

Phillips's shocking death was mourned by political progressives and the literary world alike. "He was a true patriot," declared the *New York Times*, "loving his country and his people to the point where he would put himself to serious trouble to point out her faults or assist in curing her mistakes, or to denounce what seemed to him wrong and sordid in the people's ideals. The loss of a man of such temper and conviction is a sad one indeed."[3]

Sources:

Filler, Louis. *The Muckrakers: Crusaders for American Liberalism.* Yellow Springs, OH: Antioch Press, 1964.

Filler, Louis. *Voice of the Democracy: A Critical Biography of David Graham Phillips, Journalist, Novelist, Progressive.* University Park, PA: Pennsylvania State University Press, 1978.

Streitmatter, Rodger. *Mightier than the Sword: How the News Media Have Shaped American History.* Boulder, CO: Westview Press, 1997.

Notes

1 Phillips, David Graham. "The Treason of the Senate: Aldrich, the Head of It All." *Cosmopolitan,* March 1906.

2 Quoted in Streitmatter, Rodger. *Mightier than the Sword: How the News Media Have Shaped American History.* Boulder, CO: Westview Press, 1997, p. 100.

3 Hawthorne, Hildegarde. "David Graham Phillips: A Novelist Who was Inspired by Moral Purpose and Aimed at Patriotic Ends," *New York Times,* Jan. 29, 1911, p. BR44.

Jacob Riis (1849-1914)
Photographer and Author of How the Other Half Lives

Jacob A. Riis was born in the small town of Ribe, Denmark, on May 3, 1849. His father, Niels Edward Riis, worked as a local schoolmaster. His mother, Carolina, worked as a governess before she began having children. She ultimately had fourteen children—thirteen of them boys. Jacob was the third-oldest child, and he had a strong bond with his generous and kind-hearted mother. "Mother deserves a halo" for being such a "good soul,"[1] Jacob wrote in a letter to one of his siblings.

Riis apprenticed as a carpenter in Copenhagen, Denmark, as a young man. He then returned to Ribe and proposed marriage to Elizabeth Giortz, a young woman with whom he had fallen deeply in love. But she did not feel the same way about Riis. She turned down his proposal and a short time later announced her engagement to a young Danish military officer. Her rejection, along with the poor Danish economy, convinced Riis to build a new life for himself in America.

Life as a Reporter and Reformer

Riis arrived by immigrant ship in New York City in June 1870. Unlike many other immigrants of that era, Riis could speak English and he was well-educated. But he still struggled to find steady work, and at one point he was reduced to sleeping in a graveyard and living on a diet of apples. As the months passed by he managed to improve his situation with carpentry work. But he never forgot those early months he spent in America as a penniless immigrant, desperately searching for food, clothing, and shelter.

In 1873 Riis began his career as a newspaperman, accepting a reporter position with a neighborhood paper called the *Long Island City Review*. Over the next several years he became an experienced reporter on police work and crime, mostly as a member of the staff of the *New York Tribune*. Meanwhile, he learned in 1874 that Giortz's fiancé had died. He resumed correspondence with Giortz, and in 1876 she agreed to join him in the United States. They married on March 5, 1876, and stayed together until her death in 1905.

Riis's ongoing work as a newspaper reporter on New York's police beat had a tremendous impact on the young journalist. His job took him into high-crime tenement neighborhoods were residents lived with nightmarish levels of poverty, overcrowding, disease, and filth. Riis even found himself spending time in some of the same slums and alleyways that he had wandered during his first horrible months in New York City. Riis was outraged and saddened by the suffering that he saw all around him. Yet he was also inspired by the courage and determination of the immigrant workers and families that populated these tenements.

During the 1880s Riis devoted more and more of his writings to the horrendous conditions in which so many New York residents lived—and the indifference of wealthy industrialists and politicians to their suffering. By 1888, when he began using new flash-photography technology to illustrate his articles, Riis had become a crusader for urban reform. He was determined to educate middle-class Americans about the daily horrors that poor city residents endured, and to force reforms to New York's police-operated poorhouses and city services.

Riis's dedication to improving the lives of the urban poor was also evident in his private life. He joined local civic reform groups devoted to ending child labor and toughening building codes. He also became a leading advocate of efforts to build new parks, playgrounds, and settlement houses for poor residents. But he remained best known for weaving together photography and personal stories of immigrant despair and hope that pricked the conscience of prosperous, native-born Americans.

How the Other Half Lives

In 1888 Riis moved to the *New York Evening Sun,* where he worked for the next eleven years. It was during this period that the reform-minded journalist became famous not only in New York, but all across the country. In 1889 he published an article in *Scribner's* magazine on the squalor in New York's slums. The article featured his trademark blend of sympathetic writing and dramatic photography, and it caused such a sensation that publisher Charles Scribner agreed to publish a book-length version. This expanded work—called *How the Other Half Lives: Studies among the Tenements of New York*—featured 44 of Riis's photographs. It also gave readers a tour of the slum neighborhoods of New York City, with Riis stopping at each point along the way to discuss the living conditions he encountered and the wider causes and effects of urban poverty.

Each paragraph of *How the Other Half Lives* was designed to awaken more affluent Americans to the tragic toll that tenement conditions were taking on hard-working men and women and innocent children. "Long ago it was said that 'one half of the world does not know how the other half lives,'" he wrote in the book's introduction. "That was true then. It did not know because it did not care. The half that was on top cared little for the struggles, and less for the fate, of those who were underneath, so long as it was able to hold them there and keep its own seat."[1] Riis wanted to use his notepad and his camera to change all that, and it is for that reason that he is sometimes described as America's first muckraker.

How the Other Half Lives was enormously popular and influential. The book's impact was due in part to Riis's amazing photographs, which gave readers a real sense of the misery of the urban poor. But it was also due to his ability to frame his cause as one of basic decency and Christian compassion—themes that his audience would recognize and appreciate. "In that first book, Riis employed every means he could muster to arouse his readers: curiosity, humor, shock, fear, guilt, and faith," wrote one biographer. "His passion ignited his audience, but his message was not truly incendiary.... [He was] a skillful entertainer who presented controversial ideas in a compelling but ultimately comforting manner."[2]

Chronicling Life in the American City

How the Other Half Lives made Riis both wealthy and famous. He became a highly sought-after lecturer on poverty and other urban issues, in part because his presentations featured lantern slides of his famous photographs set to music. Riis also struck up a deep and enduring friendship with New York City Police Commissioner Theodore Roosevelt, who later served as president of the United States from 1901 to 1909. Roosevelt respected Riis so much that he reportedly called him "the best American I ever knew."

But despite the dramatic improvement in his own personal circumstances, Riis did not forget the poor people of New York. Instead, he spent the

1890s and early 1900s publishing one book after another on the issues of urban poverty and reform. Notable titles of this period include *The Children of the Poor* (1892), *Out of Mulberry Street: Stories of Tenement Life in New York City* (1898), *A Ten Years' War: An Account of the Battle with the Slum in New York* (1900), and *Children of the Tenements* (1903). He also wrote a best-selling autobiography called *The Making of an American* (1901). All of these books were marred by racial stereotyping, but they also shone with sympathy for the downtrodden and optimism for the future of American cities.

In 1907 Riis married his second wife, Mary Phillips. They bought a farm in Massachusetts in 1911, and it was there that Riis spent most of his last few years. He died of a heart attack on May 25, 1914. Today, he is remembered both for his pioneering work with flash photography and his status as a forerunner of the muckraking movement.

Sources:

Alland, Alexander, Jr. *Jacob A. Riis: Photographer and Citizen.* New York: Aperture, 1974.

Buk-Sweinty, Tom. *The Other Half: The Life of Jacob Riis and the World of Immigrant America.* Translated by Annette Buk-Sweinty. New York: Norton, 2008.

Davis, Kay. "Documenting 'The Other Half': The Social Reform Photography of Jacob Riis and Lewis Hine." Available online at http://xroads.virginia.edu/~MA01/Davis/photography/home/home.html.

Lane, James B. Lane. *Jacob Riis and the American City.* New York: Kennikat Press, 1974.

Pascal, Janet B. *Jacob Riis: Reporter and Reformer.* New York: Oxford University Press, 2005.

Yochelson, Bonnie, and Daniel Czitrom. *Rediscovering Jacob Riis: Exposure Journalism and Photography in Turn of the Century New York.* New York: New Press, 2007.

Notes

[1] Quoted in Pascal, Janet B. *Jacob Riis: Reporter and Reformer.* New York: Oxford University Press, 2005, p. 11.

[2] Yochelson, Bonnie, and Daniel Czitrom. *Rediscovering Jacob Riis: Exposure Journalism and Photography in Turn of the Century New York.* New York: New Press, 2007, p. 7.

John D. Rockefeller (1839-1937)
Industrial Tycoon, Philanthropist, and Major Target of the Muckrakers

John Davison Rockefeller, Sr., was born on July 8, 1839, in Richford, a small town in upstate New York. His father, William Avery Rockefeller, was an irresponsible man who scrambled to make money as a businessman, farmer, magician, and traveling medicine salesman (the medications he sold included worthless cancer "remedies"). His long absences left Rockefeller's mother, Eliza Davison Rockefeller, as the sole caregiver for their four children for weeks at a time.

The Rockefeller family moved frequently before settling in Cleveland, Ohio, in 1853. Young Rockefeller was both serious and industrious, and he worked at a variety of after-school jobs. Rockefeller also took a keen interest in learning about all facets of business. Years later he declared that by the time that he was in his mid-teens, he knew more about the rules and principles of business than men twice his age.

Business Success at an Early Age

Rockefeller's rise to the heights of American business began modestly. In 1855 he graduated from high school and took a job as an assistant accounting clerk in a Cleveland brokerage house. Four years later, he partnered with Maurice Clark to establish a small trading company that did business in grain and other commodities. In 1864 Rockefeller married Laura Celestia Spelman, with whom he eventually had five children.

Rockefeller continued his march up the ladder of U.S. business and finance during the 1860s by hitching his star to America's fledgling oil industry. Abandoning his partnership with Clark, he made major investments in oil refineries during the waning months of the Civil War. He also found a new business partner in Henry Flagler, and on January 10, 1870, the two men established the Standard Oil Company.

Over the next several months, Rockefeller and Flagler put together a cunning plan to seize a commanding grip over America's oil refining industry, which was based in Cleveland at the time. First, they reached a secret business agreement with Thomas Scott, the powerful president of the Pennsylvania Railroad. This railroad was the largest corporation in the United States in the 1860s. The alliance with Scott gave Standard Oil new levels of access to lawmakers across the country, for as social reformer Wendell Phillips observed, when "[Scott] trailed his garments across the country the members of 20 legislatures rustled like dry leaves in a winter's wind."[1]

Operating under a shell company called the South Improvement Company (SIC), Scott and Rockefeller put together an oil shipping scheme that would give both Standard and the Pennsylvania Railroad major advantages over their competitors. When details of the plan began to emerge, however, public outrage forced Rockefeller and Scott to dissolve the SIC.

Building an Oil Empire

Undaunted by the unraveling of the SIC plan, Rockefeller carried out a campaign of economic warfare against his competitors in the Cleveland area. During February and March 1872 he used Standard's operating advantages over most other refiners to great effect, pressuring nearly two dozen operations to sell out to him. Critics of Standard Oil's ruthless business practices assailed these events as the "Cleveland Massacre," but Rockefeller proclaimed that he was actually providing a public service. He insisted that Standard Oil would be the "salvation of the oil business" because it would transform the industry from a "disgraceful, gambling, mining scheme" into a "reputable pursuit."[2]

Rockefeller acquired more competitors in the 1870s and 1880s, which enabled him to further expand his reach into profitable new markets. In 1882 he formally established the Standard Oil Trust to coordinate all exploration, refining, production, and distribution activities. This trust was essentially a giant corporation composed of numerous smaller corporations.

In the 1890s Rockefeller 's empire grew to encompass iron ore mining, shipping, and other industry sectors. Oil remained the cornerstone of the Standard Oil empire, though. By the 1890s it controlled nearly 90 percent of the oil produced in the United States. "Everything about its operation was colossal," wrote one Rockefeller biographer. "Twenty thousand wells poured their output into 4,000 miles of Standard Oil pipelines, carrying the crude to seaboard or to 5,000 Standard Oil tank cars. The combine now employed 100,000 people and superintended the export of 50,000 barrels of oil daily. Rockefeller's creation could be discussed only in superlatives: it was the biggest and richest, the most feared and admired business organization in the world."[3]

Not surprisingly, the staggering success of Rockefeller and Standard drew the admiring attention of business owners and executives all across the nation. Many corporate chiefs reshaped their own businesses to reflect the Rockefeller business model. By the close of the 1890s, corporate trusts had taken dominant positions in coal, sugar, beef, and many other U.S. industries.

Target of the Muckrakers

As the twentieth century dawned, an aura of mystery swirled around Rockefeller, who only rarely appeared in public. This was due in part to a bout with alopecia in the early 1890s. This rare medical condition caused Rockefeller to lose all the hair on his body, even including his eyebrows. But the tycoon's retirement from day-to-day management of Standard's affairs was also a factor in his withdrawal from public life. This retirement, which occurred gradually over the course of the 1890s, left direction of most Standard operations in the hands of executive John Archbold. Rockefeller never publicly announced his retirement, however, and he retained his title as president of the company until 1911.

As a result, Rockefeller remained the figure most closely associated with the Standard Oil empire. And as America's first billionaire, he ranked for many years as one of the country's leading symbols of industrial wealth. This status made him enormously controversial. Some people admired his long record of business triumphs and hailed his life as a classic example of the fulfillment of the American dream. Most working-class Americans and political reformers loathed him, however. They saw the fabulously wealthy Rockefeller as one of the worst of the "robber barons"—industrial tycoons who built their riches through decades of trickery, deceit, and exploitation of workers.

This viewpoint was fueled to a significant degree by intense scrutiny from America's muckraking journalists. Fierce criticism of Rockefeller's business practices and Standard's monopoly power had appeared in newspapers and magazines as far back as the 1870s. One of the earliest American muckrakers, journalist Henry Demarest Lloyd, was an especially bothersome critic. His 1881 *Atlantic Monthly* article "Story of a Great Monopoly," and his 1894 book *Wealth against Commonwealth,* painted extremely bleak and unattractive portraits of Standard Oil and its founder.

But the fiercest criticism of Rockefeller and Standard Oil came during the early 1900s, when the muckraking movement reached its peak. Many muckraking journalists joined progressive activists in condemning the "robber baron" Rockefeller and the fearsome Standard "octopus" he had created. The most influential of these individuals was Ida Tarbell. Her exposé of Standard was published first in *McClure's* in a nineteen-part series beginning in late 1902. She then published her report in book form in 1904 as *History of the Standard Oil Company*. Tarbell's depiction of Standard Oil and its founder as thoroughly corrupt forces in American society sparked a tremendous public uproar. In late 1904 mounting political pressure led President Theodore Roosevelt to approve a federal investigation of Standard's business practices.

The End of Standard Oil

On November 18, 1906, the U.S. government formally filed suit against Standard Oil. Federal lawyers charged that the company was a business monopoly that was operating in clear violation of American antitrust laws. A tremendous court battle ensued, but after five years of legal wrangling the federal government won the case. On May 15, 1911, the U.S. Supreme Court announced that Standard Oil had to be broken up. Over the next several months, Rockefeller's empire was carved into numerous smaller companies. The largest of these, Standard Oil, eventually became ExxonMobil; other major oil companies formed by the breakup evolved into such well-known oil companies as Chevron, Amoco, Sunoco, and the American arm of British Petroleum (BP).

Ironically, Rockefeller's personal wealth actually increased in the wake of the court-ordered dismantling of Standard. He retained big ownership stakes in most of the oil companies that came about as a result of the break-up, and these companies became hugely profitable in the 1910s and 1920s with the rise of the gasoline-guzzling automobile.

Rockefeller's reputation underwent some significant changes in his later years. During the 1910s the wealthy industrialist made huge financial contributions to charities, churches, and other philanthropic causes. His financial gifts also paid for the creation of the University of Chicago, the Rockefeller Institute for Medical Research, the Rockefeller Sanitary Commission (which played a big role in eradicating the hookworm disease from the American South), and the Rockefeller Foundation, which remains one of the world's leading philanthropic organizations in the twenty-first century. He also donated millions of dollars for libraries, schools, and the preservation of historical landmarks and nature preserves. Rockefeller spent his last few years living quietly at his compound in Ormond Beach, Florida. He suffered a heart attack and died on May 23, 1937.

Sources:

Chernow, Ron. *Titan: The Life of John D. Rockefeller, Sr.* New York: Random House, 1998.

"John D. Rockefeller Sr. 1839-1937" In *American Experience: The Rockefellers,* http://www.pbs .org/wgbh/amex/rockefellers/peopleevents/p_rock_jsr.html.

Morris, Charles R. *Tycoons: How Andrew Carnegie, John D. Rockefeller, Jay Gould, and J.P. Morgan Invented the American Supereconomy.* New York: Macmillan, 2005.

Nevins, Allan. *Study in Power: John D. Rockefeller, Industrialist and Philanthropist.* 2 vols. New York: Scribner's, 1953.

Weinberg, Steve. *Taking on the Trust: The Epic Battle Between Ida Tarbell and John D. Rockefeller.* New York: Norton, 2008.

Notes

[1] Quoted in Chernow, Ron. *Titan: The Life of John D. Rockefeller, Sr.* New York: Random House, 1998, p. 135.

[2] Quoted in Chernow, p. 154.

[3] Chernow, p. 249.

Theodore Roosevelt (1858-1919)
President of the United States, 1901-1909

Theodore "Teddy" Roosevelt was born in New York City on October 27, 1858. His father, Theodore Roosevelt, Sr., was a prosperous businessman. His mother, Martha (Bulloch) Roosevelt, devoted her days to taking care of her four children (Teddy was the second-oldest). Roosevelt's early childhood was marred by frailty and sickness, and he struggled with asthma and poor eyesight. As a young teen, though, he launched a campaign of physical self-improvement that had remarkable results. He took up boxing, weightlifting, horseback riding, hunting, mountain climbing, canoeing and rowing, and other challenging activities, and by the time he entered college he had transformed his spindly body into one of hard-packed muscle. This physical transformation—and the joy that Roosevelt took in all of these activities—gave him a lifelong passion for what he liked to call the "strenuous life."

Entering the World of Politics

Roosevelt received his early education from private tutors, and then entered Harvard College in 1876. He graduated four years later and promptly married Alice Hathaway Lee. Roosevelt developed a keen interest in politics during his years at Harvard. In 1882 he cast aside notions of a career as a lawyer or historian and instead became a Republican member of the New York state assembly. He served three one-year terms in the assembly, but his last term was darkened by the death of his wife died during childbirth.

Leaving his infant daughter Alice in the care of relatives, Roosevelt left New York for the Dakota Territory. He immediately made his mark out west as an ambitious and hard-nosed cattle rancher and sheriff. In 1886 he married Edith Kermit Carow, with whom he eventually had one daughter and four sons.

In 1889 Roosevelt returned to New York City when he was offered a position with the U.S. Civil Service Commission. He quickly became one of the city's most outspoken and effective crusaders against political corruption in city government. His dedication to the reform cause led to his appointment as New York City police commissioner in 1895.

Roosevelt's tenure as police commissioner was brief, though. National political leaders had taken note of the brash and charismatic reformer, and in the spring of 1897 he was selected to serve in Washington, D.C., as assistant secretary of the Navy. One year later, however, he resigned this position to take part in the Spanish-American War. Roosevelt personally organized and served as colonel of the First U.S. Volunteer Cavalry Regiment, which distinguished itself throughout the brief conflict. The exploits of Roosevelt and his so-called "Rough Riders" made him a military hero when he returned home to New York in the summer of 1898.

Governor and Vice President

Roosevelt and New York's Republican Party took full advantage of the young politician's mushrooming reputation as a tough and fearless reformer. Republicans nominated Roosevelt as their candidate for governor, and the newly returned war hero campaigned across the state with his usual gusto. He won a narrow victory in November 1898, in large part because voters placed greater value on his personal history than on the anti-reform, big-business reputation of the wider Republican Party.

As governor, Roosevelt bucked his own party on numerous occasions to force the passage of important new business and government reforms. He also supported labor against management in several high-profile clashes, which was very unusual for the governor of any state at that time. Some progressive activists expressed dissatisfaction that Roosevelt did not take even bolder steps to curb the power of big business, but as historian John Allen Gable noted, "Who *in office* was more radical in 1899?"[1]

In 1900 Republican President William McKinley asked Roosevelt to be his vice presidential nominee for the upcoming fall elections (his previous vice president, Garret Hobart, had died in office in November 1899). Roosevelt accepted, and the McKinley-Roosevelt ticket cruised to victory. Ten months later, however, McKinley was assassinated in Buffalo, New York, and Roosevelt was sworn in as president on September 14, 1901.

Roosevelt and the Progressive Movement

When Roosevelt took his seat in the Oval Office, he was younger than any of the other twenty-five men who had previously held the presidency. But he did not suffer from any self-doubts about his ability to do the job. To the contrary, his high energy and self-confidence was evident from the outset. Roosevelt believed that the United States was the greatest of countries, and he repeatedly praised its democratic system of government, its capitalist economic foundations, and the vitality and patriotism of its citizens. But he also believed that America's corporate giants had become too powerful—and too ruthless in their treatment of workers, smaller businesses, and natural resources.

Roosevelt's desire to pass reforms that would address these concerns was greatly aided by the Progressive Movement. This movement of concerned middle-class citizens and liberal activists gave Roosevelt the political support he needed to help working-class causes, address urban poverty, and curb the excesses of industry. Roosevelt's cause was also helped by his boisterous and energetic personality, which was a big hit with the American public. "The gift of the gods to Theodore Roosevelt was joy, joy in life," explained muckraking journalist Lincoln Steffens years later. "He took joy in everything he did, in hunting, camping, and ranching, in politics, in reforming the police or the civil service, in organizing and commanding the Rough Riders."[2]

When the November 1904 elections came around, Roosevelt easily won another four years in the White House. In his second term he pressed for even bolder reforms to various sectors of American business and society. These campaigns were applauded by progressives all across the country. "Men say he is not safe," scoffed Elihu Root, who served as Roosevelt's secretary of state for the last four years of his presidency. "He is not safe for the men who wish to prosecute selfish schemes to the public detriment [or] … who wish government to be conducted with greater reference to campaign contributions than to the public good."[3]

Clashing with the Muckrakers

Roosevelt had many triumphs during his second term that were hailed by progressives. He helped impose new laws regulating corporate behavior, attacked industry monopolies, ushered in new protections for workers and consumers, and passed the nation's first great wave of natural resource conservation laws. These developments were welcomed by many of the corruption-fighting journalists who whipped up popular support for government reforms during the early 1900s.

Yet Roosevelt's relations with these crusading members of the press became extremely tense during his second term in office. He came to feel that the stories that investigative magazines like *McClure's* and *Cosmopolitan* emphasized were eroding the public's faith in basic American institutions. The president also feared that their exposés were contributing to public support for truly radical proposals offered by Socialists, Communists, and anarchists to remake American society. In addition, Roosevelt became convinced that some of the journalists were simply taking advantage of working-class jealousy and envy of the rich to sell magazines.

In 1906 Roosevelt's frustrations finally boiled over. During one official dinner, he issued a stinging speech in which he compared America's crusading journalists to the "man with the muck-rake" in John Bunyan's famous book *Pilgrim's Progress*—a character who was interested only in raking filth, to the exclusion of all other aspects of life. Roosevelt's use of the term "muckrakers" was intended as a terrible insult, and some American journalists took it that way. But others actually thought it was a pretty good description of their work, and they embraced the term. Before long, "muckrakers" had become a common term, and it is still used today in reference to American journalists who uncover evidence of corporate greed, government corruption, and other lawlessness.

An Enduring Figure in American Politics

Roosevelt turned aside calls for him to run for re-election in 1908. Instead, he asked fellow Republicans to nominate his Secretary of War, William Howard Taft. The party promptly fell in line behind Taft, who won the 1908 election and took office in March 1909.

Roosevelt departed the Oval Office for a long hunting and scientific expedition in Africa followed by an extended tour of Europe. When he returned to the United States in mid-1910, however, he found a Republican Party at war with itself. Taft's presidency was proving more conservative and pro-business than some party members liked. Some reform-minded Republicans even accused Taft of betraying Roosevelt with his policies. Roosevelt himself expressed disappointment with Taft's performance, and he made an unsuccessful bid for the Republican nomination in 1912. When he fell short, he and his supporters formed a third political party. This party, known as the Progressive or Bull Moose Party, nominated Roosevelt as its presidential nominee.

The 1912 presidential election campaign between Roosevelt, Taft, and Democratic nominee Woodrow Wilson was a spirited battle. In the end, however, Roosevelt and Taft split the Republican vote and Wilson cruised to victory. One year later, Roosevelt undertook another major expedition, this time into the jungles of South America. He returned weakened by tropical infections contracted during his adventure but remained a feisty political presence. After World War I erupted in Europe in 1914, for example, he repeatedly called for the United States to join the war on the side of the Allies. When Wilson did take the United States into the conflict in 1917, all four of Roosevelt's sons served as soldiers in the war effort. Roosevelt died peacefully in his sleep on January 6, 1919.

Sources:
Brands, H.W. *T.R.: The Last Romantic.* New York: Basic Books, 1998.
Miller, Nathan. *Theodore Roosevelt: A Life.* New York: Quill/William Morrow, 1994.
Morris, Edmund. *Theodore Rex.* New York: Random House, 2001.

Notes

[1] Quoted in Morris, Edmund. *The Rise of Theodore Roosevelt.* New York: Modern Library, 1979, p. 773.
[2] Steffens, Lincoln. *The Autobiography of Lincoln Steffens.* 1931. Reprint. Berkeley, CA: Heyday Books, 2005, p. 502.
[3] Quoted in Roosevelt, Nicolas. *Theodore Roosevelt: The Man as I Knew Him.* New York: Dodd, Mead, 1967, p. 66.

Upton Sinclair (1878-1968)
Journalist, Political Leader, and Author of
The Jungle

Upton Beall Sinclair, Jr., was born in Baltimore, Maryland, on September 20, 1878. His father, Upton Beall Sinclair, Sr., was a liquor salesman. His mother, Priscilla Augusta Harden, was the daughter of a wealthy railroad executive. As a youngster, Upton and his family endured periods where good food, clothing, and shelter were hard to come by. These grim days were due mostly to his father's alcoholism and limited business abilities. But young Sinclair also spent considerable stretches of time with his maternal grandparents, who enjoyed a luxurious existence. These dramatic shifts in his surroundings made a big impression on Sinclair, who developed a life-long interest in the divisions between rich and poor in America.

Sinclair's family moved to New York City when he was ten years old. Sinclair was a bright and energetic student who loved literature. He excelled so much in his studies that he was able to enroll at the City College of New York (CCNY) at age fourteen. Over the next few years he paid for much of his tuition by selling stories and articles to publishers of magazines and adventure novels for young boys. Sinclair graduated from CCNY in 1897 with a bachelor's degree. He then enrolled at Columbia University, also in New York City, to continue his studies. He spent the next few semesters studying literature, law, and politics, but left the school before graduating.

Joining the Socialist Party

As the twentieth century began, Sinclair's life underwent major changes. In 1900 he married Meta H. Fuller, with whom he had one son, David, before they divorced in 1913. He also launched his career as a serious novelist during this time. Beginning with the 1901 novel *Springtime and Harvest,* Sinclair published five novels in a four-year period. None of these works proved to be a financial success, but Sinclair did not waver from his goal of becoming a successful author.

Sinclair first dove into the world of political activism in the early 1900s as well. He joined the Socialist Party in 1902, only one year after it was founded. Sinclair later explained that his strong Christian faith played an important role in his decision to become a Socialist. He believed that socialism displayed the same concern for the poor and the same regard for equality and fairness that Jesus Christ had shown in his life and teachings.

Finally, Sinclair developed an intense interest in muckraking journalism during this period. He was greatly impressed with the work of reform-minded reporters like Ida Tarbell, Ray Stannard Baker, and Lincoln Steffens. Their exposés of political corruption, corporate treachery, and misery in America's inner cities became a source of inspiration to the young Socialist.

Writing *The Jungle*

In 1904 Fred Warren, who served as editor of a Socialist magazine called *Appeal to Reason,* commissioned Sinclair to write a story about immigrant workers in the Chicago meatpacking industry. Sinclair spent nearly two months in Chicago conducting research for the assignment. He wandered the city's stockyards and meatpacking warehouses, and spent long evenings talking with the poor and miserable working families who lived in the squalid slums surrounding the factories.

When he returned to New York City, Sinclair wrote about what he had seen with barely contained fury. "I wrote with tears and anguish, pouring into the pages all that pain which life had meant to me,"[1] he recalled. He described in excruciating detail the many ways in which Chicago meatpacking companies exploited their powerless immigrant workforce. In addition, he revealed that many Americans were eating meat laced with rat carcasses, human body parts, and toxic chemicals.

Sinclair's thinly fictionalized account of life in the Chicago meat industry, which he termed "The Jungle," first appeared in several successive issues of *Appeal to Reason* in 1905. It caused an immediate stir from readers who were greatly disturbed by Sinclair's account. But Sinclair's efforts did not produce full-blown public outrage until 1906, when his manuscript was published in book form as *The Jungle* by Doubleday Publishers.

Sinclair's book was extremely popular with readers in both the United and Europe. It sold over 150,000 copies in the United States in its first few years of availability, and editions of *The Jungle* were eventually published in seventeen languages. The book also vaulted Sinclair to the top ranks of American muckrakers. "*The Jungle* attracted attention because it was obviously the most authentic and most powerful of the muckraking novels," wrote critic Alfred Kazin. "The romantic indignation of the book gave it its fierce honesty, but the facts in it gave Sinclair his reputation, for he had suddenly given an unprecedented social importance to muckraking.... Sinclair became a leading exponent of the muckraking spirit to thousands in America and Europe."[2]

The Jungle triggered a firestorm of public pressure for government to take action against the meatpacking industry. Disgusted and angered by the revelations in Sinclair's book, American consumers demanded reforms to ensure that contaminated meat would no longer be sold to unsuspecting families. Congress and the administration of President Theodore Roosevelt wasted little time in responding. Before 1906 was over, both the Pure Food and Drug Act (which established the Food and Drug Administration) and the Meat Inspection Act had become law.

Sinclair was glad that *The Jungle* prompted increased government oversight of the meatpacking industry and improvements in food safety. But he was tremendously disappointed by the book's reception in other respects. His main purpose in writing the book had been to increase public knowledge and anger about the deplorable living conditions in which Chicago's working families existed. But instead, most Americans had focused on his stomach-churning accounts of food contamination. "I aimed at the public's heart and by accident hit it in the stomach,"[3] he lamented.

Deepening Involvement in Politics

Sinclair made his first bid for public office in 1906, running for a seat in Congress in New Jersey as a Socialist. He finished in a distant third place in the balloting, with fewer than 800 votes. Around this same period, Sinclair used money earned from sales of *The Jungle* to help establish a small Socialist community in Englewood, New Jersey, called Helicon Home Colony. But it burned to the ground in March 1907 under mysterious circumstances. Sinclair blamed the fire on arson committed by anti-Socialists, but this charge was never proven.

Sinclair continued to turn out novels and other writings during the 1910s, including an anthology of political writings called *The Cry for Justice* (1915). None of these works of social protest ever approached the popularity or impact of *The Jungle,* but they further burnished his reputation with Americans who shared his radical political beliefs. In 1913 he divorced his first wife and married Mary Craig Kimbrough. They remained married until her death in 1961. A few months later Sinclair entered into his third and final marriage, to Mary Elizabeth Willis.

By the mid-1910s, Sinclair ranked as one of the best known Socialists in the entire United States. But when the United States entered World War I in 1917, he decisively split with most members of his party. Sinclair supported America's entrance into the war on the side of the Allies, which also included England, France, Russia, and Canada. He believed that the future of the world depended on defeating Germany's dreams of using military force to create a new empire in Europe. But many of Sinclair's fellow Socialists were convinced that U.S. entry into the war was causing needless death and enriching American industrialists. They responded by organizing antiwar rallies and other activities, even though they knew that authorities might arrest them for violating newly created "anti-treason" laws.

Sinclair was extremely troubled by these actions. "I know you are brave and unselfish people, making sacrifices for a great principle, but I cannot join you,"[4] he told one group. By the end of 1917 the divisions between Sinclair and the Socialist Party over World War I were so great that he regretfully submitted a formal note of resignation from the party. As the war continued, however, and hundreds of Socialists were arrested and imprisoned for opposing the war, Sinclair angrily condemned the American government for trampling on their political rights. The United States, he charged, was fighting "to win democracy abroad [while] losing it at home."[5]

Running for Governor of California

After World War I came to an end in November 1918 with an Allied victory, Sinclair gradually returned to the Socialist Party fold. He formally rejoined the party in 1920. Two years later, he represented the Socialists in an unsuccessful campaign for a California U.S. Senate seat.

In 1926 Sinclair launched the first of three election campaigns to become governor of California. In 1926 and 1930 he ran under the Socialist banner and attracted little popular support. Meanwhile, he continued to turn out novels and essays on a regular basis. One of the most notable Sinclair books from this era was *Oil* (1927), a novel about corruption and greed in the early oil industry. (Eighty years after its initial publication, this book was made into a major motion picture called *There Will Be Blood*, starring Daniel Day Lewis. Widely acclaimed by critics, it was nominated for eight Academy Awards.)

In 1934 Sinclair made a third bid for the governorship of California. This time, however, he ran as a Democrat, and his campaign attracted a lot of attention from Depression-battered Californians. The cornerstone of Sinclair's candidacy was a jobs program called EPIC (End Poverty in California). It enabled him to beat out establishment Democrat candidates to win that party's gubernatorial nomination. As the 1934 election drew closer, many observers thought that Sinclair's strong support from working-class Americans and Socialist groups gave him a fighting chance to defeat the state's sitting governor, Republican Frank Merriam.

The prospect of a Sinclair victory alarmed every mainstream business and political group in the state. They leveled vicious attacks on his candidacy with the willing cooperation of newspapers like the *Los Angeles Times*, which compared his supporters to maggots. When election day arrived, Sinclair earned nearly 900,000 votes, which amounted to about 37 percent of the total cast. But Merriam claimed more than 1.1 million votes (48 percent of the total) to win re-election.

A Prolific Writer to the End

After his loss in 1934, Sinclair never again ran for political office. But he continued to comment on political and social events in his books and articles. His outlook on the world continued to infuriate some Americans, but made him a hero to other people in America and around the world. The famed Irish playwright George Bernard Shaw, for example, wrote Sinclair a letter in 1941 that read in part, "I have regarded you, not as a novelist, but as an historian.... When people ask me what has happened in my long lifetime I do not refer them to the newspaper files and to the authorities, but to your novels."[6]

Sinclair never again reached the heights of literary influence and popularity that he experienced with *The Jungle*. But some of his most noteworthy efforts were published decades after he first burst onto the American scene with that famous muckraking epic. In 1942 his nonfiction book *Dragon's Teeth*, which covered the rise of Nazi Germany, won a Pulitzer Prize. And from 1940 to 1953 he wrote an eleven-volume "Larry Budd" series that was very popular with readers. By the time Sinclair died on November 25, 1968, he had written more than ninety books of fiction and non-fiction about American politics, economics, class, and culture.

Sources:

Arthur, Anthony. *Radical Innocent: Upton Sinclair.* New York: Random House, 2006.

Mattson, Kevin. *Upton Sinclair and the Other American Century.* New York: Wiley, 2006.

Mitchell, Greg. *The Campaign of the Century: Upton Sinclair's Race for Governor of California and the Birth of Media Politics.* New York: Random House, 1993.

Sinclair, Upton. *The Jungle.* 1906. Reprint. New York: Pocket Books, 2004.

Notes

1 Sinclair, Upton. *Autobiography of Upton Sinclair.* New York: Harcourt, Brace, 1962, p. 112.

2 Kazin, Alfred. *On Native Grounds. An Interpretation of Modern American Prose Literature.* New York: Doubleday, 1956, p. 91.

3 Sinclair, p. 53.

4 Quoted in Harris, Leon A. *Upton Sinclair: American Rebel.* New York: Crowell, 1975, p. 157.

5 Quoted in Harris, p. 226.

6 Quoted in Zinn, Howard. "Upton Sinclair and Sacci & Vanzetti," In *The Zinn Reader:Writings on Disobedience and Democracy.* New York: Seven Stories Press, 1997, p. 478.

Lincoln Steffens (1866-1936)
Journalist and Author of The Shame of the Cities

Joseph Lincoln Steffens was born on April 6, 1866, in San Francisco, California. He was the oldest of four children born to Joseph Steffens, a wealthy businessman, and Elizabeth Louisa (Symes) Steffens. In 1870 the family moved to Sacramento, where Steffens and his three younger sisters were raised in one of the city's finer mansions.

Finding a Life in Journalism

By his own account, Steffens was an adventurous but restless youngster who did not always apply himself in school. His parents emphasized the importance of study to his future, but they also recognized that their eldest son was not a shy, studious sort. "They sent me to school, they gave me teachers of music, drawing; they offered me every opportunity in their reach," Steffens recalled in his autobiography. "But also they gave me liberty and the tools of quite another life: horses, guns, dogs, and the range of an open country."[1]

After completing his elementary schooling, Steffens attended a military academy in San Mateo, California. He graduated in 1884 and one year later enrolled at the University of California in Berkeley. Steffens earned his bachelor's degree in 1889, then promptly went to Europe to continue his studies and see the world. In Germany he met a fellow American student named Josephine Bontecou. They secretly married in the fall of 1891 and returned to the United States one year later.

Steffens and his wife settled in New York City, where he found work as a reporter for the *New York Evening Post*. He found the experience of covering events on Wall Street and city hall—including a major police corruption scandal—to be both interesting and personally rewarding. These early newspaper experiences helped lay the groundwork for Steffens's lifelong interest in politics, social issues, and reform.

In 1897 Steffens left the *Evening Post* to become city editor of a fading newspaper called the *Commercial Advertiser*. The move seemed a strange one to casual observers, but Steffens was attracted by the *Advertiser's* promise of freedom in shaping the paper's content and operations. Over the next few years he brought new life to the newspaper by hiring talented young journalists and writers who emphasized stories about immigration, Jewish-American life, and other issues of interest to working-class New Yorkers.

Moving on to *McClure's*

When he was not working as city editor, Steffens was working on his own writing career. He published several magazine pieces in his spare time, including a profile of New York Governor Theodore Roosevelt that appeared in an 1899 issue of *McClure's,* one of the top magazines in the country. Publisher S.S. McClure was extremely impressed by the article, and he wrote a personal note to Steffens about the "rattling good" piece. "I could read a whole magazine of this kind of material,"[2] he added.

By 1901 Steffens had helped restore the *Commercial Advertiser* to profitability. But increased interference from the newspaper's ownership with editorial operations soured Steffens on his work at the *Advertiser.* In addition, both he and his wife suffered from bouts of poor health during this time. Finally, Steffens felt mounting frustration with a novel that he had been working on for some time. All of these factors convinced him that he needed a change of scenery, so when *McClure's* offered him an editorial position on its staff in 1901, he quickly accepted.

Steffens's move to *McClure's* in the fall of 1901 revitalized him. Within a matter of a few months, he was out on the road, investigating reports of massive political corruption in some of America's largest cities. His first report on this problem, called "Tweed Days in St. Louis," appeared in the October 1902 issue of *McClure's.* Some scholars have called this piece the first genuine "muckraking" article in U.S. magazine publishing history, in part because of the moral outrage that dripped from Steffens's pen. "Public spirit became private spirit [and] public enterprise became private greed" in late nineteenth century St. Louis, wrote Steffens:

> Public franchises and privileges were sought, not only for legitimate profit and common convenience, but for loot. Tak-

149

ing but slight and always selfish interest in the public councils, the big men misused politics. The riffraff, catching the smell of corruption, rushed into the Municipal Assembly, drove out the remaining respectable men, and sold the city—its streets, its wharves, its markets, and all that it had—to the now greedy business men and bribers. In other words, when the leading men began to devour their own city, the herd rushed into the trough and fed also.[3]

Two months later, Steffens targeted municipal corruption in Minneapolis in the January 1903 issue of *McClure's*. This article was accompanied by two other hard-hitting investigative reports—a piece by Ida Tarbell on the ruthless rise of Standard Oil and an article by Ray Stannard Baker on the war between labor and management in the Pennsylvania coal fields. Together, these three articles marked a turning point in American journalism. From this point forward, investigative reporting of social and political problems— or muckraking, as it came to be known—was seen as a legitimate pursuit for magazines and newspapers.

Leaving the Muckraking Movement Behind

Over the next few years, the muckraking movement continued to gain steam. Journalists all across the country published articles and books detailing the destructive effects of political corruption, urban poverty, and unregulated corporations on American society. The cranky but brilliant Steffens remained at the forefront of this movement, which generated broad support for progressive reforms to the nation's political and economic systems. In 1904, for example, he published *The Shame of the Cities,* a famous collection of six of his best-known *McClure's* articles. These pieces, which uncovered corruption in city governments in St. Louis, Chicago, Minneapolis, Pittsburgh, Philadelphia, and New York, remain among the most influential works of the entire muckraking movement.

In 1906 Steffens, Tarbell, and Baker all left *McClure's* because of dissatisfaction with S.S. McClure's stewardship of the magazine. They became part of a group that launched a new muckraking publication called *American Magazine,* which became a prominent reform-oriented magazine in its own right. But Steffens stayed with the magazine for only a year before departing to pursue freelance writing for a wide range of publishers.

By 1911, when his wife died, Steffens had adopted a radical perspective on American society. Increasingly attracted to Socialist and Communist political ideas, he bitterly criticized American-style capitalism. But his influence waned during this period, in part because of declining public interest in the muckraking movement with which he was so closely associated.

In the late 1910s Steffens regularly extolled the benefits of communism over American-style capitalism. He then traveled to Russia, which had become a Communist state under Vladimir Lenin. After touring Russia and interviewing Lenin, he returned to America in 1921 and declared that "I have seen the future; and it works." In 1924 he married Ella Winter, with whom he had one son.

Steffens spent most of the 1920s in Europe, where radical political views were tolerated more than they were in the United States. In 1927, though, he returned to America and settled in Carmel, California. He spent the next few years writing his memoirs, which were published in 1931 as *The Autobiography of Lincoln Steffens*. This entertaining account of his life and political views reflected disillusionment with communism, but also maintained that serious reforms were still necessary in America. The autobiography was a bestseller, and it restored him to a level of prominence in America that he had not enjoyed in many years. He spent the next few years lecturing and writing to audiences across the United States. In 1933, though, Steffens suffered a serious heart attack. He never really recovered from this setback, and he spent the next three years virtually housebound. He died in Carmel on August 6, 1936.

Sources:
Kaplan, Justin. *Lincoln Steffens, A Biography.* New York: Simon and Schuster, 2004.

Steffens, Lincoln. *The Autobiography of Lincoln Steffens.* 1931. Reprint. Berkeley, CA: Heyday Books, 2005.

Notes

1 Steffens, Lincoln. *The Autobiography of Lincoln Steffens.* 1931. Reprint. Berkeley, CA: Heyday Books, 2005, p. 111

2 Quoted in Kaplan, Justin. *Lincoln Steffens, A Biography.* New York: Simon and Schuster, 2004, p. 90.

3 Steffens, Lincoln. *The Shame of the Cities.* 1904. Reprint. New York: Hill and Wang, 1957, p. 21.

Ida M. Tarbell (1857-1944)
Journalist and Author of The History of the Standard Oil Company

Muckraking journalist Ida Minerva Tarbell was born on November 5, 1857, in rural Erie County, Pennsylvania. Her father, Franklin Tarbell, was a barrel and tank maker for local oil companies. Her mother, Esther Ann (McCullough) Tarbell, was a homemaker who cared for Ida and her two younger siblings (another child died in infancy).

Frank Tarbell's barrelmaking business thrived in the 1860s, when Pennsylvania became the center of America's oil boom. Ida's memories of her childhood surroundings, though, were grim. "No industry of man in its early days has ever been more destructive of beauty, order, decency, than the production of petroleum," she later wrote. "Every tree, every shrub, every bit of grass in the vicinity [of the oil fields] was coated with black grease and left to die."[1]

Pursuing a Career in Journalism

In 1870 the Tarbell family moved to Titusville, Pennsylvania, where young Ida attended high school. By all accounts, she was both intellectually curious and very smart, and after graduating from high school she became the first young woman to attend Allegheny College in nearby Meadville. She briefly tried school teaching after graduating in 1880, but then found work in the editorial offices of the *Chautauquan,* a monthly magazine devoted to popular education.

Tarbell worked at the magazine for eight years before relocating to Paris, France. She studied and wrote articles for American magazines for the next three years. Several of these pieces caught the attention of S.S. McClure, an ambitious American editor and businessman who was plotting to start up a new magazine that would bear his name. He convinced her to return to America in 1894 and join his editorial staff. Before long, Tarbell was publishing serialized biographies of Abraham Lincoln and Napoleon Bonaparte in the pages of *McClure's.* These efforts vaulted her to the top ranks of McClure's stable of talented writers.

In 1901 Tarbell embarked on the assignment that would make her one of the most famous journalists in American history. She decided to investigate the rise of industrialist John D. Rockefeller's Standard Oil Company, a corporate giant that had been a constant presence throughout her childhood and young adulthood in Pennsylvania. By the close of the nineteenth century, Rockefeller ranked as perhaps the most powerful industrialist in the United States. This stature was due to his ironhanded direction of Standard Oil, which had become a dominant force in all sectors of the nation's oil industry. Tarbell's plan was to trace the history of Rockefeller and his company and tell *McClure's* readers how they had achieved such wealth and power.

The History of the Standard Oil Company

Over the next two years, Tarbell dug into newspaper files and courtroom records and conducted interviews to trace the history of Rockefeller and his business empire. The finished product of her investigative journalism was a nineteen-part series on Standard Oil that appeared in *McClure's* from November 1902 through October 1904. The series was also published in book form as the two-volume *The History of the Standard Oil Company* in late 1904.

Tarbell's series was a groundbreaking event in the history of American journalism, for it caught public attention like no other investigative report ever had. This impact was due in part to the progressive spirit of the times, but it also was a testament to the writer's talent. "The breadth of her research was remarkable," observed one analysis, "but even more impressive was her ability to digest Rockefeller's complicated business maneuvers into a narrative that would be accessible and engaging to the average reader."[2]

Tarbell painted a damning picture of Rockefeller and Standard Oil. Using all sorts of evidence uncovered during her research, she described the company as a ruthless monopoly that manipulated America's political and economic systems in a never-ending quest for greater power. She never attacked American capitalism, but she summarized her feelings about Standard Oil's management by saying that they "never played fair, and that ruined their greatness for me."[3] Tarbell also offered a harsh judgment of Rockefeller himself, saying that "our national life is on every side distinctly poorer, uglier, meaner, for the kind of influence he exercises."[4]

Icon of the Muckraking Movement

Tarbell's investigation of Standard Oil played a major role in the rise of the muckraking movement of the early twentieth century. She and other reform-minded journalists, like Lincoln Steffens and Upton Sinclair, inspired numerous reporters and editors to conduct and publish their own examinations of corporate misbehavior, political corruption, and social injustice. Even a century later, Tarbell's work remained an inspiration to journalists and historians. As Tarbell biographer Steve Weinberg wrote in 2008, her techniques of gathering "information about a secretive corporation and its evasive, powerful chief executive taught me that a talented, persistent journalist can penetrate any façade through close readings of government documents, lawsuits, and interviews."[5]

The History of the Standard Oil Company also led to a federal investigation of Standard Oil to see if its operations violated antitrust laws. On November 18, 1906, the U.S. government formally filed suit against Standard Oil, charging that it was an illegal monopoly. Five years later the U.S. Supreme Court ordered the breakup of Rockefeller's business empire. Historians agree that Tarbell's documentation of Standard's business practices contributed to the Court's final decision.

Throughout that five-year court battle, Tarbell continued to write about social and political problems in America. But most of these reports appeared in magazines other than *McClure's*. In 1906 she resigned from the magazine along with fellow muckrakers Lincoln Steffens and Ray Stannard Baker and editor John S. Phillips. Frustrated by S.S. McClure's managerial policies and irresponsible personal behavior, they decided to form their own periodical, called *American Magazine*.

Tarbell wrote for *American Magazine* for the next nine years before moving on to a free-lance writing career. She remained an outspoken critic of illegal and dishonest activities by corporate America during this time, but she also became known as a strong supporter of Democratic President Woodrow Wilson. In addition, Tarbell emerged as an opponent of women's suffrage, to the surprise and disappointment of many of her old progressive colleagues.

During the 1920s and 1930s Tarbell left investigative journalism behind and concentrated on biography writing. The most notable works of this period were biographies of industrialists Elbert H. Gary and Owen D. Young, both of which cast their subjects in largely positive lights. In 1939 she published an autobiography of her life and career called *All in the Day's Work*. Tarbell died of pneumonia at her home in Bridgeport, Connecticut, on January 6, 1944.

Sources:

Brady, Kathleen. *Ida Tarbell: Portrait of a Muckraker.* Pittsburgh: University of Pittsburgh Press, 1989.

Tarbell, Ida Minerva. *All in the Day's Work: An Autobiography.* 1939. Reprint. Champaign: University of Illinois Press, 2003.

Weinberg, Steve. *Taking on the Trust: The Epic Battle between Ida Tarbell and John D. Rockefeller.* New York: Norton, 2008.

Notes

1 Tarbell, Ida Minerva. *All in the Day's Work: An Autobiography.* 1939. Reprint. Champaign: University of Illinois Press, 2003, p. 9.

2 "Ida Tarbell: 1857-1944" in *American Experience: The Rockefellers,* available online at http://www.pbs.org/wgbh/amex/rockefellers/peopleevents/p_tarbell.html.

3 Tarbell, p. 230.

4 "Ida Tarbell: 1857-1944."

5 Weinberg, Steve. *Taking on the Trust: The Epic Battle between Ida Tarbell and John D. Rockefeller.* New York: Norton, 2008.

PRIMARY SOURCES

President Theodore Roosevelt Promises Progressive Reform

Theodore Roosevelt took office as President of the United States on September 14, 1901, follow-
ing the assassination of William McKinley. On December 3, he outlined the priorities of his
administration in his first annual message to Congress. Roosevelt offered his views on a wide
range of issues facing the nation. In the section excerpted below, he acknowledges growing pub-
lic discontent with the power and influence of large corporations, and expresses a willingness to
increase federal government regulation of big business. Roosevelt thus sets the stage for the pro-
gressive reforms that he implemented during his presidency.

The tremendous and highly complex industrial development which
went on with ever accelerated rapidity during the latter half of the
nineteenth century brings us face to face, at the beginning of the twentieth, with very serious social problems. The old laws, and the old customs
which had almost the binding force of law, were once quite sufficient to regulate the accumulation and distribution of wealth. Since the industrial changes
which have so enormously increased the productive power of mankind, they
are no longer sufficient.

The growth of cities has gone on beyond comparison faster than the
growth of the country, and the upbuilding of the great industrial centers has
meant a startling increase, not merely in the aggregate of wealth, but in the
number of very large individual, and especially of very large corporate, fortunes. The creation of these great corporate fortunes has not been due to the
tariff nor to any other governmental action, but to natural causes in the business world, operating in other countries as they operate in our own.

The process has aroused much antagonism, a great part of which is
wholly without warrant. It is not true that as the rich have grown richer the
poor have grown poorer. On the contrary, never before has the average man,
the wage-worker, the farmer, the small trader, been so well off as in this country and at the present time. There have been abuses connected with the accumulation of wealth; yet it remains true that a fortune accumulated in legitimate business can be accumulated by the person specially benefited only on
condition of conferring immense incidental benefits upon others. Successful
enterprise, of the type which benefits all mankind, can only exist if the conditions are such as to offer great prizes as the rewards of success.

The captains of industry who have driven the railway systems across this
continent, who have built up our commerce, who have developed our manu-

factures, have on the whole done great good to our people. Without them the material development of which we are so justly proud could never have taken place. Moreover, we should recognize the immense importance of this material development of leaving as unhampered as is compatible with the public good the strong and forceful men upon whom the success of business operations inevitably rests. The slightest study of business conditions will satisfy anyone capable of forming a judgment that the personal equation is the most important factor in a business operation; that the business ability of the man at the head of any business concern, big or little, is usually the factor which fixes the gulf between striking success and hopeless failure....

Moreover, it cannot too often be pointed out that to strike with ignorant violence at the interests of one set of men almost inevitably endangers the interests of all. The fundamental rule in our national life—the rule which underlies all others—is that, on the whole, and in the long run, we shall go up or down together. There are exceptions; and in times of prosperity some will prosper far more, and in times of adversity, some will suffer far more, than others; but speaking generally, a period of good times means that all share more or less in them, and in a period of hard times all feel the stress to a greater or less degree. It surely ought not to be necessary to enter into any proof of this statement; the memory of the lean years which began in 1893 is still vivid, and we can contrast them with the conditions in this very year which is now closing. Disaster to great business enterprises can never have its effects limited to the men at the top. It spreads throughout, and while it is bad for everybody, it is worst for those farthest down. The capitalist may be shorn of his luxuries; but the wage-worker may be deprived of even bare necessities.

The mechanism of modern business is so delicate that extreme care must be taken not to interfere with it in a spirit of rashness or ignorance. Many of those who have made it their vocation to denounce the great industrial combinations which are popularly, although with technical inaccuracy, known as "trusts," appeal especially to hatred and fear. These are precisely the two emotions, particularly when combined with ignorance, which unfit men for the exercise of cool and steady judgment. In facing new industrial conditions, the whole history of the world shows that legislation will generally be both unwise and ineffective unless undertaken after calm inquiry and with sober self-restraint. Much of the legislation directed at the trusts would have been exceedingly mischievous had it not also been entirely ineffective. In accordance with a well-known sociological law, the ignorant or reckless agitator has been the really effective friend of the evils which he has been nominally opposing. In dealing with business interests, for the Government to undertake by crude and ill-considered legislation to do what may turn out to be bad, would be to incur the risk of such far-reaching national disaster that it would be preferable to undertake nothing at all. The men who demand the impossible or the undesirable serve as the allies of the forces with which they are nominally at war, for they hamper those who would endeavor to find out in rational fashion what the wrongs really are and to what extent and in what manner it is practicable to apply remedies.

All this is true; and yet it is also true that there are real and grave evils, one of the chief being over-capitalization because of its many baleful consequences; and a resolute and practical effort must be made to correct these evils.

There is a widespread conviction in the minds of the American people that the great corporations known as trusts are in certain of their features and tendencies hurtful to the general welfare. This springs from no spirit of envy or uncharitableness, nor lack of pride in the great industrial achievements that have placed this country at the head of the nations struggling for commercial supremacy. It does not rest upon a lack of intelligent appreciation of the necessity of meeting changing and changed conditions of trade with new methods, nor upon ignorance of the fact that combination of capital in the effort to accomplish great things is necessary when the world's progress demands that great things be done. It is based upon sincere conviction that combination and concentration should be, not prohibited, but supervised and within reasonable limits controlled; and in my judgment this conviction is right.

It is no limitation upon property rights or freedom of contract to require that when men receive from Government the privilege of doing business under corporate form, which frees them from individual responsibility, and enables them to call into their enterprises the capital of the public, they shall do so upon absolutely truthful representations as to the value of the property in which the capital is to be invested. Corporations engaged in interstate commerce should be regulated if they are found to exercise a license working to the public injury. It should be as much the aim of those who seek for social betterment to rid the business world of crimes of cunning as to rid the entire body politic of crimes of violence. Great corporations exist only because they are created and safeguarded by our institutions; and it is therefore our right and our duty to see that they work in harmony with these institutions.

The first essential in determining how to deal with the great industrial combinations is knowledge of the facts—publicity. In the interest of the public, the Government should have the right to inspect and examine the workings of the great corporations engaged in interstate business. Publicity is the only sure remedy which we can now invoke. What further remedies are needed in the way of governmental regulation, or taxation, can only be determined after publicity has been obtained, by process of law, and in the course of administration. The first requisite is knowledge, full and complete—knowledge which may be made public to the world.

Artificial bodies, such as corporations and joint stock or other associations, depending upon any statutory law for their existence or privileges, should be subject to proper governmental supervision, and full and accurate information as to their operations should be made public regularly at reasonable intervals.

The large corporations, commonly called trusts, though organized in one State, always do business in many States, often doing very little business in the State where they are incorporated. There is utter lack of uniformity in the State laws about them; and as no State has any exclusive interest in or power over their acts, it has in practice proved impossible to get adequate regulation through State action. Therefore, in the interest of the whole people, the Nation should, without interfering with the power of the States in the matter itself, also assume power of supervision and regulation over all corporations doing an interstate business. This is especially true where the corporation derives a portion of its wealth from the existence of some monopolistic element or tendency in its business. There would be no hardship in such supervision; banks are subject to it, and in their case it is now accepted as a simple matter of course. Indeed, it is probable that supervision of corporations by the National Government need not go so far as is now the case with the supervision exercised over them by so conservative a State as Massachusetts, in order to produce excellent results.

When the Constitution was adopted, at the end of the eighteenth century, no human wisdom could foretell the sweeping changes, alike in industrial and political conditions, which were to take place by the beginning of the twentieth century. At that time it was accepted as a matter of course that the several States were the proper authorities to regulate, so far as was then necessary, the comparatively insignificant and strictly localized corporate bodies of the day. The conditions are now wholly different and wholly different action is called for. I believe that a law can be framed which will enable the National Government to exercise control along the lines above indicated; profiting by the experience gained through the passage and administration of the Interstate Commerce Act. If, however, the judgment of the Congress is that it lacks the constitutional power to pass such an act, then a constitutional amendment should be submitted to confer the power.

There should be created a Cabinet officer, to be known as Secretary of Commerce and Industries, as provided in the bill introduced at the last session of the Congress. It should be his province to deal with commerce in its broadest sense; including among many other things whatever concerns labor and all matters affecting the great business corporations and our merchant marine.

The course proposed is one phase of what should be a comprehensive and far-reaching scheme of constructive statesmanship for the purpose of broadening our markets, securing our business interests on a safe basis, and making firm our new position in the international industrial world; while scrupulously safeguarding the rights of wage-worker and capitalist, of investor and private citizen, so as to secure equity as between man and man in this Republic....

The most vital problem with which this country, and for that matter the whole civilized world, has to deal, is the problem which has for one side the betterment of social conditions, moral and physical, in large cities, and for another side the effort to deal with that tangle of far-reaching questions which we group together when we speak of "labor." The chief factor in the success of each man—wage-worker, farmer, and capitalist alike—must ever be the sum total of his own individual qualities and abilities. Second only to this comes the power of acting in combination or association with others. Very great good has been and will be accomplished by associations or unions of wage-workers, when managed with forethought, and when they combine insistence upon their own rights with law-abiding respect for the rights of others. The display of these qualities in such bodies is a duty to the nation no less than to the associations themselves. Finally, there must also in many cases be action by the Government in order to safeguard the rights and interests of all. Under our Constitution there is much more scope for such action by the State and the municipality than by the nation. But on points such as those touched on above the National Government can act.

When all is said and done, the rule of brotherhood remains as the indispensable prerequisite to success in the kind of national life for which we strive. Each man must work for himself, and unless he so works no outside help can avail him; but each man must remember also that he is indeed his brother's keeper, and that while no man who refuses to walk can be carried with advantage to himself or anyone else, yet that each at times stumbles or halts, that each at times needs to have the helping hand outstretched to him. To be permanently effective, aid must always take the form of helping a man to help himself; and we can all best help ourselves by joining together in the work that is of common interest to all....

Source: Roosevelt, Theodore. "First Annual Message," December 3, 1901. In Woolley, John T., and Gerhard Peters. *The American Presidency Project.* Santa Barbara, CA: University of California, n.d. Available online at http://www.presidency.ucsb.edu/ws/index.php?pid=29542&st=&st1=.

Jacob Riis Chronicles the Struggles of the Urban Poor

One of the best-known writers to investigate the problems facing poor and working-class residents of American cities was Jacob Riis. Riis spent years exploring the tenement districts of New York City, recording his observations in a notebook and taking photographs of the residents and their surroundings. In 1890 he published the results of his work in a powerful book called How the Other Half Lives. *The following excerpt from Chapter 1 describes the dirty, overcrowded conditions he encountered in the tenements. Riis's book forced middle-class Americans and government officials to confront the problems facing people in the nation's urban slums. His exposé led to the establishment of the Tenement House Commission to improve the design of urban housing and provide safe and sanitary living conditions for the poor.*

In thirty-five years the city of less than a hundred thousand came to harbor half a million souls, for whom homes had to be found. Within the memory of men not yet in their prime, Washington had moved from his house on Cherry Hill as too far out of town to be easily reached. Now the old residents followed his example; but they moved in a different direction and for a different reason. Their comfortable dwellings in the once fashionable streets along the East River front fell into the hands of real-estate agents and boarding-house keepers; and here, says the report to the Legislature of 1857, when the evils engendered had excited just alarm, "in its beginning, the tenant-house became a real blessing to that class of industrious poor whose small earnings limited their expenses, and whose employment in workshops, stores, or about the warehouses and thoroughfares, render a near residence of much importance." Not for long, however. As business increased, and the city grew with rapid strides, the necessities of the poor became the opportunity of their wealthier neighbors, and the stamp was set upon the old houses, suddenly become valuable, which the best thought and effort of a later age have vainly struggled to efface. Their "*large* rooms were partitioned into *several smaller ones,* without regard to light or ventilation, the rate of rent being lower in proportion to space or height from the street; and they soon became filled from cellar to garret with a class of tenantry living from hand to mouth, loose in morals, improvident in habits, degraded, and squalid as beggary itself." It was thus the dark bedroom, prolific of untold depravities, came into the world. It was destined to survive the old houses. In their new role, says the old report, eloquent in its indignant denunciation of "evils more destructive than wars," "they were not intended to last. Rents were fixed high enough to cover damage and abuse from this class, from whom nothing was

165

expected, and the most was made of them while they lasted. Neatness, order, cleanliness, were never dreamed of in connection with the tenant-house system, as it spread its localities from year to year; while reckless slovenliness, discontent, privation, and ignorance were left to work out their invariable results, until the entire premises reached the level of tenant-house dilapidation, containing, but sheltering not, the miserable hordes that crowded beneath mouldering, water-rotted roofs or burrowed among the rats of clammy cellars." Yet so illogical is human greed that, at a later day, when called to account, "the proprietors frequently urged the filthy habits of the tenants as an excuse for the condition of their property, utterly losing sight of the fact that it was the tolerance of those habits which was the real evil, and that for this they themselves were alone responsible."

Still the pressure of the crowds did not abate, and in the old garden where the stolid Dutch burgher grew his tulips or early cabbages a rear house was built, generally of wood, two stories high at first. Presently it was carried up another story, and another. Where two families had lived ten moved in. The front house followed suit, if the brick walls were strong enough. The question was not always asked, judging from complaints made by a contemporary witness, that the old buildings were "often carried up to a great height without regard to the strength of the foundation walls." It was rent the owner was after; nothing was said in the contract about either the safety or the comfort of the tenants. The garden gate no longer swung on its rusty hinges. The shell-paved walk had become an alley; what the rear house had left of the garden, a "court." Plenty such are yet to be found in the Fourth Ward, with here and there one of the original rear tenements.

Worse was to follow. It was "soon perceived by estate owners and agents of property that a greater percentage of profits could be realized by the conversion of houses and blocks into barracks, and dividing their space into smaller proportions capable of containing human life within four walls.... Blocks were rented of real estate owners, or 'purchased on time,' or taken in charge at a percentage, and held for under-letting." With the appearance of the middleman, wholly irresponsible, and utterly reckless and unrestrained, began the era of tenement building which turned out such blocks as Gotham Court, where, in one cholera epidemic that scarcely touched the clean wards, the tenants died at the rate of one hundred and ninety-five to the thousand of population; which forced the general mortality of the city up from 1 in 41.83 in 1815, to 1 in 27.33 in 1855, a year of unusual freedom from epidemic disease, and which wrung from the early organizers of the Health Department this wail: "There are numerous examples of tenement-houses in which are lodged several hundred people that have a *pro rata* allotment of ground area scarcely equal to two square yards upon the city lot, court-yards and all included." The tenement-house population had swelled to half a million souls by that time, and on the East Side, in what is still the most densely populated district in all the world, China not excluded, it was packed at the rate of 290,000 to the square mile, a state of affairs wholly unexampled. The utmost cupidity [greed] of other lands and other days had never contrived to herd much more than half that number within the same space. The greatest crowding of Old London was at the rate of 175,816. Swine roamed the streets and gutters as their principal scavengers. The death of a child in a tenement was registered at the Bureau of Vital Statistics as "plainly due to suffocation in the foul air of an unventilated apartment," and the Senators, who had come down from Albany to find out what was the matter with New York, reported that "there are annually cut off from the population by disease and death enough human beings to people a city, and enough human labor to sustain it."

And yet experts had testified that, as compared with uptown, rents were from twenty-five to thirty per cent higher in the worst slums of the lower wards, with such accommodations as were enjoyed, for instance, by a "family with boarders" in Cedar Street, who fed hogs in the cellar that contained eight or ten loads of manure; or "one room 12 x 12 with five families living in it, comprising twenty persons of both sexes and all ages, with only two beds, without partition, screen, chair, or table." The rate of rent has been successfully maintained to the present day, though the hog at least has been eliminated.

Lest anybody flatter himself with the notion that these were evils of a day that is happily past and may safely be forgotten, let me mention here three very recent instances of tenement-house life that came under my notice. One was the burning of a rear house in Mott Street, from appearances one of the original tenant-houses that made their owners rich. The fire made homeless ten families, who had paid an average of $5 a month for their mean little cubby-holes. The owner himself told me that it was *fully* insured for $800, though it brought him in $600 a year rent. He evidently considered himself especially entitled to be pitied for losing such valuable property. Another was the case of a hard-working family of man and wife, young people from the old country, who took poison together in a Crosby Street tenement because they were "tired." There was no other explanation, and none was needed when I stood in the room in which they had lived. It was in the attic with sloping ceiling and a single window so far out on the roof that it seemed not to belong to the place at all. With scarcely room enough to turn around in they had been compelled to pay five dollars and a half a month in advance. There were four such rooms in that attic, and together they brought in as much as many a handsome little cottage in a pleasant part of Brooklyn. The third instance was that of a colored family of husband, wife, and baby in a wretched rear rookery in West Third Street. Their rent was eight dollars and a half for a single room on the top-story, so small that I was unable to get a photograph of it even by placing the camera outside the open door. Three short steps across either way would have measured its full extent.

There was just one excuse for the early tenement-house builders, and their successors may plead it with nearly as good right for what it is worth. "Such," says an official report, "is the lack of house- room in the city that any kind of tenement can be immediately crowded with lodgers, if there is space offered." Thousands were living in cellars. There were three hundred underground lodging-houses in the city when the Health Department was organized. Some fifteen years before that the old Baptist Church in Mulberry Street, just off Chatham Street, had been sold, and the rear half of the frame structure had been converted into tenements that with their swarming population became the scandal even of that reckless age. The wretched pile harbored no less than forty families, and the annual rate of deaths to the population was officially stated to be 75 in 1,000. These tenements were an extreme type of very many, for the big barracks had by this time spread east and west and far up the island into the sparsely settled wards. Whether or not the title was clear to the land upon which they were built was of less account than that the rents were collected. If there were damages to pay, the tenant had to foot them. Cases were "very frequent when property was in litigation, and two or three different parties were collecting rents." Of course under such circumstances "no repairs were ever made."

The climax had been reached. The situation was summed up by the Society for the Improvement of the Condition of the Poor in these words: "Crazy old buildings, crowded rear tenements in filthy yards, dark, damp basements, leaking garrets, shops, outhouses, and stables converted into dwellings, though scarcely fit to shelter brutes, are habitations of thousands of our fellow-beings in this wealthy, Christian city." "The city," says its historian, Mrs. Martha Lamb, commenting on the era of aqueduct building between 1835 and 1845, "was a general asylum for vagrants." Young vagabonds, the natural offspring of such "home" conditions, overran the streets. Juvenile crime increased fearfully year by year. The Children's Aid Society and kindred philanthropic organizations were yet unborn, but in the city directory was to be found the address of the "American Society for the Promotion of Education in Africa."

Source: Riis, Jacob. "Chapter 1: Genesis of the Tenement." In *How the Other Half Lives.* New York: Scribner's, 1890, pp. 7-14.

John Spargo Describes the Tragedy of Child Labor

Around the turn of the twentieth century, an estimated two million American children worked in the nation's factories, textile mills, coal mines, and other industrial operations. Many poor families had no choice but to send all members out in search of employment. Children often worked up to seventy hours per week—performing hard, physical labor in depressing or even dangerous work environments—and received wages of just pennies per day. The tragedy of child labor became a focus of muckraking journalists like John Spargo, whose 1907 book The Bitter Cry of the Children *generated public sympathy and outrage for the plight of these young workers. In the following excerpt, the author describes the terrible conditions faced by boys working in U.S. coal mines.*

According to the census of 1900, there were 25,000 boys under sixteen years of age employed in and around the mines and quarries of the United States. In the state of Pennsylvania alone,—the state which enslaves more children than any other,—there are thousands of little "breaker boys" employed, many of them not more than nine or ten years old. The law forbids the employment of children under fourteen, and the records of the mines generally show that the law is "obeyed." Yet in May, 1905, an investigation by the National Child Labor Committee showed that in one small borough of 7000 population, among the boys employed in breakers 35 were nine years old, 40 were ten, 45 were eleven, and 45 were twelve—over 150 boys illegally employed in one section of boy labor in one small town! During the anthracite coal strike of 1902, I attended the Labor Day demonstration at Pittston and witnessed the parade of another at Wilkesbarre. In each case there were hundreds of boys marching, all of them wearing their "working buttons," testifying to the fact that they were *bona fide* workers. Scores of them were less than ten years of age, others were eleven or twelve.

Work in the coal breakers is exceedingly hard and dangerous. Crouched over the chutes, the boys sit hour after hour, picking out the pieces of slate and other refuse from the coal as it rushes past to the washers. From the cramped position they have to assume, most of them become more or less deformed and bent-backed like old men. When a boy has been working for some time and begins to get round-shouldered, his fellows say that "He's got his boy to carry round wherever he goes." The coal is hard, and accidents to the hands, such as cut, broken, or crushed fingers, are common among the boys. Sometimes there is a worse accident: a terrified shriek is heard, and a boy is mangled and torn in the machinery, or disappears in the chute to be picked out later smothered and dead.

Clouds of dust fill the breakers and are inhaled by the boys, laying the foundations for asthma and miners' consumption. I once stood in a breaker for half an hour and tried to do the work a twelve-year-old boy was doing day after day, for ten hours at a stretch, for sixty cents a day. The gloom of the breaker appalled me. Outside the sun shone brightly, the air was pellucid [clear], and the birds sang in chorus with the trees and the rivers. Within the breaker there was blackness, clouds of deadly dust enfolded everything, the harsh, grinding roar of the machinery and the ceaseless rushing of coal through the chutes filled the ears. I tried to pick out the pieces of slate from the hurrying stream of coal, often missing them; my hands were bruised and cut in a few minutes; I was covered from head to foot with coal dust, and for many hours afterwards I was expectorating some of the small particles of anthracite I had swallowed.

I could not do that work and live, but there were boys of ten and twelve years of age doing it for fifty and sixty cents a day. Some of them had never been inside of a school; few of them could read a child's primer. True, some of them attended the night schools, but after working ten hours in the breaker the educational results from attending school were practically *nil*. "We goes fer a good time, an' we keeps de guys wots dere hoppin' all de time," said little Owen Jones, whose work I had been trying to do. How strange that barbaric patois [dialect] sounded to me as I remembered the rich, musical language I had so often heard other little Owen Joneses speak in faraway Wales. As I stood in that breaker I thought of the reply of the small boy to Robert Owen. Visiting an English coal-mine one day, Owen asked a twelve-year-old lad if he knew God. The boy stared vacantly at his questioner: "God?" he said, "God? No, I don't. He must work in some other mine." It was hard to realize amid the danger and din and blackness of that Pennsylvania breaker that such a thing as belief in a great All-good God existed.

From the breakers the boys graduate to the mine depths, where they become door tenders, switch-boys, or mule-drivers. Here, far below the surface, work is still more dangerous. At fourteen or fifteen the boys assume the same risks as the men, and are surrounded by the same perils. Nor is it in Pennsylvania only that these conditions exist. In the bituminous mines of West Virginia, boys of nine or ten are frequently employed. I met one little fellow ten years old in Mt. Carbon, W. Va., last year, who was employed as a "trap boy." Think of what it means to be a trap boy at ten years of age. It means to sit alone in a dark mine passage hour after hour, with no human soul near; to see no living creature except the mules as they pass with their loads, or a rat or two seeking to share one's meal; to stand in water or mud that covers the ankles, chilled to the marrow by the cold draughts that rush in when you open the trap-door for the mules to pass through; to work for fourteen hours—waiting—opening and shutting a door—then waiting again—for sixty cents; to reach the surface when all is wrapped in the mantle of night, and to fall to the earth exhausted and have to be carried away to the nearest "shack" to be revived before it is possible to walk to the farther shack called "home."

Boys twelve years of age may be *legally* employed in the mines of West Virginia, by day or by night, and for as many hours as the employers care to make them toil or their bodies will stand the strain. Where the disregard of child life is such that this may be done openly and with legal sanction, it is easy to believe what miners have again and again told me—that there are hundreds of little boys of nine and ten years of age employed in the coal-mines of this state.

Source: Spargo, John. *The Bitter Cry of the Children.* New York: Macmillan, 1907, pp. 163-67.

Ida Tarbell Investigates the Standard Oil Trust

The large corporations or trusts that dominated American industry at the turn of the twentieth century became a major target for muckraking journalists. These companies used their tremendous power and influence to negotiate favorable contracts with other businesses, command high prices for their products, demand concessions from their workers, derail proposed government regulations, and build huge fortunes for their owners. One of the earliest and most famous muckraking attacks on the trusts was journalist Ida M. Tarbell's groundbreaking investigation of the Standard Oil Company, which was owned by the wealthy industrialist John D. Rockefeller. In the following excerpt from her 1904 book The History of the Standard Oil Company, *Tarbell explains the strategy and tactics Rockefeller used to bring 90 percent of U.S. oil production under his control.*

Mr. Rockefeller was certainly now in an excellent condition to work out his plan of bringing under his own control all the refineries of the country. The Standard Oil Company owned in each of the great refining centres, New York, Pittsburg and Philadelphia, a large and aggressive plant run by the men who had built it up. These works were, so far as the public knew, still independent and their only relation that of the "Central Association." As a matter of fact they were the "Central Association." Not only had Mr. Rockefeller brought these powerful interests into his concern; he had secured for them a rebate of ten per cent, on a rate which should always be as low as any one of the [rail]roads gave any of his competitors. He had done away with middlemen, that is, he was "paying nobody a profit." He had undeniably a force wonderfully constructed for what he wanted to do and one made practically impregnable as things were in the oil business then, by virtue of its special transportation rate.

As soon as his new line was complete the work of acquiring all outside refineries began at each of the oil centres. Unquestionably the acquisitions were made through persuasion when this was possible. If the party approached refused to lease or sell, he was told firmly what Mr. Rockefeller had told the Cleveland refiners when he went to them in 1872 with the South Improvement contracts, that there was no hope for him; that a combination was in progress which was bound to work; and that those who stayed out would inevitably go to the wall. Naturally the first fruits to fall into the hands of the new alliance were those refineries which were embarrassed or discouraged by the conditions which Mr. [H.H.] Rogers [a defender of Rockefeller's combination plan] explains above....

Those who felt the hard times and had any hope of weathering them resisted at first. With many of them the resistance was due simply to their love for their business and their unwillingness to share its control with outsiders. The thing which a man has begun, cared for, led to a healthy life, from which he has begun to gather fruit, which he knows he can make greater and richer, he loves as he does his life. It is one of the fruits of his life. He is jealous of it—wishes the honour of it, will not divide it with another. He can suffer heavily his own mistakes, learn from them, correct them. He can fight opposition, bear all—so long as the work is his. There were refiners in 1875 who loved their business in this way. Why one should love an oil refinery the outsider may not see; but to the man who had begun with one still and had seen it grow by his own energy and intelligence to ten, who now sold 500 barrels a day where he once sold five, the refinery was the dearest spot on earth save his home. He walked with pride among its evil-smelling places, watched the processes with eagerness, experimented with joy and recounted triumphantly every improvement. To ask such a man to give up his refinery was to ask him to give up the thing which, after his family, meant most in life to him.

To Mr. Rockefeller this feeling was a weak sentiment. To place love of independent work above love of profits was as incomprehensible to him as a refusal to accept a rebate because it was *wrong!* Where persuasion failed then, it was necessary, in his judgment, that pressure be applied—simply a pressure sufficient to demonstrate to these blind or recalcitrant individuals the impossibility of their long being able to do business independently. It was a pressure varied according to locality. Usually it took the form of cutting their market. The system of "predatory competition" was no invention of the Standard Oil Company. It had prevailed in the oil business from the start. Indeed, it was one of the evils Mr. Rockefeller claimed his combination would cure, but until now it had been used spasmodically. Mr. Rockefeller never did anything spasmodically. He applied underselling for destroying his rivals' market with the same deliberation and persistency that characterised all his efforts, and in the long run he always won. There were other forms of pressure. Sometimes the independents found it impossible to get oil; again, they were obliged to wait days for cars to ship in; there seemed to be no end to the ways of making it hard for men to do business, of discouraging them until they would sell or lease, and always at the psychological moment a purchaser was at their side.

Take as an example the case of the Harkness refinery in Philadelphia [condensed from testimony before a U.S. House of Representatives antitrust investigating committee]:

"I was the originator of the enterprise," said William W. Harkness, "believing that there was no better place than Philadelphia to refine oil, particularly for export. We commenced then, as near as I can now recollect, about 1870, and we made money up to probably 1874. We managed our business very close and did not speculate in oil. We bought and we sold, and we paid a great deal of attention to the statistical part of our business so as to save waste, and we did a nice business. But we found in some years that probably five months out of a year we could not sell our oil unless it would be at a positive loss, and then we stopped. Then when we could sell our oil, we found a difficulty about getting cars. My brother would complain of it, but I believed that the time would come when that would be equalised. I had no idea of the iniquity that was going on; I could not conceive it. I went on in good faith until about 1874, and then the trouble commenced. We could not get our oil and were compelled to sell at a loss. Then Warden, Frew and Company formed some kind of running arrangement where they supplied the crude, and we seemed to get along a little better. After a while the business got complicated, and I got tired and handed it over to my brother; I backed out. That was about 1875. I was dissatisfied and wanted to do an independent business, or else I wanted to give it up. In 1876—I recollect that very well, because it was the year of the Centennial Exposition—we were at the Centennial Exposition. I was sitting in front of the great Corliss engine, admiring it, and he told me there was a good opportunity to get out. Warden, Frew and Company, he said, were prepared to buy us out, and I asked him whether he considered that as the best thing to do; whether we had not better hold on and fight it through, for I believed that these difficulties would not continue; that we would get our oil. I knew he was a competent refiner, and I wanted to continue business, but he said he thought he had better make this arrangement, and I consented, and we got our investment back."

Here we have a refiner discouraged by the conditions which Mr. Rockefeller claims his aggregation will cure. Under the Rutter circular [a private agreement with James H. Rutter, freight agent of the New York Central Railroad] and the discrimination in freight to the Standard which followed, his difficulty in getting oil increases, and he consents to a running arrangement with Mr. Rockefeller's partner in Philadelphia, but he wants to do an "independent business." Impossible. As he sits watching the smooth and terrible power of that famous Corliss engine of 1876, an engine which showed to thousands for the first time what great power properly directed means, he realised that something very like it was at work in the oil business—something resistless, silent, perfect in its might—and he sold out to that something. Everywhere men did the same. The history of oil refining on Oil Creek from 1875 to 1879 is almost uncanny. There were at the beginning of that period twenty-seven plants in the region, most of which were in a fair condition, considering the difficulties in the business. During 1873 the demand for refined oil had greatly increased, the exports nearly doubling over those of 1872. The average profit on refined that year in a well-managed refinery was not less than three cents a gallon. During the first half of 1874 the oil business had been depressed, but the oil refiners were looking for better times when the Rutter circular completely demoralised them by putting fifty cents extra freight charges on their shipments without an equivalent raise on competitive points. It was not only this extra charge, enough to cut off their profits, as business then stood, but it was that the same set of men who had thrown their business into confusion in 1872 was again at work. The announcement of the Central Association with Mr. Rockefeller's name at its head confirmed their fears. Nevertheless at first none of the small refiners would listen to the proposition to sell or lease made them in the spring of 1875 by the representative first sent out by the Central Association. They would have nothing to do, they said bluntly, with any combination engineered by John D. Rockefeller. The representative withdrew and the case was considered. In the mean time conditions on the creek grew harder. All sorts of difficulties began to be strewn in their way—cars were hard to get, the markets they had built up were cut under them—a demoralising conviction was abroad in the trade that this new and mysterious combination was going to succeed; that it was doing rapidly what its members were reported to be saying daily: "We mean to secure the entire refining business of the world."

Such was the state of things on the creek when in the early fall of 1875 an energetic young refiner and oil buyer well known in the Oil Regions, J. D. Archbold, appeared in Titusville as the representative of a new company, the Acme Oil Company, a concern which everybody believed to be an offshoot of the Standard Oil Company of Cleveland, though nobody could prove it. As a matter of fact the Acme was capitalised and controlled entirely by Standard men, its stockholders being, in addition to Mr. Archbold, William Rockefeller, William G. Warden, Frank Q. Barstow, and Charles Pratt. It was evident at once that the Acme Oil Company had come into the Oil Regions for the purpose of absorbing the independent interests as Mr. Rockefeller and his colleagues were absorbing them elsewhere. The work was done with a promptness and despatch which do great credit to the energy and resourcefulness of the engineer of the enterprise. In three years, by 1878, all but two of the refineries of Titusville had "retired from the business gloriously," as Mr. Archbold, flushed with victory, told the counsel of the Commonwealth of Pennsylvania in 1879, when the state authorities were trying to find what was at work in the oil interests to cause such a general collapse. Most of the concerns were bought outright, the owners being convinced that it was impossible for them to do an independent business, and being unwilling to try combination. All down the creek the little refineries which for years had faced every difficulty with stout hearts collapsed. "Sold out," "dismantled," "shut down," is the melancholy record of the industry during these four years. At the end practically nothing was left in the Oil Regions but the Acme of Titusville and the Imperial of Oil City, both of them now under Standard management. To the oil men this sudden wiping out of the score of plants with which they had been familiar for years seemed a crime which nothing could justify. Their bitterness of heart was only intensified by the sight of the idle refiners thrown out of business by the sale of their factories. These men had, many of them, handsome sums to invest, but what were they to put them in? They were refiners, and they carried a pledge in their pockets not to go into that business for a period of ten years. Some of them tried the discouraged oil man's fatal resource, the market, and as a rule left their money there. One refiner who had, according to popular report, received $200,000 for his business, speculated the entire sum away in less than a year. Others tried new enterprises, but men of forty learn new trades with difficulty, and failure followed many of them. The scars left in the Oil Regions by the Standard Combination of 1875-1879 are too deep and ugly for men and women of this generation to forget them.

Source: Tarbell, Ida Minerva. *The History of the Standard Oil Company.* New York: McClure, Phillips and Co., 1904, pp. 154-60.

Upton Sinclair Exposes Problems in the Meatpacking Industry

The Jungle by Upton Sinclair is one of the most famous works of muckraking literature. Published in 1906, it grew out of the author's undercover investigation of working conditions in Chicago's meatpacking plants. Sinclair wove his observations of disgusting, unsanitary facilities and dangerous, dehumanizing jobs into a story about a fictional meatpacking industry worker named Jurgis Rudkos. Rudkos was a Lithuanian immigrant who endured everything Sinclair had witnessed in the plants and the surrounding tenement district known as Packingtown. The following excerpt from Chapter 14 of The Jungle describes the methods used to disguise spoiled meat so it can be sold to unsuspecting consumers. It also demonstrates the terrible toll the work took on Rudkos and his family.

With one member trimming beef in a cannery, and another working in a sausage factory, the family had a first-hand knowledge of the great majority of Packingtown swindles. For it was the custom, as they found, whenever meat was so spoiled that it could not be used for anything else, either to can it or else to chop it up into sausage. With what had been told them by Jonas, who had worked in the pickle rooms, they could now study the whole of the spoiled-meat industry on the inside, and read a new and grim meaning into that old Packingtown jest—that they use everything of the pig except the squeal.

Jonas had told them how the meat that was taken out of pickle would often be found sour, and how they would rub it up with soda to take away the smell, and sell it to be eaten on free-lunch counters; also of all the miracles of chemistry which they performed, giving to any sort of meat, fresh or salted, whole or chopped, any color and any flavor and any odor they chose. In the pickling of hams they had an ingenious apparatus, by which they saved time and increased the capacity of the plant—a machine consisting of a hollow needle attached to a pump; by plunging this needle into the meat and working with his foot, a man could fill a ham with pickle in a few seconds. And yet, in spite of this, there would be hams found spoiled, some of them with an odor so bad that a man could hardly bear to be in the room with them. To pump into these the packers had a second and much stronger pickle which destroyed the odor—a process known to the workers as "giving them thirty per cent." Also, after the hams had been smoked, there would be found some that had gone to the bad. Formerly these had been sold as "Number Three Grade," but later on some ingenious person had hit upon a new device, and now they would extract the bone, about which the bad part generally lay, and insert in the hole a white-hot iron. After this invention there was no longer Number One, Two, and Three Grade—there was only Number One Grade. The packers were always originating such schemes—they had what they called "boneless hams," which were all the odds and ends of pork stuffed into casings; and "California hams," which were the shoulders, with big knuckle joints, and nearly all the meat cut out; and fancy "skinned hams," which were made of the oldest hogs, whose skins were so heavy and coarse that no one would buy them—that is, until they had been cooked and chopped fine and labeled "head cheese!"

It was only when the whole ham was spoiled that it came into the department of Elzbieta. Cut up by the two-thousand-revolutions-a-minute flyers, and mixed with half a ton of other meat, no odor that ever was in a ham could make any difference. There was never the least attention paid to what was cut up for sausage; there would come all the way back from Europe old sausage that had been rejected, and that was moldy and white—it would be dosed with borax and glycerine, and dumped into the hoppers, and made over again for home consumption. There would be meat that had tumbled out on the floor, in the dirt and sawdust, where the workers had tramped and spit uncounted billions of consumption germs. There would be meat stored in great piles in rooms; and the water from leaky roofs would drip over it, and thousands of rats would race about on it. It was too dark in these storage places to see well, but a man could run his hand over these piles of meat and sweep off handfuls of the dried dung of rats. These rats were nuisances, and the packers would put poisoned bread out for them; they would die, and then rats, bread, and meat would go into the hoppers together. This is no fairy story and no joke; the meat would be shoveled into carts, and the man who did the shoveling would not trouble to lift out a rat even when he saw one— there were things that went into the sausage in comparison with which a poisoned rat was a tidbit. There was no place for the men to wash their hands before they ate their dinner, and so they made a practice of washing them in the water that was to be ladled into the sausage. There were the butt-ends of smoked meat, and the scraps of corned beef, and all the odds and ends of the waste of the plants, that would be dumped into old barrels in the cellar and left there. Under the system of rigid economy which the packers enforced, there were some jobs that it only paid to do once in a long time, and among these was the cleaning out of the waste barrels. Every spring they did it; and in the barrels would be dirt and rust and old nails and stale water—and cart-load after cartload of it would be taken up and dumped into the hoppers with fresh meat, and sent out to the public's breakfast. Some of it they would make into "smoked" sausage—but as the smoking took time, and was therefore expensive, they would call upon their chemistry department, and preserve it with borax and color it with gelatine to make it brown. All of their sausage came out of the same bowl, but when they came to wrap it they would stamp some of it "special," and for this they would charge two cents more a pound.

* * *

Such were the new surroundings in which Elzbieta was placed, and such was the work she was compelled to do. It was stupefying, brutalizing work; it left her no time to think, no strength for anything. She was part of the machine she tended, and every faculty that was not needed for the machine was doomed to be crushed out of existence. There was only one mercy about the cruel grind—that it gave her the gift of insensibility. Little by little she sank into a torpor—she fell silent. She would meet Jurgis and Ona in the evening, and the three would walk home together, often without saying a word. Ona, too, was falling into a habit of silence—Ona, who had once gone about singing like a bird. She was sick and miserable, and often she would barely have strength enough to drag herself home. And there they would eat what they had to eat, and afterward, because there was only their misery to talk of, they would crawl into bed and fall into a stupor and never stir until it was time to get up again, and dress by candlelight, and go back to the machines. They were so numbed that they did not even suffer much from hunger, now; only the children continued to fret when the food ran short.

Yet the soul of Ona was not dead—the souls of none of them were dead, but only sleeping; and now and then they would waken, and these were cruel times. The gates of memory would roll open—old joys would stretch out their arms to them, old hopes and dreams would call to them, and they would stir beneath the burden that lay upon them, and feel its forever immeasurable weight. They could not even cry out beneath it; but anguish would seize them, more dreadful than the agony of death. It was a thing scarcely to be spoken—a thing never spoken by all the world, that will not know its own defeat.

They were beaten; they had lost the game, they were swept aside. It was not less tragic because it was so sordid, because it had to do with wages and grocery bills and rents. They had dreamed of freedom; of a chance to look about them and learn something; to be decent and clean, to see their child grow up to be strong. And now it was all gone—it would never be! They had played the game and they had lost. Six years more of toil they had to face before they could expect the least respite, the cessation of the payments upon the house; and how cruelly certain it was that they could never stand six years of such a life as they were living! They were lost, they were going down—and there was no deliverance for them, no hope; for all the help it gave them the vast city in which they lived might have been an ocean waste, a wilderness, a desert, a tomb. So often this mood would come to Ona, in the nighttime, when something wakened her; she would lie, afraid of the beating of her own heart, fronting the blood-red eyes of the old primeval terror of life. Once she cried aloud, and woke Jurgis, who was tired and cross. After that she learned to weep silently—their moods so seldom came together now! It was as if their hopes were buried in separate graves.

Jurgis, being a man, had troubles of his own. There was another specter following him. He had never spoken of it, nor would he allow any one else to speak of it—he had never acknowledged its existence to himself. Yet the battle with it took all the manhood that he had—and once or twice, alas, a little more. Jurgis had discovered drink.

He was working in the steaming pit of hell; day after day, week after week—until now, there was not an organ of his body that did its work without pain, until the sound of ocean breakers echoed in his head day and night, and the buildings swayed and danced before him as he went down the street. And from all the unending horror of this there was a respite, a deliverance—he could drink! He could forget the pain, he could slip off the burden; he would see clearly again, he would be master of his brain, of his thoughts, of his will. His dead self would stir in him, and he would find himself laughing and cracking jokes with his companions—he would be a man again, and master of his life.

Source: Sinclair, Upton. *The Jungle*. New York: Doubleday, 1906, pp. 188-93.

Lincoln Steffens Reveals the Shame of the Cities

During the Progressive Era, corrupt city governments came under investigation by muckraking journalists like Lincoln Steffens. After joining the staff of McClure's *magazine in 1902, Steffens compiled a series of articles about the ways in which bribery, backroom deals, and political favors drove the governments of virtually every major American city. The first installment in his "Shame of the Cities" series, entitled "Tweed Days in St. Louis," is excerpted below. Steffens describes the lonely battle waged by a newly elected district attorney, Joseph Folk, to clean up corruption in St. Louis, Missouri.*

S t. LOUIS, the fourth city in size in the United States, is making two announcements to the world: one that it is the worst-governed city in the land; the other that it wishes all men to come there and see it. It isn't our worst-governed city; Philadelphia is that. But St. Louis is worth examining while we have it inside out.

There is a man at work there, one man, working all alone, but he is the Circuit (district or state) Attorney, and he is "doing his duty." That is what thousands of district attorneys and other public officials have promised to do and boasted of doing. This man has a literal sort of mind. He is a thin-lipped, firm-mouthed, dark little man, who never raises his voice, but goes ahead doing, with a smiling eye and a set jaw, the simple thing he said he would do. The politicians and reputable citizens who asked him to run urged him when he declined. When he said that if elected he would have to do his duty, they said, "Of course." So he ran, they supported him, and he was elected. Now some of these politicians are sentenced to the penitentiary, some are in Mexico. The Circuit Attorney, finding that his "duty" was to catch and convict criminals, and that the biggest criminals were some of these same politicians and leading citizens, went after them. It is magnificent, but the politicians declare it isn't politics.

The corruption of St. Louis came from the top. The best citizens—the merchants and big financiers—used to rule the town, and they ruled it well. They set out to outstrip Chicago. The commercial and industrial war between these two cities was at one time a picturesque and dramatic spectacle such as is witnessed only in our country. Businessmen were not mere merchants and the politicians were not mere grafters; the two kinds of citizens got together and wielded the power of banks, railroads, factories, the prestige of the city and the spirit of its citizens to gain business and population. And it was a close race. Chicago, having the start, always led, but St. Louis had pluck, intelligence, and tremendous energy. It pressed Chicago hard. It excelled in a sense of civic beauty and good government; and there are those who think yet it might have won. But a change occurred. Public spirit became private spirit, public enterprise became private greed.

Along about 1890, public franchises and privileges were sought, not only for legitimate profit and common convenience, but for loot. Taking but slight and always selfish interest in the public councils, the big men misused politics. The riffraff, catching the smell of corruption, rushed into the Municipal Assembly, drove out the remaining respectable men, and sold the city— its streets, its wharves, its markets, and all that it had—to the now greedy businessmen and bribers. In other words, when the leading men began to devour their own city, the herd rushed into the trough and fed also.

So gradually has this occurred that these same citizens hardly realize it. Go to St. Louis and you will find the habit of civic pride in them; they still boast. The visitor is told of the wealth of the residents, of the financial strength of the banks, and of the growing importance of the industries, yet he sees poorly paved, refuse-burdened streets, and dusty or mud-covered alleys; he passes a ramshackle firetrap crowded with the sick, and learns that it is the City Hospital; he enters the "Four Courts," and his nostrils are greeted by the odor of formaldehyde used as a disinfectant, and insect powder spread to destroy vermin; he calls at the new City Hall, and finds half the entrance boarded with pine planks to cover up the unfinished interior. Finally, he turns a tap in the hotel, to see liquid mud flow into wash basin or bathtub.

The St. Louis charter vests legislative power of great scope in a Municipal Assembly, which is composed of a Council and a House of Delegates. Here is a description of the latter by one of Mr. Folk's grand juries:

"We have had before us many of those who have been, and most of those who are now, members of the House of Delegates. We found a number of these utterly illiterate and lacking in ordinary intelligence, unable to give a better reason for favoring or opposing a measure than a desire to act with the majority. In some, no trace of mentality or morality could be found; in others, a low order of training appeared, united with base cunning, groveling instincts, and sordid desires. Unqualified to respond to the ordinary requirements of life, they are utterly incapable of comprehending the significance of an ordinance, and are incapacitated, both by nature and training, to be the makers of laws. The choosing of such men to be legislators makes a travesty of justice, sets a premium on incompetency, and deliberately poisons the very source of the law."

These creatures were well organized. They had a "combine"—a legislative institution—which the grand jury described as follows:

"Our investigation, covering more or less fully a period of ten years, shows that, with few exceptions, no ordinance has been passed wherein valuable privileges or franchises are granted until those interested have paid the legislators the money demanded for action in the particular case. Combines in both branches of the Municipal Assembly are formed by members sufficient in number to control legislation. To one member of this combine is delegated the authority to act for the combine, and to receive and to distribute to each member the money agreed upon as the price of his vote in support of, or opposition to, a pending measure. So long has this practice existed that such members have come to regard the receipt of money for action on pending measures as a legitimate perquisite of a legislator."

One legislator consulted a lawyer with the intention of suing a firm to recover an unpaid balance on a fee for the grant of a switchway. Such difficulties rarely occurred, however. In order to insure a regular and indisputable revenue, the combine of each house drew up a schedule of bribery prices for all possible sorts of grants, just such a list as a commercial traveler takes out on the road with him. There was a price for a grain elevator, a price for a short switch; side tracks were charged for by the linear foot, but at rates which varied according to the nature of the ground taken; a street improvement cost so much; wharf space was classified and precisely rated. As there was a scale for favorable legislation, so there was one for defeating bills. It made a difference in the price if there was opposition, and it made a difference whether the privilege asked was legitimate or not. But nothing was passed free of charge. Many of the legislators were saloonkeepers—it was in St. Louis that a practical joker nearly emptied the House of Delegates by tipping a boy to rush into a session and call out, "Mister, your saloon is on fire"—but even the saloonkeepers of a neighborhood had to pay to keep in their inconvenient locality a market which public interest would have moved.

From the Assembly, bribery spread into other departments. Men empowered to issue peddlers' licenses and permits to citizens who wished to erect an awning or use a portion of the sidewalk for storage purposes charged an amount in excess of the prices stipulated by law, and pocketed the difference. The city's money was loaned at interest, and the interest was converted into private bank accounts. City carriages were used by the wives and children of city officials. Supplies for public institutions found their way to private tables; one itemized account of food furnished the poorhouse included California jellies, imported cheeses, and French wines! A member of the Assembly caused the incorporation of a grocery company, with his sons and daughters the ostensible stockholders, and succeeded in having his bid for city supplies accepted although the figures were in excess of his competitors'. In return for the favor thus shown, he indorsed a measure to award the contract for city printing to another member, and these two voted aye on a bill granting to a third the exclusive right to furnish city dispensaries with drugs.

Men ran into debt to the extent of thousands of dollars for the sake of election to either branch of the Assembly. One night, on a street car going to the City Hall, a new member remarked that the nickel he handed the conductor was his last. The next day he deposited $5,000 in a savings bank. A member of the House of Delegates admitted to the grand jury that his dividends from the combine netted $25,000 in one year; a councilman stated that he was paid $50,000 for his vote on a single measure....

The blackest years were 1898, 1899, and 1900. Foreign corporations came into the city to share in its despoliation, and home industries were driven out by blackmail. Franchises worth millions were granted without one cent of cash to the city, and with provision for only the smallest future payment; several companies which refused to pay blackmail had to leave; citizens were robbed more and more boldly; payrolls were padded with the names of nonexistent persons; work on public improvements was neglected, while money for them went to the boodlers.

Some of the newspapers protested, disinterested citizens were alarmed, and the shrewder men gave warnings, but none dared make an effective stand. Behind the corruptionists were men of wealth and social standing, who, because of special privileges granted them, felt bound to support and defend the looters. Independent victims of the far-reaching conspiracy submitted in silence, through fear of injury to their business. Men whose integrity was never questioned, who held high positions of trust, who were church members and teachers of Bible classes, contributed to the support of the dynasty—became blackmailers, in fact—and their excuse was that others did the same, and that if they proved the exception it would work their ruin. The system became loose through license and plenty till it was as wild as that of Tweed in New York.

Then the unexpected happened—an accident. There was no uprising of the people, but they were restive; and the Democratic party leaders, thinking to gain some independent votes, decided to raise the cry "reform" and put up a ticket of candidates different enough from the usual offerings of political parties to give color to their platform. These leaders were not in earnest. There was little difference between the two parties in the city; but the rascals that were in had been getting the greater share of the spoils, and the "outs" wanted more than was given to them. "Boodle" was not the issue, no exposures were made or threatened, and the bosses expected to control their men if elected. Simply as part of the game, the Democrats raised the slogan, "reform" and "no more Ziegenheinism."

Mayor Ziegenhein, called "Uncle Henry," was a "good fellow," "one of the boys," and though it was during his administration that the city grew ripe and went to rot, his opponents talked only of incompetence and neglect, and repeated such stories as that of his famous reply to some citizens who complained because certain street lights were put out: "You have the moon yet—ain't it?"

When somebody mentioned Joseph W. Folk for Circuit Attorney the leaders were ready to accept him. They didn't know much about him. He was a young man from Tennessee; had been president of the Jefferson Club, and arbitrated the railroad strike of 1898. But Folk did not want the place. He was a civil lawyer, had had no practice at the criminal bar, cared little about it, and a lucrative business as counsel for corporations was interesting him. He rejected the invitation. The committee called again and again, urging his duty to his party, and the city, etc.

"Very well," he said, at last, "I will accept the nomination, but if elected I will do my duty. There must be no attempt to influence my actions when I am called upon to punish lawbreakers."

The committeemen took such statements as the conventional platitudes of candidates. They nominated him, the Democratic ticket was elected, and Folk became Circuit Attorney for the Eighth Missouri District.

Three weeks after taking the oath of office his campaign pledges were put to the test. A number of arrests had been made in connection with the recent election, and charges of illegal registration were preferred against men of both parties. Mr. Folk took them up like routine cases of ordinary crime. Political bosses rushed to the rescue. Mr. Folk was reminded of his duty to his party, and told that he was expected to construe the law in such a manner that repeaters and other election criminals who had hoisted democracy's flag and helped elect him might be either discharged or receive the minimum punishment. The nature of the young lawyer's reply can best be inferred from the words of that veteran political leader, Colonel Ed Butler, who, after a visit to Mr. Folk, wrathfully exclaimed, "D—n Joe! He thinks he's the whole thing as Circuit Attorney."

The election cases were passed through the courts with astonishing rapidity; no more mercy was shown Democrats than Republicans, and before winter came a number of ward heelers and old-time party workers were behind the bars in Jefferson City. He next turned his attention to grafters and straw bondsmen with whom the courts were infested, and several of these leeches are in the penitentiary today. The business was broken up because of his activity. But Mr. Folk had made little more than the beginning....

Mr. Folk has shown St. Louis that its bankers, brokers, corporation officers—its businessmen—are the sources of evil, so that from the start it will know the municipal problem in its true light. With a tradition for public spirit, it may drop Butler and its runaway bankers, brokers and brewers, and pushing aside the scruples of the hundreds of men down in blue book, and red book, and church register, who are lying hidden behind the statutes of limitations, the city may restore good government. Otherwise the exposures by Mr. Folk will result only in the perfection of the corrupt system. For the corrupt can learn a lesson when the good citizens cannot....

This is St. Louis' one great chance. But, for the rest of us, it does not matter about St. Louis any more than it matters about Colonel Butler et al. The point is, that what went on in St. Louis is going on in most of our cities, towns and villages. The problem of municipal government in America has not been solved. The people may be tired of it, but they cannot give it up—not yet.

Source: Steffens, Lincoln. "Tweed Days in St. Louis." *McClure's*, October 1902. Reprinted in Weinberg, Lila Shaffer. *The Muckrakers*. Chicago: University of Illinois Press, 2001, pp. 122-27.

David Graham Phillips Blasts Corrupt U.S. Senators

Among the most controversial muckraking reports is the "Treason of the Senate" series by David Graham Phillips. In this nine-part series on federal government corruption, Phillips profiled twenty-one U.S. Senators whom he claimed had inappropriate relationships with corporate interests. The first installment, which is excerpted below, appeared in Cosmopolitan *magazine in March 1906. It accuses the two senators from New York, Thomas Platt (served 1897-1909) and Chauncey Depew (served 1899-1911), of being under the control of wealthy industrialists.*

Although the "Treason of the Senate" series encouraged lawmakers across the country to enact important political reforms, it also severely strained the relationship between President Theodore Roosevelt and the muckrakers. Phillips's reports targeted a number of the president's friends, allies, and supporters. The month after the first article was published, Roosevelt made a famous speech denouncing the journalists for being too negative and ignoring the many positive aspects of American society and government.

Politics does not determine prosperity. But in this day of concentrations, politics does determine *the distribution of prosperity*. Because the people have neglected politics, have not educated themselves out of credulity to flimsily plausible political lies and liars, because they will not realize that *it is not enough to work, it is also necessary to think*, they remain poor, or deprived of their fair share of the products, though they have produced an incredible prosperity. The people have been careless and unwise enough in electing every kind of public administrator. When it comes to the election of the Senate, how describe their stupidity, how measure its melancholy consequences? The Senate is the most powerful part of our public administration. It has vast power in the making of laws. It has still vaster power through its ability to forbid the making of laws and in its control over the appointment of the judges who say what the laws mean. It is, in fact, *the final arbiter of the sharing of prosperity*. The laws it permits or compels, the laws it refuses to permit, the interpreters of laws it permits to be appointed—these factors determine whether the great forces which modern concentration has produced shall operate to distribute prosperity equally or with shameful inequality and cruel and destructive injustice. The United States Senate is a larger factor than your labor or your intelligence, you average American, in determining your income. And the Senate is a traitor to you.

The treason of the Senate! Treason is a strong word, but not too strong, rather too weak, to characterize the situation in which the Senate is the eager, resourceful, indefatigable agent of interests as hostile to the American people as any invading army could be, and vastly more dangerous; interests that manipulate the prosperity produced by all, so that it heaps up riches for the few; interests whose growth and power can only mean the degradation of the people, of the educated into sycophants, of the masses toward serfdom.

A man cannot serve two masters. The senators are not elected by the people; they are elected by the "interests." A servant obeys him who can punish and dismiss. Except in extreme and rare and negligible instances, can the people either elect or dismiss a senator? The senator, in the dilemma which the careless ignorance of the people thrusts upon him, chooses to be comfortable, placed and honored, and a traitor to oath and people rather than to be true to his oath and poor and ejected into private life.

New York's Misrepresentatives

Let us begin with the state which is first in population, in wealth, in organization of industries. As we shall presently see, the nine states that contain more than half the whole American people send to the Senate eighteen men, no less than ten of whom are notorious characters, frankly the servants of the interests the American people have decided must be destroyed, unless they themselves are to be crushed down. And of these servants of the plutocracy none is more candid in obsequiousness, in treachery to the people, than are the two senators from the state which contains one-tenth of our population and the strong financial citadel-capital of the plutocracy.

Thomas Collier Platt! Chauncey Mitchell Depew!

Probably Platt's last conspicuous appearance will have been that on the witness stand in the insurance investigation, where he testified that he had knowingly received thousands of dollars of the stolen goods of the insurance thieves. He confessed this with obvious unconsciousness of his own shame.

We shall come across this phenomenon frequently in our course through the Senate—this shamelessness that has lost all sense of moral distinctions. Our Platts and Burtons have no more moral sense than an ossified man has feeling. Then, there are those of our public men who, through fear or lack of opportunity or some instinct of personal self-respect, sit inactive, silent or only vaguely murmurous spectators, while the treasons are plotted and executed. These men have been corrupted by association. The public man meets the people only in masses, at political gatherings. His associations

189

are altogether with other public men and with the class that is either fattening on the people or quite cynical about corruption of that kind. Hence, his sense of shame becomes paralyzed, atrophied.

The very "interests" that are ruining the people come to stand in his mind for the people themselves, and in his confused mind prostitution becomes a sort of patriotism.

Platt cannot live long. His mind is already a mere shadow. The other day a friend found him crying like a child because Roosevelt was unable to appoint for him to a federal district attorneyship a man who had been caught stealing trust funds, and insisted that he must select some henchman wearing the brand less conspicuously. "Platt was like an unreasonable child," said his friend....

But let us not linger upon Platt—Platt, with his long, his unbroken record of treachery to the people in legislation of privilege and plunder promoted and in decent legislation prevented. Let us leave him, not because he is sick and feeble; for death itself without repentance or restitution deserves no consideration; but because he needs no extended examination to be understood and entered under his proper heading in the record. Wherever Platt is known, to speak of him as a patriot would cause wonder if not open derision. The most that could be said of him is that, wherever the interests of the people do not conflict with the interests of the "interests" or with his own pocket, which includes that of his family, Platt has been either inactive or not positively in opposition.

Let us turn to the other of the two representatives whom the people of New York suffer to sit and cast the other of their two votes in the body that arbitrates the division of the prosperity of the country, the wages and the prices. At this writing Depew has just given out a flat refusal to resign. "Why should I resign?" he cried out hysterically. "Has anybody put forward any good reason why I should resign?" And he added, "As soon as I have completed my resignation from certain companies, I shall give all my time to my senatorial duties."

What are his senatorial duties? What does he do in the body that is now as much an official part of the plutocracy as the executive council of a Rockefeller or a Ryan? No one would pretend for an instant that he sits in the Senate for the people. Indeed, why should he, except because he took an oath to do so—and among such eminent respectabilities as he an oath is a mere formality, a mere technicality. Did the people send him to the Senate? No! The

Vanderbilt interests ordered Platt to send him the first time; and when he came up for a second term the Vanderbilt-Morgan interests got, not without difficulty, Harriman's O.K. on an order to Odell to give it to him....

It was ... when Depew was but thirty-two years old that he took "personal and official" service with the Vanderbilt family. And ever since then they have owned him, mentally and morally; they have used him, or rather, he, in his eagerness to please them, has made himself useful to them to an extent which he does not realize nor do they. So great is his reverence for wealth and the possessors of wealth, so humble is he before them, that he probably does not appreciate how much of the Vanderbilt fortune his brain got for that family....

And, for reward, the Vanderbilts have given him scant and contemptuous crumbs. After forty years of industrious, faithful, and, to his masters, enormously profitable self-degradation he has not more than five millions, avaricious and saving though he has been. And they tossed him the senatorship as if it had been a charity. Of all the creatures of the Vanderbilts, none has been more versatile, more willing or more profitable to his users than Depew. Yet he has only five million dollars and a blasted name to console his old age, while his users are in honor and count their millions by the score.

Source: Phillips, David Graham. "The Treason of the Senate." *Cosmopolitan*, March 1906.

Roosevelt Calls Crusading Journalists "Muckrakers"

During his second term in office, President Theodore Roosevelt voiced growing concerns about the trends he saw in American journalism. The investigative reports that had dominated national magazines for much of his presidency had often served to generate public support for his progressive reforms. But Roosevelt felt that the articles had become more sensational, unfair, bitter, and personal over time. He expressed his views in a speech entitled "The Man with the Muck-Rake," delivered on April 14, 1906, at a ceremony laying the foundation for a new congressional office building. In this famous speech, which is excerpted below, the president describes the crusading journalists as "muckrakers" and warns that their excessive focus on the negative could damage the country.

Over a century ago Washington laid the corner stone of the Capitol in what was then little more than a tract of wooded wilderness here beside the Potomac. We now find it necessary to provide by great additional buildings for the business of the government.

This growth in the need for the housing of the government is but a proof and example of the way in which the nation has grown and the sphere of action of the national government has grown. We now administer the affairs of a nation in which the extraordinary growth of population has been outstripped by the growth of wealth in complex interests. The material problems that face us today are not such as they were in Washington's time, but the underlying facts of human nature are the same now as they were then. Under altered external form we war with the same tendencies toward evil that were evident in Washington's time, and are helped by the same tendencies for good. It is about some of these that I wish to say a word today.

In Bunyan's *Pilgrim's Progress* you may recall the description of the Man with the Muck Rake, the man who could look no way but downward, with the muck rake in his hand; who was offered a celestial crown for his muck rake, but who would neither look up nor regard the crown he was offered, but continued to rake to himself the filth of the floor.

In *Pilgrim's Progress* the Man with the Muck Rake is set forth as the example of him whose vision is fixed on carnal instead of spiritual things. Yet he also typifies the man who in this life consistently refuses to see aught that is lofty, and fixes his eyes with solemn intentness only on that which is vile and debasing.

Now, it is very necessary that we should not flinch from seeing what is vile and debasing. There is filth on the floor, and it must be scraped up with the muck rake; and there are times and places where this service is the most needed of all the services that can be performed. But the man who never does anything else, who never thinks or speaks or writes, save of his feats with the muck rake, speedily becomes, not a help but one of the most potent forces for evil.

There are in the body politic, economic and social, many and grave evils, and there is urgent necessity for the sternest war upon them. There should be relentless exposure of and attack upon every evil man, whether politician or business man, every evil practice, whether in politics, business, or social life. I hail as a benefactor every writer or speaker, every man who, on the platform or in a book, magazine, or newspaper, with merciless severity makes such attack, provided always that he in his turn remembers that the attack is of use only if it is absolutely truthful.

The liar is no whit better than the thief, and if his mendacity takes the form of slander he may be worse than most thieves. It puts a premium upon knavery untruthfully to attack an honest man, or even with hysterical exaggeration to assail a bad man with untruth.

An epidemic of indiscriminate assault upon character does no good, but very great harm. The soul of every scoundrel is gladdened whenever an honest man is assailed, or even when a scoundrel is untruthfully assailed.

Now, it is easy to twist out of shape what I have just said, easy to affect to misunderstand it, and if it is slurred over in repetition not difficult really to misunderstand it. Some persons are sincerely incapable of understanding that to denounce mud slinging does not mean the endorsement of whitewashing; and both the interested individuals who need whitewashing and those others who practice mud slinging like to encourage such confusion of ideas.

One of the chief counts against those who make indiscriminate assault upon men in business or men in public life is that they invite a reaction which is sure to tell powerfully in favor of the unscrupulous scoundrel who really ought to be attacked, who ought to be exposed, who ought, if possible, to be put in the penitentiary. If Aristides is praised overmuch as just, people get tired of hearing it; and overcensure of the unjust finally and from similar reasons results in their favor.

Any excess is almost sure to invite a reaction; and, unfortunately, the reactions instead of taking the form of punishment of those guilty of the excess, is apt to take the form either of punishment of the unoffending or of

193

giving immunity, and even strength, to offenders. The effort to make financial or political profit out of the destruction of character can only result in public calamity. Gross and reckless assaults on character, whether on the stump or in newspaper, magazine, or book, create a morbid and vicious public senti-ment, and at the same time act as a profound deterrent to able men of normal sensitiveness and tend to prevent them from entering the public service at any price....

At the risk of repetition let me say again that my plea is not for immuni-ty to, but for the most unsparing exposure of, the politician who betrays his trust, of the big business man who makes or spends his fortune in illegitimate or corrupt ways. There should be a resolute effort to hunt every such man out of the position he has disgraced. Expose the crime, and hunt down the crimi-nal; but remember that even in the case of crime, if it is attacked in sensation-al, lurid, and untruthful fashion, the attack may do more damage to the pub-lic mind than the crime itself.

It is because I feel that there should be no rest in the endless war against the forces of evil that I ask the war be conducted with sanity as well as with resolution. The men with the muck rakes are often indispensable to the well being of society; but only if they know when to stop raking the muck, and to look upward to the celestial crown above them, to the crown of worthy endeavor. There are beautiful things above and round about them; and if they gradually grow to feel that the whole world is nothing but muck, their power of usefulness is gone.

If the whole picture is painted black there remains no hue whereby to single out the rascals for distinction from their fellows. Such painting finally induces a kind of moral color blindness; and people affected by it come to the conclusion that no man is really black, and no man really white, but they are all gray.

In other words, they neither believe in the truth of the attack, nor in the honesty of the man who is attacked; they grow as suspicious of the accusation as of the offense; it becomes well nigh hopeless to stir them either to wrath against wrongdoing or to enthusiasm for what is right; and such a mental atti-tude in the public gives hope to every knave, and is the despair of honest men. To assail the great and admitted evils of our political and industrial life with such crude and sweeping generalizations as to include decent men in the gen-eral condemnation means the searing of the public conscience. There results a general attitude either of cynical belief in and indifference to public corruption or else of a distrustful inability to discriminate between the good and the bad. Either attitude is fraught with untold damage to the country as a whole.

The fool who has not sense to discriminate between what is good and what is bad is well nigh as dangerous as the man who does discriminate and yet chooses the bad. There is nothing more distressing to every good patriot, to every good American, than the hard, scoffing spirit which treats the allegation of dishonesty in a public man as a cause for laughter. Such laughter is worse than the crackling of thorns under a pot, for it denotes not merely the vacant mind, but the heart in which high emotions have been choked before they could grow to fruition. There is any amount of good in the world, and there never was a time when loftier and more disinterested work for the betterment of mankind was being done than now. The forces that tend for evil are great and terrible, but the forces of truth and love and courage and honesty and generosity and sympathy are also stronger than ever before. It is a foolish and timid, no less than a wicked thing, to blink the fact that the forces of evil are strong, but it is even worse to fail to take into account the strength of the forces that tell for good.

Hysterical sensationalism is the poorest weapon wherewith to fight for lasting righteousness. The men who with stern sobriety and truth assail the many evils of our time, whether in the public press, or in magazines, or in books, are the leaders and allies of all engaged in the work for social and political betterment. But if they give good reason for distrust of what they say, if they chill the ardor of those who demand truth as a primary virtue, they thereby betray the good cause and play into the hands of the very men against whom they are nominally at war....

At this moment we are passing through a period of great unrest—social, political, and industrial unrest. It is of the utmost importance for our future that this should prove to be not the unrest of mere rebelliousness against life, of mere dissatisfaction with the inevitable inequality of conditions, but the unrest of a resolute and eager ambition to secure the betterment of the individual and the nation.

So far as this movement of agitation throughout the country takes the form of a fierce discontent with evil, of a determination to punish the authors of evil, whether in industry or politics, the feeling is to be heartily welcomed as a sign of healthy life.

If, on the other hand, it turns into a mere crusade of appetite against appetite, of a contest between the brutal greed of the "have nots" and the brutal greed of the "haves," then it has no significance for good, but only for evil. If it seeks to establish a line of cleavage, not along the line which divides good men from bad, but along that other line, running at right angles thereto, which divides those who are well off from those who are less well off, then it will be fraught with immeasurable harm to the body politic....

More important than aught else is the development of the broadest sympathy of man for man. The welfare of the wage worker, the welfare of the tiller of the soil, upon these depend the welfare of the entire country; their good is not to be sought in pulling down others; but their good must be the prime object of all our statesmanship.

Materially we must strive to secure a broader economic opportunity for all men, so that each shall have a better chance to show the stuff of which he is made. Spiritually and ethically we must strive to bring about clean living and right thinking. We appreciate that the things of the body are important; but we appreciate also that the things of the soul are immeasurably more important.

The foundation stone of national life is, and ever must be, the high individual character of the average citizen.

Source: Roosevelt, Theodore. "The Man with the Muck-Rake," April 14, 1906. Presidential Rhetoric Program, Texas A&M University, n.d. Available online at http://www .presidentialrhetoric.com/historicspeeches/roosevelt_theodore/muckrake.html.

The *Washington Post* Gives Wounded Veterans a Voice

The 2007 Washington Post *article excerpted below provides an example of modern-day muck-raking journalism. It is the first installment of a Pulitzer Prize-winning investigative series by Dana Priest and Anne Hull entitled "The Other Walter Reed." The series called attention to the poor outpatient medical care provided to wounded veterans of the wars in Iraq and Afghanistan at Walter Reed Army Medical Center in Washington, D.C. In this article, Priest and Hull reveal that U.S. military personnel were forced to recover from serious injuries in rundown, unsanitary facilities, and that they were confronted with a frustrating array of administrative hassles. These revelations led to a Congressional investigation and contributed to the resignation of several key military officials.*

Behind the door of Army Spec. Jeremy Duncan's room, part of the wall is torn and hangs in the air, weighted down with black mold. When the wounded combat engineer stands in his shower and looks up, he can see the bathtub on the floor above through a rotted hole. The entire building, constructed between the world wars, often smells like greasy carry-out. Signs of neglect are everywhere: mouse droppings, belly-up cockroaches, stained carpets, cheap mattresses.

This is the world of Building 18, not the kind of place where Duncan expected to recover when he was evacuated to Walter Reed Army Medical Center from Iraq last February with a broken neck and a shredded left ear, nearly dead from blood loss. But the old lodge, just outside the gates of the hospital and five miles up the road from the White House, has housed hundreds of maimed soldiers recuperating from injuries suffered in the wars in Iraq and Afghanistan.

The common perception of Walter Reed is of a surgical hospital that shines as the crown jewel of military medicine. But 5 1/2 years of sustained combat have transformed the venerable 113-acre institution into something else entirely—a holding ground for physically and psychologically damaged outpatients. Almost 700 of them—the majority soldiers, with some Marines—have been released from hospital beds but still need treatment or are awaiting bureaucratic decisions before being discharged or returned to active duty.

They suffer from brain injuries, severed arms and legs, organ and back damage, and various degrees of post-traumatic stress. Their legions have grown so exponentially—they outnumber hospital patients at Walter Reed 17 to 1—that they take up every available bed on post and spill into dozens of nearby hotels and apartments leased by the Army. The average stay is 10 months, but some have been stuck there for as long as two years.

Not all of the quarters are as bleak as Duncan's, but the despair of Building 18 symbolizes a larger problem in Walter Reed's treatment of the wounded, according to dozens of soldiers, family members, veterans aid groups, and current and former Walter Reed staff members interviewed by two *Washington Post* reporters, who spent more than four months visiting the outpatient world without the knowledge or permission of Walter Reed officials. Many agreed to be quoted by name; others said they feared Army retribution if they complained publicly.

While the hospital is a place of scrubbed-down order and daily miracles, with medical advances saving more soldiers than ever, the outpatients in the Other Walter Reed encounter a messy bureaucratic battlefield nearly as chaotic as the real battlefields they faced overseas.

On the worst days, soldiers say they feel like they are living a chapter of "Catch-22." The wounded manage other wounded. Soldiers dealing with psychological disorders of their own have been put in charge of others at risk of suicide.

Disengaged clerks, unqualified platoon sergeants and overworked case managers fumble with simple needs: feeding soldiers' families who are close to poverty, replacing a uniform ripped off by medics in the desert sand or helping a brain-damaged soldier remember his next appointment.

"We've done our duty. We fought the war. We came home wounded. Fine. But whoever the people are back here who are supposed to give us the easy transition should be doing it," said Marine Sgt. Ryan Groves, 26, an amputee who lived at Walter Reed for 16 months. "We don't know what to do. The people who are supposed to know don't have the answers. It's a non-stop process of stalling."

Soldiers, family members, volunteers and caregivers who have tried to fix the system say each mishap seems trivial by itself, but the cumulative effect wears down the spirits of the wounded and can stall their recovery.

"It creates resentment and disenfranchisement," said Joe Wilson, a clinical social worker at Walter Reed. "These soldiers will withdraw and stay in their rooms. They will actively avoid the very treatment and services that are meant to be helpful."

Danny Soto, a national service officer for Disabled American Veterans who helps dozens of wounded service members each week at Walter Reed, said soldiers "get awesome medical care and their lives are being saved," but, "Then they get into the administrative part of it and they are like, 'You saved me for what?' The soldiers feel like they are not getting proper respect. This leads to anger."

This world is invisible to outsiders. Walter Reed occasionally showcases the heroism of these wounded soldiers and emphasizes that all is well under the circumstances. President Bush, former defense secretary Donald H. Rumsfeld and members of Congress have promised the best care during their regular visits to the hospital's spit-polished amputee unit, Ward 57.

"We owe them all we can give them," Bush said during his last visit, a few days before Christmas. "Not only for when they're in harm's way, but when they come home to help them adjust if they have wounds, or help them adjust after their time in service."

Along with the government promises, the American public, determined not to repeat the divisive Vietnam experience, has embraced the soldiers even as the war grows more controversial at home. Walter Reed is awash in the generosity of volunteers, businesses and celebrities who donate money, plane tickets, telephone cards and steak dinners.

Yet at a deeper level, the soldiers say they feel alone and frustrated. Seventy-five percent of the troops polled by Walter Reed last March said their experience was "stressful." Suicide attempts and unintentional overdoses from prescription drugs and alcohol, which is sold on post, are part of the narrative here.

Vera Heron spent 15 frustrating months living on post to help care for her son. "It just absolutely took forever to get anything done," Heron said. "They do the paperwork, they lose the paperwork. Then they have to redo the paperwork. You are talking about guys and girls whose lives are disrupted for the rest of their lives, and they don't put any priority on it."

Family members who speak only Spanish have had to rely on Salvadoran housekeepers, a Cuban bus driver, the Panamanian bartender and a Mexican floor cleaner for help. Walter Reed maintains a list of bilingual staffers, but they are rarely called on, according to soldiers and families and Walter Reed staff members.

Evis Morales's severely wounded son was transferred to the National Naval Medical Center in Bethesda for surgery shortly after she arrived at Walter Reed. She had checked into her government-paid room on post, but she slept in the lobby of the Bethesda hospital for two weeks because no one told her there is a free shuttle between the two facilities. "They just let me off the bus and said 'Bye-bye,'" recalled Morales, a Puerto Rico resident.

Morales found help after she ran out of money, when she called a hotline number and a Spanish-speaking operator happened to answer.

"If they can have Spanish-speaking recruits to convince my son to go into the Army, why can't they have Spanish-speaking translators when he's injured?" Morales asked. "It's so confusing, so disorienting."

Soldiers, wives, mothers, social workers and the heads of volunteer organizations have complained repeatedly to the military command about what one called "The Handbook No One Gets" that would explain life as an outpatient. Most soldiers polled in the March survey said they got their information from friends. Only 12 percent said any Army literature had been helpful.

"They've been behind from Day One," said Rep. Thomas M. Davis III (R-Va.), who headed the House Government Reform Committee, which investigated problems at Walter Reed and other Army facilities. "Even the stuff they've fixed has only been patched."

Among the public, Davis said, "there's vast appreciation for soldiers, but there's a lack of focus on what happens to them" when they return. "It's awful."

Maj. Gen. George W. Weightman, commander at Walter Reed, said in an interview last week that a major reason outpatients stay so long, a change from the days when injured soldiers were discharged as quickly as possible, is that the Army wants to be able to hang on to as many soldiers as it can, "because this is the first time this country has fought a war for so long with an all-volunteer force since the Revolution."

200

Acknowledging the problems with outpatient care, Weightman said Walter Reed has taken steps over the past year to improve conditions for the outpatient army, which at its peak in summer 2005 numbered nearly 900, not to mention the hundreds of family members who come to care for them. One platoon sergeant used to be in charge of 125 patients; now each one manages 30. Platoon sergeants with psychological problems are more carefully screened. And officials have increased the numbers of case managers and patient advocates to help with the complex disability benefit process, which Weightman called "one of the biggest sources of delay."

And to help steer the wounded and their families through the complicated bureaucracy, Weightman said, Walter Reed has recently begun holding twice-weekly informational meetings. "We felt we were pushing information out before, but the reality is, it was overwhelming," he said. "Is it fail-proof? No. But we've put more resources on it."

He said a 21,500-troop increase in Iraq has Walter Reed bracing for "potentially a lot more" casualties.

Bureaucratic Battles

The best known of the Army's medical centers, Walter Reed opened in 1909 with 10 patients. It has treated the wounded from every war since, and nearly one of every four service members injured in Iraq and Afghanistan.

The outpatients are assigned to one of five buildings attached to the post, including Building 18, just across from the front gates on Georgia Avenue. To accommodate the overflow, some are sent to nearby hotels and apartments. Living conditions range from the disrepair of Building 18 to the relative elegance of Mologne House, a hotel that opened on the post in 1998, when the typical guest was a visiting family member or a retiree on vacation.

The Pentagon has announced plans to close Walter Reed by 2011, but that hasn't stopped the flow of casualties. Three times a week, school buses painted white and fitted with stretchers and blackened windows stream down Georgia Avenue. Sirens blaring, they deliver soldiers groggy from a pain-relief cocktail at the end of their long trip from Iraq via Landstuhl Regional Medical Center in Germany and Andrews Air Force Base.

Staff Sgt. John Daniel Shannon, 43, came in on one of those buses in November 2004 and spent several weeks on the fifth floor of Walter Reed's hospital. His eye and skull were shattered by an AK-47 round. His odyssey in the Other Walter Reed has lasted more than two years, but it began when someone handed him a map of the grounds and told him to find his room across post.

A reconnaissance and land-navigation expert, Shannon was so disoriented that he couldn't even find north. Holding the map, he stumbled around outside the hospital, sliding against walls and trying to keep himself upright, he said. He asked anyone he found for directions.

Shannon had led the 2nd Infantry Division's Ghost Recon Platoon until he was felled in a gun battle in Ramadi. He liked the solitary work of a sniper; "Lone Wolf" was his call name. But he did not expect to be left alone by the Army after such serious surgery and a diagnosis of post-traumatic stress disorder. He had appointments during his first two weeks as an outpatient, then nothing.

"I thought, 'Shouldn't they contact me?'" he said. "I didn't understand the paperwork. I'd start calling phone numbers, asking if I had appointments. I finally ran across someone who said: 'I'm your case manager. Where have you been?'

"Well, I've been here! Jeez Louise, people, I'm your hospital patient!"

Like Shannon, many soldiers with impaired memory from brain injuries sat for weeks with no appointments and no help from the staff to arrange them. Many disappeared even longer. Some simply left for home.

One outpatient, a 57-year-old staff sergeant who had a heart attack in Afghanistan, was given 200 rooms to supervise at the end of 2005. He quickly discovered that some outpatients had left the post months earlier and would check in by phone. "We called them 'call-in patients,'" said Staff Sgt. Mike McCauley, whose dormant PTSD from Vietnam was triggered by what he saw on the job: so many young and wounded, and three bodies being carried from the hospital.

Life beyond the hospital bed is a frustrating mountain of paperwork. The typical soldier is required to file 22 documents with eight different commands—most of them off-post—to enter and exit the medical processing world, according to government investigators. Sixteen different information systems are used to process the forms, but few of them can communicate with one another. The Army's three personnel databases cannot read each other's files and can't interact with the separate pay system or the medical recordkeeping databases.

The disappearance of necessary forms and records is the most common reason soldiers languish at Walter Reed longer than they should, according to soldiers, family members and staffers. Sometimes the Army has no record that a soldier even served in Iraq. A combat medic who did three tours had to bring in letters and photos of herself in Iraq to show she that had been there, after a clerk couldn't find a record of her service.

Shannon, who wears an eye patch and a visible skull implant, said he had to prove he had served in Iraq when he tried to get a free uniform to replace the bloody one left behind on a medic's stretcher. When he finally tracked down the supply clerk, he discovered the problem: His name was mistakenly left off the "GWOT list"—the list of "Global War on Terrorism" patients with priority funding from the Defense Department.

He brought his Purple Heart to the clerk to prove he was in Iraq.

Lost paperwork for new uniforms has forced some soldiers to attend their own Purple Heart ceremonies and the official birthday party for the Army in gym clothes, only to be chewed out by superiors.

The Army has tried to re-create the organization of a typical military unit at Walter Reed. Soldiers are assigned to one of two companies while they are outpatients—the Medical Holding Company (Medhold) for active-duty soldiers and the Medical Holdover Company for Reserve and National Guard soldiers. The companies are broken into platoons that are led by platoon sergeants, the Army equivalent of a parent.

Under normal circumstances, good sergeants know everything about the soldiers under their charge: vices and talents, moods and bad habits, even family stresses.

At Walter Reed, however, outpatients have been drafted to serve as platoon sergeants and have struggled with their responsibilities. Sgt. David Thomas, a 42-year-old amputee with the Tennessee National Guard, said his platoon sergeant couldn't remember his name. "We wondered if he had mental problems," Thomas said. "Sometimes I'd wear my leg, other times I'd take my wheelchair. He would think I was a different person. We thought, 'My God, has this man lost it?'"

Civilian care coordinators and case managers are supposed to track injured soldiers and help them with appointments, but government investigators and soldiers complain that they are poorly trained and often do not understand the system.

One amputee, a senior enlisted man who asked not to be identified because he is back on active duty, said he received orders to report to a base in Germany as he sat drooling in his wheelchair in a haze of medication. "I went to Medhold many times in my wheelchair to fix it, but no one there could help me," he said.

Finally, his wife met an aide to then-Deputy Defense Secretary Paul D. Wolfowitz, who got the erroneous paperwork corrected with one phone call. When the aide called with the news, he told the soldier, "They don't even know you exist."

"They didn't know who I was or where I was," the soldier said. "And I was in contact with my platoon sergeant every day."

The lack of accountability weighed on Shannon. He hated the isolation of the younger troops. The Army's failure to account for them each day wore on him. When a 19-year-old soldier down the hall died, Shannon knew he had to take action.

The soldier, Cpl. Jeremy Harper, returned from Iraq with PTSD after seeing three buddies die. He kept his room dark, refused his combat medals and always seemed heavily medicated, said people who knew him. According to his mother, Harper was drunkenly wandering the lobby of the Mologne House on New Year's Eve 2004, looking for a ride home to West Virginia. The next morning he was found dead in his room. An autopsy showed alcohol poisoning, she said.

"I can't understand how they could have let kids under the age of 21 have liquor," said Victoria Harper, crying. "He was supposed to be right there at Walter Reed hospital.... I feel that they didn't take care of him or watch him as close as they should have."

The Army posthumously awarded Harper a Bronze Star for his actions in Iraq.

Shannon viewed Harper's death as symptomatic of a larger tragedy—the Army had broken its covenant with its troops. "Somebody didn't take care of him," he would later say. "It makes me want to cry."

Shannon and another soldier decided to keep tabs on the brain injury ward. "I'm a staff sergeant in the U.S. Army, and I take care of people," he said. The two soldiers walked the ward every day with a list of names. If a name dropped off the large white board at the nurses' station, Shannon would hound the nurses to check their files and figure out where the soldier had gone.

Sometimes the patients had been transferred to another hospital. If they had been released to one of the residences on post, Shannon and his buddy would pester the front desk managers to make sure the new charges were indeed there. "But two out of 10, when I asked where they were, they'd just say, 'They're gone,'" Shannon said.

Even after Weightman and his commanders instituted new measures to keep better track of soldiers, two young men left post one night in November and died in a high-speed car crash in Virginia. The driver was supposed to be restricted to Walter Reed because he had tested positive for illegal drugs, Weightman said.

Part of the tension at Walter Reed comes from a setting that is both military and medical. Marine Sgt. Ryan Groves, the squad leader who lost one leg and the use of his other in a grenade attack, said his recovery was made more difficult by a Marine liaison officer who had never seen combat but dogged him about having his mother in his room on post. The rules allowed her to be there, but the officer said she was taking up valuable bed space.

"When you join the Marine Corps, they tell you, you can forget about your mama. 'You have no mama. We are your mama,'" Groves said. "That training works in combat. It doesn't work when you are wounded."

Source: Priest, Dana, and Anne Hull. "Soldiers Face Neglect, Frustration at Army's Top Medical Facility." *Washington Post*, February 18, 2007, p. A1.

Pete Hamill Explains the Importance of Investigative Journalism

During his long career as a journalist, Pete Hamill served as editor-in-chief of the New York Daily News *and the* New York Post. *In the following essay, Hamill discusses the important role that muckraking journalism has played throughout American history. "Without criticism, no modern society can endure," he explains, "and investigative journalism is essentially a form of criticism."*

The reporter is the member of the tribe who is sent to the back of the cave to find out what's there. The report must be accurate. If there's a rabbit hiding in the darkness it cannot be transformed into a dragon. Bad reporting, after all, could deprive people of shelter and warmth and survival on an arctic night. But if there is, in fact, a dragon lurking in the dark it can't be described as a rabbit. The survival of the tribe could depend upon that person with the torch.

In certain basic ways, the modern investigative reporter is only a refinement of that primitive model. The tools of the trade are now extraordinary: the astonishing flood of documents on the Internet, the speed of other forms of communication, local and international, and, perhaps most important, the existence of a tradition.

Much of that tradition comes from work done over many decades in the United States, where a splendid variety of men and women took advantage of the First Amendment to the Constitution and made that specific freedom real by practicing it. In many ways, they had a simple task: to note the difference between what the United States promised and what the United States delivered. Those reporters were the first to dig into the system that seemed beyond any laws. They took their torches to the back of the cave and in newspapers and magazines they told the citizenry what they found.

Their basic search was for an explanation of what all could plainly see: rotting city slums, child labor, widespread prostitution, exploitation of immigrant labor. They knew that thousands were dying in cities like New York because there was not enough water. There were not enough hospitals. There were few schools. There were no libraries open to the poor. Thousands died each summer of cholera and smallpox. Others, broken in spirit, found

---

degraded refuge in alcohol or petty crime. Clearly, the gaudy promises of America were not being kept, and those early investigative reporters saw a common root to all our ills: corruption.

This was not a case of a few isolated thieves. Much corruption was systemic. When the *New York Times* brought down William M. Tweed in 1871 (with the immense help of *Harper's Weekly* cartoonist Thomas Nast), it was by publishing documents that showed the way the system worked. The records were provided by an unhappy low-level politico who had been bypassed in his own quest for some of the swag. On one level, they proved what almost everybody suspected: Boss Tweed and his Ring were stealing millions through a system that involved kickbacks from municipal contractors. But they also showed that the system was wider than anyone had thought. Tweed was corrupt, but his corruption had a purpose beyond personal enrichment: as a New York Democrat he needed cash to bribe the upstate Republicans who controlled the city from Albany. If he wanted to get water to his constituents, or build a school in the Five Points (services essential to maintaining his personal power), Tweed needed cash to bribe the Republicans. That was the system he had inherited from his predecessors; when he was gone, the system persisted, in newer, subtler, more respectable clothing.

The reporters and their editors understood that one victory was not the end of the campaign. Exposure in the press was soon an essential part of a process that all knew must continue for as long as there was a United States. After the Civil War, the cycles were established: corruption, then exposure, then reform, followed by a slow drift back into corruption. They continue today. In a way, those cycles are an almost comforting expression of the eternal American verities. They are infuriating, and can certainly hurt human beings, but they remind us of the endless capacity of human beings for larceny and folly, and assure us that the nation will never achieve the dubious perfection of utopia. In the twentieth century, we all learned that the promise of utopia almost always leads to mounds of corpses.

Across the years from the 1870s to the present, investigative reporters have become a mainstay of American journalism.... They are a special breed. They don't require the indifference to physical danger of the great war correspondents (although they do, in fact, sometimes risk their lives). They don't need the instinct for celebration that is essential to the greatest sportswriters.

They don't often display the entertaining cynicism of veteran police reporters. But they share one absolutely essential quality: an almost obsessive tenacity.

That sometimes ferocious tenacity is what serves as the motor for all of their other skills. Day after day, they go on. They batter at closed doors and they gnaw away at hidden redoubts. The quarry is often clever and always elusive. They examine documents designed to be obtuse, studying them like archaeologists examining Mayan hieroglyphs, looking for patterns, for buried facts, for implied verbs. Most of us would see such work as tedium; they do it with growing excitement. They meet in remote coffee shops with people who might be persuaded to tell the real story. They go back to sources once fruitlessly interviewed, hoping for illumination on the second, third, or fifth try. They go on and on.

They are not, of course, cops. They carry no guns. They have no subpoena power. Sometimes they are helped by good cops who suspect felonies that they cannot prove in court. Sometimes they are in pursuit of the cops themselves. But like the best police detectives, they have a gift for imagining themselves into the minds of felons. They try to think the way the bad guys think, imagining their strengths and weaknesses, creating a number of possible scenarios. They're not simply clerking crimes against the citizens; they must first imagine them.

They pick up the spoor of stories in a variety of ways. They see the announcement of some major municipal contract—school books, parking meters, road construction—and experience urges them to examine the fine print. They search the names of contractors, dig out past records, match names with campaign contributions, demand lists of subcontractors. They always suspect that some piece of the cost to taxpayers will include payoffs to hoodlums, or diversions of money to personal bank accounts. The investigation begins.

On other occasions, they receive anonymous phone calls, whispering of nefarious schemes. Or they are in a bar with reporters and lawyers and they pick up a rumor. They begin to check out these tips, knowing, as one great newspaper editor told me years ago, "If you want it to be true, it usually isn't." Sometimes the rumors turn out to be false, planted by political opponents or personal enemies. The reporters acknowledge that they've hit a "dry hole," from which nothing will flow, and they close the file. More often, they follow the trail of one possible story and discover that it leads to a completely different destination, much richer or more nefarious than the first.

In that sense, most investigative reporters resemble prosecutors. Indeed, their labors often force previously indifferent prosecutors to actually prosecute, that is, to put the right people in jail. But there are many investigators who also serve as unofficial counsel for the defense. They work valiantly to get the wrongfully accused out of jail. They use their tenacious gifts to defend the weak from those with careless power. They go after union leaders who make sweetheart deals at the expense of their members, while looting the pension plans on the side. They go after vicious slumlords who create misery among their poor tenants. They expose businesses that defraud investors and employees.

But they are also surprising people. In my experience, most of today's investigative reporters have vague politics. In that sense, they don't resemble the great generation of muckrakers at the turn of the nineteenth and twentieth centuries, who were men and women with an idealistic, mainly socialist vision of the America that would emerge from their labors. Today's investigators have an almost permanent skepticism about human virtue, political or otherwise. If they are pursuing a crooked judge, they don't much care whether he is a Democrat or a Republican, a liberal or a conservative, or a man who gives alms to orphans and bellows "God Bless America" most loudly on the fourth of July. If he's a crook, they want to nail him. As the great Washington columnist Lars-Erik Nelson once said to me, "The enemy isn't liberalism. The enemy isn't conservatism. The enemy is bullshit."

To be sure, however, most investigative journalism—no matter what the personal politics of its practitioners—aids the progressive side of American politics. It's part of the process of reform, of improving the lot of at least some citizens, incrementally leading toward the goal of elemental social justice that has always belonged to the left. Exposure of corruption usually leads to punishment of big shots (not always, of course). Sometimes the ratholes are actually plugged by legislation. Sometimes (again, not always) there is even a clear moral lesson: power does not always guarantee immunity. Many of us have lived through a time when even a president of the United States fell before the tenacity of investigative reporters.

In this country, and in most others, there is no great tradition of right-wing investigative reporting (William Safire of the *New York Times* is an exception). Most right-wing governments, from that of Francisco Franco to that of Saddam Hussein, have smothered all attempts at exposure, sometimes with violence. The Soviet Union, in spite of all its official socialist rhetoric, was essentially a right-wing state, and feared a free press almost as much as it feared its own citizens. Reporters for *Pravda* and Tass were chosen on the basis of ideological rigidity, and such people make poor reporters. They substitute dogma for curiosity, certainty for doubt. Skepticism, of course, was a crime. In the service of the armed Stalinist bureaucracy, the Soviet reporters asked no questions. Asking questions, after all, could lead to the basement of the Lubyanka prison.

Communism failed for a number of reasons, but one was certainly the absence of an independent press. There was no pain-in-the-ass reporter shining a light upon the slippery privileges of the nomenklatura. There was no fearless weekly making sardonic fun of the difference between what was being said by the leadership and what was actually delivered. No Soviet reporter cast a word of doubt or rage on the processes of the Purge Trials or asked why the Kulaks died or raised arguments against the pact with Hitler. Forgive the apparent absurdity, but there was no Soviet equivalent of the *Wall Street Journal,* explaining that a certain ball-bearing plant in Minsk was inefficient because the managers were relatives of some big shot in Moscow and were essentially thieves or brutes or both. Soviet inefficiency and corruption were never scrutinized in public. Finally, the whole wormy structure crumpled into the rubbish heap of history.

That dismal, murderous example should remind us of how crucial the press is to our own imperfect system. Without criticism, no modern society can endure, and investigative journalism is essentially a form of criticism. Every journalist knows that great journalism is impossible without great publishers; no Katharine Graham, no Woodward and Bernstein. Publishers must provide both money and patience while their reporters do their work, and then they must publish their findings. That truth has to be learned again in every generation. When newspapers and magazine publishers turn timid— usually out of fear of the readers or fear of the advertisers—the news package itself gets softer and flabbier. One result: the readers become increasingly indifferent. Worse, the larger society itself becomes stagnant, and the thieves and scoundrels get bolder.

But even timidity is part of the recurring American cycle of advance and retreat. As I write, there's an atmosphere of triumphant right-wing vindication in the air over the war in Iraq, and a sneering dismissal of those who refuse to embrace the conventional pieties. But even the story of the war remains hidden, incomplete, buried behind the image-mongering. We should be reassured by one thing: investigative reporters are at work, methodically separating myth from fact, propaganda from actuality. The full story will come out, as it always does, because someone is heading into the cave with a torch.

Source: Hamill, Pete. "Foreword." In Shapiro, Bruce. *Shaking the Foundations: 200 Years of Investigative Journalism in America.* New York: Nation Books, 2003, pp. vii-xii.

Modern-Day Muckrakers Face Major Challenges

The article reprinted below originally appeared in a 2008 special issue of Nieman Reports *dedicated to "Twenty-First Century Muckrakers."* Nieman Reports *is published by the Nieman Foundation for Journalism at Harvard University. The article outlines some of the challenges facing investigative journalism in America, and it emphasizes the continuing need for modern-day muckrakers to expose government corruption and corporate abuses of the public trust. The author of the article, longtime investigative reporter Florence Graves, is the founding director of the Schuster Institute for Investigative Journalism at Brandeis University. Her organization is part of a growing network of journalism nonprofits that are helping to fill the gaps in coverage left by the mainstream media.*

Once upon a time, the nation was crawling with brave and well-funded investigative reporters who found and exposed wrongdoing wherever it occurred. From Ida Tarbell to Bob Woodward, journalists crusading for truth bravely defended democracy from the incursions of corruption and undue influence. Alas, how we have fallen from those mighty days! As newsrooms slash budgets and publishers demand higher profits, investigative journalism is under attack.

It's a great narrative. But it's a myth.

The profit pressures on journalism are very real. In fact, that is one reason I founded the Schuster Institute for Investigative Journalism in 2004, as one of the emerging nonprofit models for investigative journalism. And the urgent need to expose undue influence, tainted decision-making, and hidden malfeasance is real. Those are among the main goals of the Schuster Institute at Brandeis University, and it's also why I founded and ran *Common Cause Magazine* with a focus on investigative reporting during the 1980s. We can admire—and aim at—this goal without believing the myth. The truth: Even when news organizations were flush, in-depth investigative reporting has been more an ideal than a reality.

Consider the research done by Michael Schudson, professor at the University of California at San Diego and at the Graduate School of Journalism of Columbia University, and published in his books *The Power of News* and *Watergate in American Memory: How We Remember, Forget and Reconstruct the Past.*

- In *The Power of News*, Schudson wrote, "The muckraking theme has been powerful in American journalism for a century, even though its practice is the exception, not the rule." He points out that "in the time

212

between Lincoln Steffens, Ida Tarbell, and Ray Stannard Baker in 1904 and Woodward and Bernstein in 1972 and 1973," muckraking had "no culturally resonant, heroic exemplars."

- In analyzing myths generated by Watergate, Schudson concluded that "the press as a whole during Watergate was—as before and since—primarily an establishment institution with few ambitions to rock establishment bonds." While he concluded that many news organizations' commitments to investigative reporting began to increase in the 1960s—before Watergate—that commitment was already dissipating early in the Reagan years.

Government Watchdog

The myth of journalists doggedly uncovering all the facts is both important—and dangerous. "What is most important to journalism is not the spate of investigative reporting or the recoil from it after Watergate," wrote Schudson, "but the renewal, reinvigoration, and remythologization of muckraking." This helps all of us aim higher and dig even more deeply.

Here's the danger: Many Americans naively believe that Watergate spawned hordes of investigative reporters who are urgently ferreting out all waste, fraud and abuse of power in the public interest. This fosters a false and complacent public impression that if there is any wrongdoing by government or corporate officials, heroic journalists are doing everything they can to track it down and report it.

While the Washington press corps has grown mightily, is it adequate? Most medium-sized newspapers have a Washington presence, but these reporters often focus on the same few issues and the same few people at the top—leaving significant issues and agencies uncovered. Those U.S. news organizations that do assign a full-time reporter to an agency "beat," usually assign them only to a handful of big beats such as the Pentagon, Department of Justice, Department of State, and Treasury. Those "beats" usually involve tracking major policy decisions and rarely leave enough time for reporters to make connections between these policies and relevant influence-peddlers or to dig deeply into other agency business. It is extremely difficult, if not impossible, for these reporters—as well as those who are assigned to cover several agencies at one time—to cover the "official" daily news and the insider machinations about decisions and also track the influence of hundreds of well-paid lobbyists and well-staffed PR firms dedicated to protecting huge corporations' interests and who have vast access to policymakers. This doesn't even take into account the increased difficulties reporters confront when facing the recent and unprecedented government clampdown on the release of information and deliberate slowdowns in response to Freedom of Information Act (FOIA) requests, the increasing trend of the government issuing subpoenas to journalists to disclose their confidential sources, and the threat posed by libel suits.

Contrary to the myth, only a skeleton crew of reporters is trying to find out how Americans' daily lives—what they eat, the medicines they take, the products they use, and the environmental conditions in which they live—are being affected by hundreds of lobbyists, dozens of partisan and "Astroturf" [fake or industry-funded] think-tanks, scores of federal agencies, and hundreds of officials all defended by the ironically named "public information officers" who prevent the flow of many important facts out of their offices.

To get a sense of just how bad the problem was becoming, in 2001 the Project on the State of the American Newspaper surveyed newspapers and wire-services to determine which ones "regularly cover" 19 federal departments and agencies. The survey found that apart from the major departments such as defense, state, justice and treasury—which are comparatively well covered by reporters—a surprising number of agencies with huge budgets had either no reporters or just a few, including the following:

- No full-time reporter: Veterans Affairs ($46 billion budget) and the Nuclear Regulatory Commission ($482 million budget)

- Two full-time reporters: Department of Interior ($10 billion budget)

- Three full-time reporters: Agriculture ($73 billion budget), Environmental Protection Agency ($8 billion budget), and Social Security Administration ($7 billion budget)

- Four full-time reporters: Labor Department ($39 billion budget) and Internal Revenue Service ($9 billion budget).

Congress is where laws are passed, but it is within these agencies that the laws are shaped into realities that affect our lives. Are only three full-time reporters enough to oversee all of the government's decision-making about environmental protection and monitor all of what lobbyists do to shape those regulations behind closed doors? Consider, too, the spectacular growth in sophistication and influence of a vast number of power centers—multinational corporations, global financial institutions, international governments, and nongovernmental organizations. Then there is coverage of local and state news, when editors and publishers are subjected to even greater pressure from special interests—commercial and otherwise—in their community.

Increasingly bereft of key resources—time, people and money—to do in-depth reporting, journalists have become much more dependent on leaks and tips from people who usually have an agenda that might not always be so obvious. One resulting paradox is that while more reporters than ever are covering Washington, we really know less about many very important things. Consider the press's spectacular failure to find out the truth about the [George W. Bush] administration's claims about Iraq. Or how long it took to unmask Congressmen Tom DeLay and Randy (Duke) Cunningham. Or the overlooked warnings about today's subprime [mortgage] crisis—and in earlier years the Savings & Loan crisis, the Department of Housing and Urban Development scandal, and the Iran-contra arms deals.

This is not to say that investigative reporters have been failing. Press investigations have recently revealed unacceptable conditions for Iraq War veterans at Walter Reed Army Medical Center, the CIA's abuses in prisoner interrogations, the use of warrantless wiretaps of citizens' phones by the U.S. government, and other memorable watchdog stories. We can find plenty of other examples of superb investigative journalism—likely more and better than a decade ago—but that doesn't mean there's enough of it.

In our news media's daily practice and performance, watchdog reporting is not keeping pace with the growing need. While powerful institutions—government, corporate and nonprofit, both U.S. and global—that need to be watched are multiplying and getting richer and more sophisticated, precisely the opposite is happening in journalism: The number and availability of reporters who have the time, institutional backing, and resources to be effective watchdogs are getting pinched. Nor does it seem that this trend is about to change given the faltering financial resources available at most news organizations—and the ways in which these resources are being used in this era of celebrity and entertainment journalism.

Uncovering Corporate Malfeasance

Meanwhile, news organizations have never been very committed to exposing corporate wrongdoing. A convincing argument could be made that today corporations effectively run the country—including what happens in Washington, D.C.—through their campaign contributions, opposition research, careful spin-doctoring, sophisticated public influence campaigns, heavy-hitting lobbyists, and still more tools. Arguably, corporate titans might be in a better position to abuse the public trust than many government officials. While numerous outlets cover business and report on corporate news, most of what reaches the public is aimed at investors, usually indicating whose business is up and whose is down. The *New York Times* then-media reporter Felicity Barringer pointed out a few years ago that "more than 250 Pulitzers in journalism have been awarded since 1978. Business figures prominently in about 10." She then asked, "But what about corporations and industries? Are there some comfortable folk there who could do with some afflicting?"

Our own survey of the Pulitzers revealed that out of the 90 Pulitzers given for public service journalism, only about a handful involved primarily an investigation of corporate power. And of the 25 Pulitzer Prizes awarded for investigative journalism, in just two of them did the reporters focus specifically on situations involving corporations.

Even in flush times, the job of systematically and thoroughly covering the government, the corporate sector, and the nonprofit sector would have been a mammoth David-takes-on-Goliath effort. But these are not flush times for the news business. And that's why there's such an urgent need for what Chuck Lewis, founder of the Center for Public Integrity, has been calling the new nonprofit journalism. Each of us who launched one of these new nonprofit models did so independently, albeit with similar reckonings about the need. None of us pretend to be the solution to the ongoing financial crisis that has led many newspapers to eliminate or cut back their investments in investigative reporting. But all of us want to contribute to the solution—albeit in slightly different ways and with somewhat different areas of focus.

Schuster Institute for Investigative Journalism

The Schuster Institute for Investigative Journalism is the nation's first—and only—investigative reporting center based at a university (in our case, Brandeis University) that is intended to help fill the increasing void in high-quality public interest and investigative journalism. As journalists, we research, report, place and publish or broadcast our work. Our ongoing interaction with students comes in working closely with those we hire to assist us with our investigations; we get superb research assistance, while we mentor them and offer an intimate sense of what is required to do in-depth reporting. We also reveal to them the value this kind of reporting holds for our nation. No matter what these students end up doing, whether it's journalism, law, business or politics, they take with them an understanding of—and appreciation for—the importance of a free and unfettered press in a democracy.

Our goal is to explore in-depth significant social and political problems and uncover corporate and government abuses of power and reveal what we find through "impact journalism," in which our in-depth projects break important news and jump-start public policy discussions about underreported social and political injustices important to a democracy. The three prime areas of our interest are:

1. Political and Social Justice

2. Gender and Justice

3. The Justice Brandeis Innocence Project.

Our investigations reach the public via broadcast, the Web, and in newspapers and magazines that have a proven ability to inform the public. In collaboration with the *Washington Post,* I explored a whistleblower lawsuit against Boeing. In reporting that story, we found that Boeing—with what seemed like almost a wink from the Federal Aviation Administration (FAA)—was installing unapproved (and potentially dangerous) parts on its planes. With the freedom I have through my association with this institute, I was able to delve deeply for months. Few reporters would have had the time to study the FAA's regulations and requirements deeply enough to be able to challenge its spin. "Boeing Parts and Rules Bent, Whistle-Blowers Say," appeared as an above-the-fold Page One story in April 2006 and was picked up around the world. While reporting the story, I discovered many indications that Boeing and the FAA have a tighter relationship than any citizen would want to exist, and I uncovered half a dozen other stories I'd like to pursue when I have more time.

There are certainly other ways to do this work—and plenty of room for many more news organizations and journalists to commit to doing it. The breadth of global "beats" is only going to expand, while it appears likely that crucial stories simply are not going to be done. Last fall, the *Columbia Journalism Review* editorialized that, "As newsroom resources continue to contract— foreign bureaus close, staffs shrink, travel budgets evaporate—producing a broad, deep and authoritative news report day in and day out may in some cases require that news operations join forces." The Schuster Institute alone— or even in concert with every other nonprofit investigative journalism entity in existence today—will never be able to fill the growing gap. Doing so is going to require innovative ideas matched with unprecedented cooperation and collaboration among journalists and a commitment to this job by all of us.

Source: Graves, Florence. "Watchdog Reporting: Exploring Its Myth." *Nieman Reports,* Spring 2008. Available online at http://www.nieman.harvard.edu/reportsitem.aspx ?id=100065.

IMPORTANT PEOPLE, PLACES, AND TERMS

Baker, Ray Stannard (1870-1946)
Muckraking journalist who is best known for exploring race relations in his book *Following the Color Line*.

Bernstein, Carl (1944-)
Investigative journalist whose reporting of the Watergate scandal contributed to the resignation of President Richard M. Nixon.

Boss
A corrupt official who controls a city government and awards municipal jobs and contracts on the basis of bribery, connections, and political favors.

Capitalism
An economic system that emphasizes free enterprise, competition, and private ownership of property as keys to prosperity.

Carnegie, Andrew (1835-1919)
Businessman who made a fortune in the steel industry and later gave away much of his money to support philanthropic causes.

Carson, Rachel (1907-1964)
Biologist and writer who exposed the environmental damage resulting from the unregulated use of pesticides in her 1962 book *Silent Spring*.

Civil War
A military conflict (1861-65) between the northern and southern parts of the United States over slavery and other issues.

Conservative
A political philosophy that favors lowering taxes and government spending, reducing government regulation of business, and limiting the role of government in society.

Great Depression
A severe economic downturn in the 1930s that was marked by bank failures, financial losses, business closures, and high unemployment.

Hamilton, Alice (1869-1970)
Physician and occupational health pioneer who investigated industrial illnesses and their social consequences.

Hersh, Seymour (1937-)
Investigative journalist who uncovered the 1969 My Lai massacre during the Vietnam War and also reported on the abuse of Iraqi prisoners by U.S. military personnel at Abu Ghraib Prison in Baghdad in 2004.

Industrial Revolution
A period during the 1800s when a series of important advances in technology, communication, transportation, energy, and commerce brought fundamental changes to American society.

Investigative journalism
A type of reporting that emphasizes uncovering problems and bringing them to public attention.

Labor Union
An organization that represents workers in negotiations with employers for shorter work hours, better wages, safer working conditions, and other benefits.

McClure, S.S. (1857-1949)
Progressive owner and editor who turned *McClure's* magazine into a leader of the muckraking movement.

McKinley, William (1843-1901)
President of the United States from 1897 until his assassination in 1901.

Monopoly
A situation in which one individual, corporation, or group of related companies controls a product or industry without viable competition.

Moore, Michael (1954-)
Controversial documentary filmmaker who has examined such issues as gun violence, the health care crisis, and U.S. policy toward Iraq.

Muckrakers
A term used to describe crusading journalists who conduct investigations, uncover problems, raise public awareness, and generate calls for reform.

Murrow, Edward R. (1908-1965)
Broadcast journalist who famously challenged the anti-communist "witch hunts" of Senator Eugene McCarthy on his CBS News television program *See It Now.*

Nader, Ralph (1934-)
Attorney, consumer advocate, political activist, and author whose 1965 book *Unsafe at Any Speed* raised public awareness of automobile and highway safety issues.

New Deal
A set of progressive reforms designed to help struggling Americans and stimulate the economy during the Great Depression.

Norris, Frank (1870-1902)
Author best known for his 1901 novel *The Octopus,* which revolved around a deadly real-life confrontation between railroad companies and settlers over land rights.

Patent medicines
Pills and potions of dubious medical value that were widely advertised as cures for a variety of ailments; they became a target for consumer advocates and muckraking journalists during the Progressive Era.

Phillips, David Graham (1867-1911)
Muckraking journalist best known for writing the "Treason of the Senate" series for *Cosmopolitan* magazine in 1906.

Progressive
A political philosophy that supports government intervention to address social, political, and economic problems.

Progressive Era
A period in American history (roughly from the 1890s through the 1910s) that was marked by reform of various social, political, and economic institutions that had been transformed by industrialization.

Prohibition
> The period from 1920 to 1933 when the manufacture, distribution, and sale of alcohol was banned in the United States.

Riis, Jacob (1849-1914)
> Journalist and photographer who is best known for chronicling poverty and squalor in American cities in his 1890 book *How the Other Half Lives*.

Robber Barons
> A term used by critics to describe the small group of wealthy businessmen who dominated the American banking, railroad, oil, and steel industries at the turn of the twentieth century.

Rockefeller, John D. (1839-1937)
> Wealthy businessman and philanthropist whose ruthless business practices as owner of the Standard Oil Company made him a major target of the muckrakers.

Roosevelt, Franklin D. (1882-1945)
> President of the United States (served 1933-1945) who enacted progressive New Deal policies to help the nation recover from the Great Depression.

Roosevelt, Theodore (1858-1919)
> President of the United States (served 1901-1909) whose policies launched the Progressive Era.

Sherman Antitrust Act
> Passed in 1890, this legislation gave the federal government power to prevent large corporations from gaining monopoly control over entire industries.

Sinclair, Upton (1878-1968)
> Muckraking journalist best known for his 1906 book *The Jungle*, an exposé of the meatpacking industry that drew national attention to the issue of food safety.

Social Darwinism
> A theory that explains the gulf between wealthy and impoverished Americans by claiming that rich people are genetically superior in terms of intelligence and ambition.

Socialism

An economic system that emphasizes collective ownership of business and other property as a means to distribute wealth fairly among all members of a society.

Spargo, John (1876-1966)

Muckraking writer best known for exploring the tragedy of child labor in his 1906 book *The Bitter Cry of the Children.*

Standard Oil Company

A powerful trust, owned by John D. Rockefeller, that became known as "the Octopus" because its influence spread into so many different areas of business and government.

Steffens, Lincoln (1866-1936)

Muckraking journalist who is best known for uncovering government corruption in his 1904 book *The Shame of the Cities.*

Suffrage

The right to vote.

Taft, William Howard (1857-1930)

President of the United States from 1908 to 1913.

Tarbell, Ida M. (1857-1944)

Muckraking journalist who is best known for her 1904 book *The History of the Standard Oil Company,* which exposed the ruthless business practices of John D. Rockefeller and contributed to the passage of new antitrust laws.

Tenement

A type of urban housing used by poor and working-class residents; these buildings were often dirty, airless, and overcrowded, and served as breeding grounds for crime and disease.

Trust

A large corporation or group of related companies that dominated various industries and exerted a great deal of control over the U.S. economy at the turn of the twentieth century.

Trust-busting

Government efforts to break up large corporations or trusts that hold monopoly power over certain industries.

Woodward, Bob (1943-)

Investigative journalist whose reporting of the Watergate scandal contributed to the resignation of President Richard M. Nixon.

CHRONOLOGY

1690

The first newspaper in the American colonies, *Publick Occurrences Both Forreign and Domestick,* is published in Boston. *See p. 22.*

1704

The *Boston News-Letter* becomes the first ongoing newspaper in the American colonies. *See p. 22.*

1721

Brothers James and Benjamin Franklin launch a newspaper called the *New England Courant.* *See p. 22.*

1740s

The first magazines appear in the American colonies. *See p. 27.*

1765

British authorities pass the Stamp Act, which requires all legal documents, books, and newspapers printed in the American colonies to appear on specially stamped paper; American newspapers refuse to pay the high tax on stamped paper, and the act is repealed. *See p. 22.*

1769

The steam engine, one of the great inventions of the Industrial Revolution, is unveiled in England. *See p. 8.*

1776

American newspapers help shape public opinion in favor of independence from English rule. *See p. 24.*

1787

The First Amendment to the U.S. Constitution guarantees freedom of the press. *See p. 24.*

1830s

The invention of the cylinder press makes newspaper publishing faster and cheaper. *See p. 24.*

1833

Editor Benjamin H. Day launches the *New York Sun*. *See p. 25.*

1835

Editor James Gordon Bennett launches the *New York Herald*. *See p. 25.*

1851

The *New York Times* publishes its first edition. *See p. 26.*

1870

John D. Rockefeller forms the Standard Oil Company. *See p. 53.*

1880

A deadly confrontation takes place between railroad company representatives and settlers over land rights in California; known as the Battle at Mussel Slough, the incident later forms the centerpiece of Frank Norris's novel *The Octopus*. *See p. 65.*

1883

Renowned publisher Joseph Pulitzer focuses on investigative reporting at the *New York World*. *See p. 26.*

The Pendleton Act of 1883 puts measures in place to prevent elected officials from appointing their friends and supporters to fill government jobs at the expense of more qualified applicants. *See p. 76.*

1886

The rise of nationally distributed, general-interest, monthly magazines begins when *Cosmopolitan* publishes its first issue. *See p. 27.*

1887

The Interstate Commerce Act creates the first federal regulatory agency, the Interstate Commerce Commission, to oversee the operations of the nation's railroads. *See p. 17.*

1888

Collier's magazine is introduced. *See p. 27.*

1889

Reformer Jane Addams launches the settlement house movement by founding Hull House, which offers a variety of services and assistance to immigrant families in Chicago. *See p. 39.*

1890

The Sherman Antitrust Act gives the federal government power to prevent large corporations from gaining monopoly control over entire industries. *See p. 17.*

Journalist and photographer Jacob Riis chronicles the struggles of the urban poor in *How the Other Half Lives*. *See p. 38.*

1891

A national political party called the People's Party or Populists forms with the goals of limiting the power of large corporations and reducing corruption in government. *See p. 18.*

1892

Publisher William Randolph Hearst launches a trend toward "yellow journalism" at the *New York Morning Journal. See p. 26.*

1893

Editor S.S. McClure launches his namesake monthly journal. *See p. 32.*

1894

The federal government sides with wealthy railroad owners over labor union members in breaking up the Pullman Palace Car strike. *See p. 14.*

1899

Everybody's joins the parade of new general-interest magazines. *See p. 27.*

Activist Florence Kelley founds the National Consumers' League, an organization which fought to pass food safety laws and end the exploitation of female workers. *See p. 45.*

1901

Following the assassination of President William McKinley in September, Theodore Roosevelt takes office. *See p. 19.*

The Octopus, a novel by Frank Norris, condemns corporate greed and its impact on the lives of working-class Americans. *See p. 64.*

1902

President Roosevelt intervenes on behalf of United Mine Workers members to resolve a bitter strike against the large corporations that control Pennsylvania coal mines. *See p. 66.*

Muckraking journalist Lincoln Steffens publishes "Tweed Days in St. Louis," the first installment of his famous "Shame of the Cities" series on government corruption, in the October issue of *McClure's. See p. 71.*

The first article in Ida M. Tarbell's famous investigative series on the Standard Oil Company runs in the November issue of *McClure's. See p. 53.*

1903

The January issue of *McClure's* features investigative reports by Tarbell, Steffens, and Ray Stannard Baker that expose serious problems in American business, government, and society; it is generally considered the start of the muckraking movement in American journalism. *See p. 32.*

1904

Sociologist Robert Hunter calls public attention to the plight of the urban poor in his influential book *Poverty. See p. 40.*

Ida M. Tarbell publishes her landmark book *The History of the Standard Oil Company.* *See p. 54.*

Lincoln Steffens collects his articles on municipal corruption in the book *Shame of the Cities.* *See p. 73.*

Roosevelt wins reelection in a landslide, with 57 percent of the popular vote. *See p. 67.*

1905

Samuel Hopkins Adams attacks the patent medicine industry in a series of articles for *Collier's* entitled "The Great American Fraud." *See p. 63.*

William Randolph Hearst purchases *Cosmopolitan* with the goal of turning it into a muckraking journal. *See p. 74.*

Upton Sinclair's novel *The Jungle* appears in serial form in *Appeal to Reason* magazine. *See p. 60.*

1906

Cosmopolitan publishes a series of articles by Edwin Markham detailing the grim existence of child workers in textile mills. *See p. 43.*

John Spargo publishes *The Bitter Cry of the Children,* which further raises public awareness of the tragedy of child labor. *See p. 42.*

The Jungle, Upton Sinclair's influential novel about the meatpacking industry, is published in book form. *See p. 62.*

Increased public concerns about food safety lead to the passage of the Pure Food and Drug Act of 1906. *See p. 62.*

The Hepburn Act empowers the Interstate Commerce Commission to increase its regulation of the nation's railroads. *See p. 67.*

David Graham Phillips publishes the first installment of his "Treason of the Senate" series in the March issue of *Cosmopolitan.* *See p. 74.*

On April 14, Roosevelt makes a famous speech describing investigative journalists as "muckrakers" and calling upon the national magazines to offer more balanced reporting. *See p. 79.*

A group of prominent journalists leave the staff of *McClure's* to form their own journal, *American Magazine,* which publishes its first issue in October. *See p. 82.*

1907

The U.S. Congress charters the National Child Labor Committee to investigate the use of child labor and make recommendations for laws restricting it. *See p. 43.*

1908

Ray Stannard Baker publishes *Following the Color Line,* a book exploring racial prejudice in the United States. *See p. 48.*

1909

President Theodore Roosevelt leaves office and is succeeded by fellow Republican William Howard Taft. *See p. 104.*

Lewis Hine's published photographs of children at work in factories increases public demand for child labor protection laws. *See p. 44.*

1910

Journalist and activist Rheta Childe Dorr publishes an influential book about the growing movement for women's rights called *What Eight Million Women Want*. *See p. 45.*

The Mann-Elkins Act of 1910 establishes federal regulation of the telephone, telegraph, cable, and railroad industries. *See p. 104.*

1911

John A. Fitch's article "Old Age at Forty," criticizing twelve-hour work shifts in the steel industry, appears in the March issue of *American Magazine*. *See p. 58.*

In May, a fire destroys the Triangle Shirtwaist Factory in New York City, taking the lives of 146 young female textile workers. *See p. 58.*

S.S. McClure retires as editor of *McClure's* magazine. *See p. 122.*

The U.S. Supreme Court orders the breakup of the Standard Oil Company. *See p. 67.*

1912

Running as the candidate of the Progressive Party, Theodore Roosevelt loses the presidential election to Democrat Woodrow Wilson. *See p. 105.*

1913

The Seventeenth Amendment to the Constitution provides for the direct election of U.S. Senators by popular vote. *See p. 75.*

The Federal Reserve Act of 1913 regulates the U.S. banking industry and helps stabilize the value of the dollar. *See p. 105.*

1914

In April, a strike by miners in Ludlow, Colorado, ends in violence when troops under the direction of company management attack a tent city full of workers and their families; twenty people are killed in the tragedy, which further tarnishes the public reputation of company owner John D. Rockefeller. *See p. 59.*

The Clayton Antitrust Act of 1914 outlaws a number of unfair business practices and protects the rights of workers to organize and engage in peaceful labor protests. *See p. 105.*

The Federal Trade Commission Act of 1914 creates a new government regulatory agency to enforce antitrust laws. *See p. 105.*

World War I erupts in Europe. *See p. 105.*

1916

The Adamson Act of 1916 establishes an eight-hour workday for interstate railroad employees. *See p. 105.*

1917

The United States enters World War I. *See p. 106.*

1918

World War I ends in victory for the United States and its allies. *See p. 106.*

1919

An investigation of gambling in professional sports, prompted by a *New York World* story by Hugh Fullerton, reveals that several players with the Chicago White Sox deliberately lost the World Series as part of a betting scheme.

1920

The Eighteenth Amendment to the U.S. Constitution bans the manufacture, distribution, and sale of alcohol in the United States, initiating the era known as Prohibition. *See p. 46.*

American women gain the right to vote with the passage of the Nineteenth Amendment to the Constitution. *See p. 45.*

The election of pro-business Republican Warren G. Harding to the presidency marks a shift back toward conservative political ideas. *See p. 106.*

1929

A sudden crash in the value of the U.S. stock market pitches the nation into the Great Depression. *See p. 107.*

1932

Democrat Franklin D. Roosevelt is elected president; after taking office, his New Deal policies shift the nation back toward progressive ideas. *See p. 107.*

1933

Prohibition is repealed with the passage of the Twenty-First Amendment to the Constitution. *See p. 47.*

1935

Progressives achieve a longstanding goal with the passage of the Social Security Act, which creates a safety net of federal assistance for poor, disabled, and elderly Americans. *See p. 108.*

1938

George Seldes writes about the dangers of cigarette smoking in his weekly newspaper *In Fact.*

1939

John Steinbeck's novel *The Grapes of Wrath* raises public awareness of the hardships faced by migrant farm workers.

1952

Reader's Digest publishes "Cancer by the Carton," a hard-hitting article by Roy Norr about the health risks associated with cigarette smoking.

1954

Journalist Edward R. Murrow challenges the anti-communist "witch hunt" of Senator Eugene McCarthy on his CBS television news program *See It Now*. *See p. 89.*

1962

Biologist Rachel Carson publishes *Silent Spring*, a groundbreaking expose of the environmental hazards associated with the unregulated use of pesticides. *See p. 90.*

1963

President Lyndon B. Johnson launches a number of progressive reforms that come to be known as the Great Society programs. *See p. 110.*

Self-described "queen of the muckrakers" Jessica Mitford exposes fraudulent practices in the funeral industry in her book *The American Way of Death*.

1965

Consumer advocate Ralph Nader publishes *Unsafe at Any Speed*, which raises concerns about automobile safety. *See p. 91.*

1966

Partly in response to *Unsafe at Any Speed*, the U.S. Congress passes the Traffic and Motor Vehicle Safety Act of 1966. *See p. 91.*

1969

Investigative journalist Seymour Hersh uncovers the My Lai massacre, an incident in the Vietnam War in which U.S. troops raided a village and killed hundreds of civilians. *See p. 92.*

1971

New York Times reporter Neil Sheehan reveals the existence of the Pentagon Papers, a secret study of U.S. policy in southeast Asia and conduct of the Vietnam War. *See p. 94.*

1972

Partly due to the public outcry over *Silent Spring*, the U.S. Congress bans the pesticide DDT from use in the United States. *See p. 90.*

In June, *Washington Post* reporters Bob Woodward and Carl Bernstein are assigned to cover a suspicious break-in at the offices of the Democratic National Committee in the Watergate Hotel in Washington, D.C.; their investigation lasts two years and plays a vital role in uncovering the Nixon administration's involvement in the burglary. *See p. 95.*

Associated Press reporter Jean Heller uncovers a secret U.S. military medical experiment in which syphilis was left untreated in African-American soldiers without the patients' knowledge or consent.

1974

President Richard M. Nixon chooses to resign from office rather than face impeachment for his role in the Watergate scandal. *See p. 96.*

1980

The election of President Ronald Reagan marks a return to conservative policies. *See p. 110.*

1985

The *National Catholic Reporter* launches an investigation into child abuse by priests.

1997

In his book *One World, Ready or Not,* modern-day muckraker William Greider explains how globalization brings old problems like child labor and exploitation of factory workers to the doorsteps of American consumers. *See p. 96.*

2001

Journalist Eric Schlosser revisits the meatpacking industry and food safety issues in his book *Fast Food Nation: The Dark Side of the All-American Meal. See p. 97.*

2004

The American media uncovers the systematic abuse of Iraqi prisoners by U.S. soldiers at Abu Ghraib prison in Baghdad. *See p. 99.*

2007

Washington Post reporters Dana Priest and Anne Hull reveal mistreatment of wounded veterans at the Walter Reed Army Medical Center in Washington, D.C. *See p. 197.*

SOURCES FOR FURTHER STUDY

Andrews, Peter. "The Press." *American Heritage,* October 1994. This *American Heritage* cover story traces the history of journalism in the United States and outlines major criticisms of the twenty-first century American media.

Bausum, Ann. *Muckrakers: How Ida Tarbell, Upton Sinclair, and Lincoln Steffens Helped Expose Scandal, Inspire Reform, and Invent Investigative Journalism.* New York: National Geographic Books, 2007. This readable book for students relates the history of the muckraking movement through the stories of three journalists who made important contributions to it.

Jensen, Carl. *Stories that Changed America: Muckrakers of the 20th Century.* New York: Seven Stories Press, 2000. This collection features excerpts from major muckraking books and articles, ranging from Upton Sinclair's *The Jungle* to Bob Woodward and Carl Bernstein's Watergate reporting.

Serrin, Judith, and William Serrin, eds. *Muckraking: The Journalism That Changed America.* New York: New Press, 2002. This collection includes examples of investigative reporting on a wide range of social and political topics—including poverty, public health and safety, women's rights, and conservation—from throughout American history.

Shapiro, Bruce, ed. *Shaking the Foundations: 200 Years of Investigative Journalism in America.* New York: Thunder's Mouth Press/Nation Books, 2003. Arranged by historical era, this collection of investigative reports follows the development of muckraking journalism through the nineteenth and twentieth centuries.

"Twenty-First Century Muckrakers." *Nieman Reports,* Spring 2008. Available online at http://www.nieman.harvard.edu/reports.aspx?id=100000. This special issue of *Nieman Reports,* based upon a year-long research project, examines some of the challenges facing investigative journalists in the modern era.

University of Kansas, School of Journalism and Mass Communications. "History of American Journalism." Available online at http://history.journalism.ku.edu/1900/1900.shtml. Compiled as part of a graduate program in journalism, this informative web site offers a decade-by-decade history of the most important trends, stories, and personalities in American media in the twentieth century.

Weinberg, Arthur, and Lila Weinberg, eds. *The Muckrakers.* Champaign: University of Illinois Press, 2001. This collection includes excerpts from many of the best-known muckraking exposés of the early twentieth century.

BIBLIOGRAPHY

Books

Baker, Ray Stannard. *American Chronicle: The Autobiography of Ray Stannard Baker.* New York: Charles Scribner's Sons, 1945.

Baker, Ray Stannard. *Following the Color Line: An Account of Negro Citizenship in the American Democracy.* New York: Doubleday, 1908.

Bausum, Ann. *Muckrakers: How Ida Tarbell, Upton Sinclair, and Lincoln Steffens Helped Expose Scandal, Inspire Reform, and Invent Investigative Journalism.* New York: National Geographic Books, 2007.

Bliss, Edward Jr. *In Search of Light: The Broadcasts of Edward R. Murrow.* New York: Knopf, 1967.

Chalmers, David Mark. *The Muckrake Years.* New York: D. Van Nostrand, 1974.

Cook, Fred J. *The Muckrakers: Crusading Journalists Who Changed America.* New York: Doubleday, 1972.

DeNevi, Don. *Muckrakers and Robber Barons: The Classic Era, 1902-1912.* New York: Replica Books, 1973.

Downie, Leonard Jr., and Robert G. Kaiser. *The News about the News: American Journalism in Peril.* New York: Knopf, 2002.

Gallagher, Aileen. *The Muckrakers: American Journalism during the Age of Reform.* New York: Rosen Publishing, 2006.

Greider, William. *One World, Ready or Not.* New York: Simon and Schuster, 1997.

Hersh, Seymour. *My Lai 4: A Report on the Massacre and Its Aftermath.* New York: Random House, 1970.

Hunter, Robert. *Poverty.* New York: Macmillan, 1904.

Jensen, Carl. *Stories that Changed America: Muckrakers of the 20th Century.* New York: Seven Stories Press, 2000.

Lippmann, Walter. *Drift and Mastery: An Attempt to Diagnose the Current Unrest.* H. Holt and Company, 1914.

McClure, Samuel Sidney, with Willa Cather. *My Autobiography.* New York: Frederick A. Stokes, 1914.

McGerr, Michael. *A Fierce Discontent: The Rise and Fall of the Progressive Movement in America.* New York: Oxford University Press, 2005.

Mott, Frank Luther. *American Journalism: A History 1690-1960.* New York: Macmillan, 1962.

Mumford, Lewis, and Bryan S. Turner. *The Culture of Cities.* New York: Routledge, 1997.

Nader, Ralph. *Unsafe at Any Speed.* New York: Grossman, 1965.

"Progressive Movement." In Kutler, Stanley I., ed. *Dictionary of American History,* 3d ed. New York: Charles Scribner's Sons, 2003.

Riis, Jacob. *How the Other Half Lives.* New York: Scribner's, 1890.

Roosevelt, Theodore. *Theodore Roosevelt: An Autobiography.* New York: Macmillan, 1913.

Serrin, Judith, and William Serrin, eds. *Muckraking: The Journalism That Changed America.* New York: New Press, 2002.

Shapiro, Bruce, ed. *Shaking the Foundations: 200 Years of Investigative Journalism in America.* New York: Thunder's Mouth Press/Nation Books, 2003.

Sinclair, Upton. *The Autobiography of Upton Sinclair.* New York: Harcourt, Brace and World, 1962.

Sinclair, Upton. *The Jungle.* New York: 1906.

Spargo, John. *The Bitter Cry of the Children.* New York: Macmillan, 1906.

Steffens, Lincoln. *The Autobiography of Lincoln Steffens.* New York: Harcourt, Brace and Company, 1931.

Tarbell, Ida M. *All in the Day's Work.* New York: 1938.

Tarbell, Ida M. *The History of the Standard Oil Company.* New York: McClure, Phillips and Company, 1904.

Tebbel, John, and Mary Ellen Zuckerman. *The Magazine in America, 1741-1990.* New York: Oxford University Press, 1991.

Traxel, David. *Crusader Nation: The United States in Peace and the Great War, 1898-1920.* New York: Alfred A. Knopf, 2006.

Weinberg, Arthur, and Lila Weinberg, eds. *The Muckrakers.* Champaign: University of Illinois Press, 2001.

Wilson, Harold S. *McClure's Magazine and the Muckrakers.* Princeton, NJ: Princeton University Press, 1970.

Periodicals

Andrews, Peter. "The Press." *American Heritage,* October 1994.

Bok, Edward. "The Patent-Medicine Curse." *Ladies' Home Journal,* 1904.

Dorman, Jessica. "Where Are Muckraking Journalists Today?" *Nieman Reports*, Summer 2000.

Fitch, John A. "Old Age at Forty." *American Magazine*, March 1911.

Giles, Bob. "The Vital Role of the Press in a Time of National Crisis." *Nieman Reports*, Winter 2002.

Gillmor, Dan. "Bloggers and Mash: When Everybody Can Be a Journalist or a Filmmaker, What Happens to the Media?" *New Scientist*, March 15, 2008.

Graves, Florence. "Watchdog Reporting: Exploring Its Myth." *Nieman Reports*, Spring 2008.

Guthrie, Marisa. "Investigative Journalism under Fire." *Broadcasting and Cable*, June 23, 2008.

Markham, Edwin. "The Hoe-Man in the Making." *Cosmopolitan*, September 1906.

Roosevelt, Theodore. "The Man with the Muck-Rake." *Putnam's Monthly and the Critic*, October 1906.

Rosenberg, Simon, and Peter Leyden. "The 50-Year Strategy: A New Progressive Era." *Mother Jones*, October 31, 2007.

Sheehan, Neil, and Hedrick Smith. "Vast Review of War Took a Year." *New York Times*, June 13, 1971.

Shepherd, William G. "Eyewitness at Triangle." United Press, May 27, 1911.

Steffens, Lincoln. "The Shame of Minneapolis," *McClure's*, January 1903.

Steiger, Paul E. "Going Online with Watchdog Journalism." *Nieman Reports*, Spring 2008, p. 30.

Weinberg, Steve. "Publisher, Editor, and Reporter: The Investigative Formula Looking Back to the Early 1900s—to Ida Tarbell and S.S. McClure—Offers Valuable Lessons for Watchdog Journalism in the Twenty-First Century." *Nieman Reports*, Spring 2008.

Woodward, Bob, and Carl Bernstein. "GOP Security Aide among Five Arrested in Bugging Affair." *Washington Post*, June 17, 1972.

Online

Borosage, Robert. "A New Progressive Era?" *Huffington Post*, October 28, 2008. Available online at http://www.huffingtonpost.com/robert-l-borosage/a-new-progressive-era_b _138718.html.

Library of Congress. "Rise of Industrial America: Immigration to the United States, 1851-1900." Available online at http://www.loc.gov/teachers/classroommaterials /presentationsandactivities/presentations/timeline/riseind/immgnts/immgrnts.html.

Pavis, Theta. "Modern Day Muckrakers: The Rise of the Independent Media Center Movement." *Online Journalism Review*, April 3, 2002. Available online at http://www.ojr.org /ojrbusiness/1017866594.php.

University of Kansas, School of Journalism and Mass Communications. "History of American Journalism." Available online at http://history.journalism.ku.edu/1900/1900.shtml.

PHOTO AND ILLUSTRATION CREDITS

Cover and Title Page: Photograph attributed to Lewis Wickes Hine on provenance, National Child Labor Committee Photograph Collection, Prints and Photographs Division, Library of Congress, LC-DIG-nclc-02146.

Chapter One: John C. H. Grabill Collection, Prints and Photographs Division, Library of Congress, LC-DIG-ppmsc-02615 (p. 9); Harris & Ewing Collection, Prints and Photographs Division, Library of Congress, LC-DIG-hec-03941 (p. 11); Prints and Photographs Division, Library of Congress, LC-USZ62-56650 (p. 12); Illustration by William Balfour Ker, Prints and Photographs Division, Library of Congress, LC-USZ62-45985 (p. 15); National Photo Company Collection, Prints and Photographs Division, Library of Congress, LC-USZ62-131913 (p. 18).

Chapter Two: Photo by Lewis Wickes Hine based on provenance, Prints and Photographs Division, Library of Congress, LC-DIG-nclc-03734 (p. 23); Prints and Photographs Division, Library of Congress, LC-USZ62-68945 (p. 25); Art & Architecture Collection, Miriam and Ira D. Wallach Division of Art, Prints and Photographs, The New York Public Library, Astor, Lenox and Tilden Foundations (p. 27); George Grantham Bain Collection, Prints and Photographs Division, Library of Congress, LC-DIG-ggbain-12529 (p. 29); Brown Brothers, Sterling, PA (p. 33).

Chapter Three: Detroit Publishing Company Photograph Collection, Prints and Photographs Division, Library of Congress, LC-USZC4-1584 (p. 37); Photograph by Jacob A. Riis, Prints and Photographs Division, Library of Congress, LC-USZ62-39057 (p. 39); Lewis Wickes Hine based on provenance, Prints and Photographs Division, Library of Congress, LC-DIG-nclc-05394 (p. 42); George Grantham Bain Collection, Prints and Photographs Division, Library of Congress, LC-DIG-ggbain-10997 (p. 44); Prints and Photographs Division, Library of Congress, LC-USZ62-67628 (p. 46).

Chapter Four: Prints and Photographs Division, Library of Congress, LC-USZ62-68572 (p. 53); Lithograph by Udo J. Keppler, Prints and Photographs Division, Library of Congress, LC-USZC4-435 (p. 54); Prints and Photographs Division, Library of Congress, LC-USZ62-75205 (p. 59); Prints and Photographs Division, Library of Congress, LC-USZ62-97323 (p. 61); Prints and Photographs Division, Library of Congress, LC-USZ62-58861 (p. 63).

INDEX

A

Abu Ghraib prisoner abuse scandal, 99-100
Academy Awards, 96, 99, 146
Adams, John, 24
Adams, Samuel, 24
Adams, Samuel Hopkins, 63
Adamson Act of 1916, 105
Addams, Jane, 39
Agricultural Adjustment Act of 1933, 107
Aldrich, Nelson, 125
All in the Day's Work (Tarbell), 154
All the President's Men (Woodward and
　Bernstein), 96
All-Story, 86
*American Chronicle: The Autobiography of Ray
　Stannard Baker,* 118
"American Crisis" (Paine), 24
American Magazine, 58, 82, 117, 122, 150
Ames, Albert Alonzo "Doc," 72-73
Appeal to Reason, 60, 62, 143
Archbold, John D., 134, 176
Atlantic Monthly, 27, 134
Autobiography of Lincoln Steffens, The, 151
automobile safety, 91

B

Baker, Ray Stannard, 35, 48, 78, 85, 87 (ill.),
　115 (ill.), 143, 213
　American magazine and, 82, 122, 154
　biography, 115-18

January 1903 *McClure's* and, 30, 31, 32,
　121, 150
relationship with Theodore Roosevelt,
　77, 79
Barringer, Felicity, 216
Battle at Mussel Slough, 65
Bennett, James Gordon, 25
Bernstein, Carl, 95 (ill.), 95-96, 210, 213
"Birth of an Industry, The" (Tarbell), 53
Bitter Cry of the Children, The (Spargo), 40,
　42-43
　excerpt, 170-72
"Boeing Parts and Rules Bent, Whistle-
　Blowers Say" (Graves), 217
Bok, Edward, 63-64
Bonaparte, Napoleon, 152
Boston News-Letter, 22
Bowling for Columbine (Moore), 98, 99
Bradford III, William, 23
Brandeis University, 212, 216
Bryan, William Jennings, 18
Bull Moose Party. *See* Progressive Party
Bunyan, John, 80-81, 140, 192
Bush, George W., 99, 112, 199, 215
Butler, Ed, 70-71, 187

C

Calley, William, 92-94
Campbell, John, 22
Carnegie, Andrew, 10, 11 (ill.), 17, 52
Carson, Rachel, 90-91

Cather, Willa, 120, 122

CCC. *See* Civilian Conservation Corps (CCC)

CDC. *See* U.S. Centers for Disease Control (CDC)

Center for Investigative Reporting, 101

Center for Public Integrity, 101, 216

Century, 120

Chautauquan, 152

Chicago, Illinois, 11-12, 39

Chicago News-Record, 115

child labor, 40, 42-44, 107, 170-72
  See also labor unions; working conditions

Children of the Poor, The (Riis), 131

Children of the Tenements (Riis), 131

CIA. *See* U.S. Central Intelligence Agency (CIA)

Cincinnati Times-Star, 124

Civil Rights Act of 1964, 110

civil rights movement, 110

Civilian Conservation Corps (CCC), 108

Clayton Antitrust Act of 1914, 105

Cleveland, Grover, 14

Clinton, Bill, 111

Collier's, 27, 63, 121

Colorado Fuel and Iron Company, 59

Columbia Journalism Review, 217

Commercial Advertiser, 149

communism, 89, 106, 140, 151, 210

conservation movement, 47, 91, 104, 139

conservative political principles, 107, 109, 110-11, 112

Constitution. *See* U.S. Constitution

Consumer Product Safety Commission (CPSC), 92

corporate abuses, 51-52, 54-57, 58-60, 62-65, 215-16

corruption. *See* government corruption

Cosmopolitan, 27, 121, 140
  major muckraking articles in, 43, 74, 79, 125, 188

Cover-Up: The Army's Secret Investigation of the Massacre of My Lai 4 (Hersh), 94

Coxey's Army, 115

CPSC. *See* Consumer Product Safety Commission (CPSC)

Crane, Stephen, 28, 120

Cry for Justice, The (Sinclair), 144

Cunningham, Randy "Duke," 215

D

Darwin, Charles, 16-17

Dateline NBC, 100

Davis III, Thomas M., 200

Day, Benjamin H., 25

DeLay, Tom, 215

Deluge, The (Phillips), 125

Depew, Chauncey Mitchell, 188, 189-91

Disabled American Veterans, 199

Dispatch News Service, 93

Dorr, Rheta Childe, 45

Downsize This! (Moore), 99

Doyle, Arthur Conan, 28

Dragon's Teeth (Sinclair), 146

Dude, Where's My Country (Moore), 99

E

Ellsberg, Daniel, 94

Environmental Protection Agency (EPA), 92

EPA. *See* Environmental Protection Agency (EPA)

Everybody's, 27, 45

evolution, Darwin's theory of, 16-17

Exploring the Dangerous Trades (Hamilton), 57

F

FAA. *See* Federal Aviation Administration (FAA)

Fahrenheit 9/11 (Moore), 99

Farm Security Administration, 107

Fashionable Adventures of Joshua Craig, The (Phillips), 125, 126

Fast Food Nation: The Dark Side of the All-American Meal (Schlosser), 97-98

FDA. *See* U.S. Food and Drug Administration (FDA)

FDIC. *See* Federal Deposit Insurance Corporation (FDIC)

Federal Aviation Administration (FAA), 217

Federal Deposit Insurance Corporation (FDIC), 108

Federal Reserve Act of 1913, 105

Federal Trade Commission Act of 1914, 105

Fitch, John A., 58

Flagler, Henry, 132

Folk, Joseph, 70-71, 182, 186-87

Following the Color Line (Baker), 48, 117

food safety, 60-62, 97-98, 143-44, 178-81

Franco, Francisco, 209

Franklin, Benjamin, 22

Franklin, James, 22

G

Gable, Clark, 125

Garbo, Greta, 125

Gary, Elbert H., 154

General Motors (GM), 91, 98

G.I. Bill, 110

GM. *See* General Motors (GM)

Godey's Lady's Book, 27

Goldsborough, Fitzhugh, 126

government corruption, 69-75, 95-96, 125-26, 149-50, 182-91, 207, 213-15

Graham, Katharine, 210

Grange movement, 14

Graves, Florence, 212-18

Grayson, David. *See* Baker, Ray Stannard

"Great American Fraud, The" (Adams), 63

Great Depression, 86, 103, 107-08

Great God Success, The (Phillips), 124

Great Society programs, 110

Greeley, Horace, 25

Greider, William, 96-97

Gridiron Club, 79

H

Hamill, Pete, 206-11

Hamilton, Alice, 56-57

Hancock, John, 24

Harding, Warren G., 106

Harkness, William W., 175

Harper's Weekly, 27, 207

Harris, Benjamin, 22

Hearst, William Randolph, 25 (ill.), 26, 86

Henry, O., 28

Hepburn Act of 1906, 67

Hersh, Seymour, 92-94, 93 (ill.), 100

Hine, Lewis, 42 (ill.), 44

History of the Standard Oil Company, The (Tarbell), 30, 32, 54, 135, 153, 154

excerpt, 173-77

Hobart, Garret, 138

Hoffman, Dustin, 96

Hoover, Herbert, 107

How the Other Half Lives (Riis), 38-39, 130

excerpt, 165-69

Hull, Anne, 197-205

Hull House, 39-40

Hungry Heart, The (Phillips), 125

Hunter, Robert, 40

Hussein, Saddam, 209

I

ICC. *See* Interstate Commerce Commission (ICC)

immigrants, 11, 36, 41

Independent, The, 121

Industrial Poisons in the United States (Hamilton), 57

Industrial Revolution, 7, 8-9, 24

impact on American society, 10-13, 35-37

Internet, 88, 100-01

Interstate Commerce Act of 1887, 17, 163
Interstate Commerce Commission (ICC), 17, 67, 104
Iraq War, 99-100, 197, 210, 215

J

James, Henry, 120
Jim Crow laws, 36, 47-48
Johnson, Hiram, 75
Johnson, Lyndon B., 110 (ill.)
journalism
    challenges facing, 100, 212-18
    history of, 21-28, 86-89, 206-11
    See also muckrakers
Jungle, The (Sinclair), 51, 62, 65, 91, 98, 143-44
    excerpt, 178-81

K

Kelley, Florence, 45
Kipling, Rudyard, 28, 120

L

La Follette, Robert M., 3, 4-6, 75, 117
labor unions, 14, 55-58, 66, 108
    See also child labor; working conditions
Ladies' Home Journal, 63-64
"Larry Budd" series (Sinclair), 146
Lenin, Vladimir, 151
Lewis, Chuck, 216
Lewis, Daniel Day, 146
Life, 86
Light-Fingered Gentry (Phillips), 125
Lincoln, Abraham, 152
Lippmann, Walter, 52
Lloyd, Henry Demarest, 134
London, Jack, 120
Long Island City Review, 128
Look, 86
Los Angeles Times, 146

Luce, Henry, 86
Ludlow Massacre, 59

M

magazines, development of modern, 27-28
Making of an American, The (Riis), 131
"Man with the Muck-Rake, The" (Roosevelt), 192-96
Mann-Elkins Act of 1910, 104
Markham, Edwin, 43
McCarthy, Eugene, 89-90
McClure, Samuel Sidney (S.S.), 21, 32, 33 (ill.), 70, 119 (ill.), 149, 152
    biography, 119-23
    January 1903 editorial, 30-31, 33
    loses writers to *American* magazine, 82, 154
    relationship with Theodore Roosevelt, 77-78
McClure's, 53, 70, 77, 81-82, 135, 140
    founding of, 27, 32, 120
    January 1903 issue, 30-33, 116, 121-22, 150
McKinley, William, 18, 19, 138, 159
Meat Inspection Act of 1906, 144
meatpacking industry, 60-62, 97-98, 143, 178-81
Medicaid, 110
Medicare, 110
Merriam, Frank, 146
Minneapolis, Minnesota, 30, 31, 33, 72-73, 116
Moore, Michael, 98-99
Morgan, John Pierpont (J.P.), 10, 52, 66, 116
Mother Jones, 98
muckrakers
    challenges facing future, 100-01
    corporate abuses and, 51-54, 58-65, 134-35, 143-46, 153-54, 173-81
    government corruption and, 69-75, 125-26, 149-50, 182-91

impact on American society, 3-5, 19, 30-32, 35, 65-67, 104, 206-11

journalistic movement, 28-30, 32-33, 81-83, 121-22

modern-day, 85, 89-100, 197-205, 212-18

origin of term, 4, 79-81, 140, 192-96

relationship with Theodore Roosevelt, 3-4, 77-79, 125-26, 130, 139-40

social issues and, 37-39, 42-48, 129-31, 165-72

See also journalism

Munsey's, 121

Murrow, Edward R., 89 (ill.), 89-90

Mussel Slough, Battle at, 65

My Lai 4: A Report on the Massacre and Its Aftermath (Hersh), 94

My Lai massacre, 92-94

N

Nader, Ralph, 91-92

Nast, Thomas, 207

National Child Labor Committee (NCLC), 43-44

National Consumers' League, 45, 57

National Industrial Recovery Act of 1933, 107

National Institute for Occupational Safety and Health, 57

National Labor Relations Act of 1935, 108

Native American: The Book of My Youth (Baker), 118

NCLC. *See* National Child Labor Committee (NCLC)

Nelson, Lars-Erik, 209

New Deal, 103, 107-09

New England Courant, 22

New York Evening Post, 148

New York Evening Sun, 129

New York Herald, 25

New York Morning Journal, 26

New York Sun, 25, 124

New York Times, 26, 94, 207, 209, 216

New York Tribune, 25, 128

New York World, 26, 124

New Yorker, 100

newspapers

challenges facing, 86, 88, 212-18

development of modern, 24-26

Nieman Reports, 212

Nixon, Richard M., 88, 94, 96

Norris, Frank, 64-65

O

Obama, Barack, 103, 112

occupational health and safety, 56-57

Occupational Safety and Health Commission (OSHA), 92

Octopus, The (Norris), 64-65

Oil (Sinclair), 145-46

"Old Age at Forty" (Fitch), 58

On the Origin of Species (Darwin), 16-17

One World, Ready or Not (Greider), 96-97

OSHA. *See* Occupational Safety and Health Commission (OSHA)

"Other Walter Reed, The" (Priest and Hull), 197-205

Out of Mulberry Street: Stories of Tenement Life in New York (Riis), 131

Outcault, Richard F., 26

P-Q

Paine, Thomas, 24

patent medicines, 62-65

PBS Frontline, 100

Pendleton Act of 1883, 76-77

Pennsylvania Journal, 23, 24

Pennsylvania Railroad, 133

Pentagon Papers, 94

People's Party. *See* Populist Party

Phillips, David Graham, 74 (ill.), 74-75, 79-80, 124 (ill.), 188-91

biography, 124-27

Phillips, John S., 154

photojournalism, 86

Pilgrim's Progress, The (Bunyan), 80-81, 140, 192

Platt, Thomas Collier, 125, 188, 189-90

Plum Tree, The (Phillips), 125

political corruption. *See* government corruption

Pope, Albert, 119

Populist Party, 18

Poverty (Hunter), 40

Power of News, The (Schudson), 212-13

Priest, Dana, 197-205

Progressive Era, 4, 7, 19, 103-07, 112
early reform efforts, 13-14, 16-18, 39-40
political reforms, 70, 75-77

progressive movement, 17, 19, 28, 44-48, 104, 121, 139
efforts to reform corporate practices, 51, 55-56, 62, 64-67
Great Society reforms, 110
New Deal reforms, 103, 107-09

Progressive Party, 105, 140

Prohibition, 45-47

Project on the State of the American Newspaper, 214

ProPublica, 101

Public Papers of Woodrow Wilson (Baker), 118

Publick Occurrences Both Forreign and Domestick, 22

Pulitzer Center on Crisis Reporting, 101

Pulitzer, Joseph, 26, 29, 124

Pulitzer Prize, 93, 96, 118, 146, 197

Pullman Palace Car Company, 14

Pullman strike of 1894, 14, 115

Pure Food and Drug Act of 1906, 62, 65, 104, 144

R

racial equality, 47-48

radio, 86

Reagan, Ronald, 110-11, 111 (ill.)

Redford, Robert, 96

"Right to Work, The" (Baker), 30, 32

Riis, Jacob, 38-39, 39 (ill.), 128 (ill.), 165-69
biography, 128-31

robber barons, 10, 52, 134

Rockefeller Foundation, 135-36

Rockefeller Institute for Medical Research, 135

Rockefeller, John D., 10, 67, 104, 132 (ill.)
biography, 132-36
target of muckrakers, 52-54, 59, 153, 173-77

Roger and Me (Moore), 98

Roosevelt, Franklin D., 103, 106 (ill.), 107, 108, 109

Roosevelt, Theodore, 18 (ill.), 78 (ill.), 105, 107, 116, 137 (ill.), 149
biography, 137-41
calls journalists "muckrakers," 79-81, 192-96
leads progressive reform movement, 21, 28, 33, 62, 66-67, 135
political philosophy, 19, 45, 47, 159-64
relationship with muckrakers, 3-4, 77-79, 122, 125-26, 130, 188

Root, Elihu, 139

Rough Riders, 138

Rumsfeld, Donald, 199

S

Safire, William, 209

St. Louis, Missouri, 70-71, 149-50, 182-87

Saturday Evening Post, 27, 125

Schlosser, Eric, 97-98

Schudson, Michael, 212

Schuster Institute for Investigative Journalism, 212, 216-18

Scott, Thomas, 133

Scribner's, 129

SEC. *See* Securities and Exchange Commission (SEC)

Securities and Exchange Commission (SEC), 108

See It Now, 89-90

settlement houses, 39-40

"Shame of Minneapolis, The" (Steffens), 30, 31, 33, 72-73, 116

"Shame of the Cities" series (Steffens), 70-73
    excerpt, 182-87

Shame of the Cities, The (Steffens), 73, 150

Shaw, George Bernard, 146

Sheehan, Neil, 94

Shepherd, William G., 59

Sherman Antitrust Act of 1890, 17, 66, 67, 104

SIC. *See* South Improvement Company (SIC)

Sicko (Moore), 99

Silent Spring (Carson), 90-91

Sinclair, Upton, 85, 142 (ill.), 154
    biography, 142-47
    The Jungle, 51, 60-62, 91, 98, 178-81

60 Minutes, 100

Smith, Roger, 98

Social Darwinism, 16-17

Social Security Act of 1935, 108

socialism, 57-58, 61, 77, 117, 140, 151

Socialist Party, 61, 143, 144, 145

South Improvement Company (SIC), 133

Southern Pacific Railroad Company, 65

Soviet Union, 209-10

Spanish-American War, 138

Spargo, John, 40, 42-43, 170-72

Spencer, Herbert, 16

Springtime and Harvest (Sinclair), 142

Stamp Act of 1765, 22-23

Standard Oil Company, 132-34
    government breakup of, 67, 104, 135, 154
    investigation by muckraker Ida M. Tarbell, 52-54, 116, 121, 135, 150, 153, 173-77

Steffens, Lincoln, 85, 87 (ill.), 120, 148 (ill.), 213
    American magazine and, 82, 122, 154
    biography, 148-51
    January 1903 *McClure's* and, 33, 121
    relationship with Theodore Roosevelt, 79, 80, 139
    "Shame of the Cities" series, 70-73, 116, 182-87

Stevenson, Robert Louis, 28, 120

"Story of a Great Monopoly" (Lloyd), 134

Stupid White Men (Moore), 99

Success, 125

Sumner, William Graham, 16

Susan Lenox: Her Rise and Fall (Phillips), 125

T

Taft, William Howard, 104-05, 140, 141

Tarbell, Ida M., 53 (ill.), 85, 87 (ill.), 120, 143, 152 (ill.), 212, 213
    American magazine and, 82, 122
    biography, 152-55
    investigation of Standard Oil Company, 52-54, 135, 173-77
    January 1903 *McClure's* and, 30, 31, 32, 116, 121, 150

television, 87-88

temperance movement, 45-47

Ten Year's War: An Account of the Battle with the Slum in New York, A (Riis), 131

Tenement House Commission, 38, 165

tenement housing, 13, 36-38, 129, 130, 165-69

Tennessee Valley Authority (TVA), 108

There Will Be Blood, 146

Time, 86

Traffic and Motor Vehicle Safety Act of 1966, 91

"Treason of the Senate, The" (Phillips), 74-75, 77, 79-80, 125-26
    excerpt, 188-91

Triangle Shirtwaist Factory fire, 58-59, 96

True Story, 86
TVA. *See* Tennessee Valley Authority (TVA)
Twain, Mark, 28
"Tweed Days in St. Louis" (Steffens), 71, 149-50
    excerpt, 182-87
Tweed, William M. "Boss," 70, 207

U

United Mine Workers, 66
United States, immigration to, 11, 36, 41
Unsafe at Any Speed (Nader), 91-92
urban problems, 11-13, 35-40, 129, 165-69
U.S. Centers for Disease Control (CDC), 57
U.S. Central Intelligence Agency (CIA), 94
U.S. Constitution
    Eighteenth Amendment, 46, 106
    First Amendment, 24, 206
    Nineteenth Amendment, 45, 106
    Seventeenth Amendment, 75, 104, 126
    Sixteenth Amendment, 104
    Twenty-First Amendment, 47
U.S. Food and Drug Administration (FDA), 144
U.S. Senate, 73-75, 188
U.S. senators, direct election of, 74, 75, 126
U.S. Steel Corporation, 52

V

Vanderbilt, Cornelius, 10, 52, 191
Vietnam War, 88, 92-95
Voting Rights Act of 1965, 110

W-X

Wagner Act of 1935, 108
Walter Reed Army Medical Center, 197, 215

Warren, Fred, 143
Washington Post, 95-96, 197, 217
Watergate in American Memory (Schudson), 212, 213
Watergate scandal, 95-96, 213
Wealth against Commonwealth (Lloyd), 134
Weightman, George W., 200-01
Wells, Ida B., 48
What Eight Million Women Want (Dorr), 45
Wheelman, 119
White, William Allen, 7
Whitman, Walt, 120
Wilson, Harold S., 85
Wilson, Woodrow, 105, 106, 117-18, 140-41, 154
Women's Christian Temperance Movement, 46
women's suffrage movement, 45, 154
Woodrow Wilson and World Settlement (Baker), 118
Woodrow Wilson: Life and Letters (Baker), 118
Woodward, Bob, 95 (ill.), 95-96, 210, 212, 213
working conditions, 13, 51, 55, 58-59, 96-98, 178-81
    See also child labor; labor unions
Works Progress Administration (WPA), 108
World War I, 82, 86, 105-06, 141, 145
World War II, 86-87, 89, 108
WPA. *See* Works Progress Administration (WPA)

Y-Z

yellow journalism, 26
"Yellow Kid, The" (Outcault), 26
Young, Owen D., 154